BURT FRANKLIN: RESEARCH & SOURCE WORKS SERIES 411
Essays in Literature & Criticism 43

MONTAIGNE AND SHAKESPEARE

MONTAIGNE

AND

SHAKESPEARE

AND OTHER ESSAYS
ON COGNATE QUESTIONS

BY

JOHN M. ROBERTSON, M.P.

**BURT FRANKLIN
NEW YORK**

Published by BURT FRANKLIN
235 East 44th St., New York, N.Y. 10017
Originally Published: 1909
Reprinted: 1969
Printed in the U.S.A.

Library of Congress Card Catalog No.: 70-108429
Burt Franklin: Research and Source Works Series 411
Essays in Literature & Criticism 43

NOTE

OF the following essays, the first originally appeared as a series of magazine articles in 1896, and thereafter, revised and expanded, as a separate volume in 1897. That having been for years out of print, the essay is now again revised and considerably expanded, the thesis being strengthened by new parallels; while there is raised a fresh problem of some little interest, as to a point of apparent intellectual contact between Shakespeare and Bacon—not, of course, in the sense of the current Bacon-Shakespeare theorem.

The paper on "The Originality of Shakespeare" discusses and answers a number of the criticisms passed on the first essay in 1897-98, and appeared as a magazine article. In view of later criticisms, and in particular of the positions taken up by the late Professor Churton Collins in his *Studies in Shakespeare* (1904), I have sought to clear up the

applicable critical principles in a general Introduction. And as Mr. Collins brought fresh
learning to the support of the opinion combated
by me in the further essay on "The Learning of
Shakespeare," which first appeared as a magazine
article in 1898, I have inserted in that a discussion
of his arguments on this head, in addition to what
I have said on the subject in the Introduction.
The problems discussed in the three essays being
interdependent, they are here grouped together,
and so submitted to the candid attention of
Shakespeare students.

JOHN M. ROBERTSON.

May 1909.

CONTENTS

MONTAIGNE AND SHAKESPEARE—

MONTAIGNE AND SHAKESPEARE

INTRODUCTION

GIVEN the probability of a literary influence exercised upon a given writer by one or more previous writers, or by any course of culture, by what kind of evidence shall it be proved to have taken place ?

This problem, necessarily present to the writer's mind when the following treatise was separately published, has since been pressed upon him with a new clearness by the essays of the late Professor Churton Collins, collected under the title of STUDIES IN SHAKESPEARE. Discussing, among other things, "Shakespeare as a Classical Scholar," "Shakespeare and Montaigne," and, under the heading of "Shakespearean Paradoxes," the point of the authorship of TITUS ANDRONICUS, they raise from three sides the question under notice. The first cited essay claims to prove Shakespeare's familiarity with Latin literature, and with Plato and the Greek tragedians in Latin translations ; the second challenges much of the evidence offered in the following pages to show that Shakespeare was much influenced by Montaigne ; and the third claims to prove, as against the main line of English criticism, that Shakespeare really wrote the disputed play named.

With the last thesis I have dealt fully in my book DID SHAKESPEARE WRITE "TITUS ANDRONICUS" ? published during Mr. Collins's lifetime ; and the conclusions therein reached bear directly upon the first issue as to Shakespeare's classical scholarship. Much of Mr. Collins's case on that head turns upon classical quotations and allusions found in TITUS and in plays long held, like that, to contain much that is not Shakespeare's work, albeit more affected than TITUS by his touch. Thus, before we can come to a conclusion as to all the literary influences undergone by Shakespeare, we must form an opinion as to what is and what is not genuine in the mass of matter which goes under his name. Upon this head there will be found some comment in the paper on " The Originality of Shakespeare " in the present volume. So far as this discussion is concerned, however, it is still left in large part an open question. While it is claimed that the non-Shakespearean authorship of TITUS is proved, it is admitted that the old question as to the HENRY VI group and RICHARD

III; the survival of alien matter in TROILUS, TIMON, ROMEO AND JULIET, the TAMING OF THE SHREW, and the COMEDY OF ERRORS; and the probability of pre-Shakespearean forms of RICHARD II, the TWO GENTLEMEN, ALL'S WELL, and MEASURE FOR MEASURE have still to be systematically dealt with. I should add that for many years I have been convinced that some of the matter in LOVE'S LABOUR'S LOST to which Mr. Collins and others point for proof of Shakespeare's classical knowledge was the work of one or more collaborators, probably not professional playwrights.

Such an avowal, of course, suggests the retort that I have reasoned in a circle, settling in advance that matter which showed classical knowledge was not Shakespeare's. In point of fact, however, it is only in regard to LOVE'S LABOUR'S LOST that I have ever so reasoned. The whole of TITUS, much of the HENRY VI plays, and most of the SHREW, was for me non-Shakespearean from the first study, in respect of everything that made Shakespeare distinguishable from other men. Instead, therefore, of begging the question, I have been led to my conclusions as to the learning of Shakespeare by a general induction from the matter which, upon the main and primary grounds of genuineness, was certificated to me as his. The fact that the distinct traces of classical knowledge in his imputed works are to be found mainly in those which, for many readers through many generations, have always been under veto or suspicion on grounds of style, is in itself a fact of obvious critical importance.

This said, I leave for another time, or to other hands, the systematic discussion as to what is and is not genuine in the Shakespeare plays. That these problems must and will be grappled with, I am assured. The recent confident deliverance of Mr. C. F. Tucker Brooke, that " all attempts to deprive the poet of a large interest in any of the thirty-six plays . . . have failed," [1] is only a suggestion to the effect that, despite such admirable critical work as Professor Bradley's, little contribution to the undertaking from English academic sources is now to be looked for beyond the useful item of careful collation of texts. Our problems, however, must be handled in detail ; and it is possible to isolate for the time being the general question of critical method, and that of a particular literary influence.

A perusal of Mr. Collins's essays will show that on the one hand, while admitting an influence exercised by Montaigne on Shakespeare, he denies

[1] Introduction to *The Shakespeare Apocrypha*, 1908, p. xii.

the validity of much of the evidence hereinafter given to prove that influence ; and that on the other hand he affirms a general influencing of Shakespeare by the Greek and Latin classics—this upon grounds not distinguishable in kind, though, as I think, very different in strength, from those put forward in my treatise. The final difficulty is, to know what weight Mr. Collins ascribed to either his general thesis or his particular propositions. In the preface to his volume of STUDIES he writes as to his " parallel illustrations " :

" It must not be supposed that I have any wish to attach undue weight to them. As a rule such illustrations belong rather to the trifles and curiosities of criticism, to its *tolerabiles nugae*, rather than to anything approaching importance. But . . . cumulatively they are remarkable."

I should add that they are very interesting in themselves to students of literary causation and evolution. No one, I think, has ever put together so many parallelisms of expression between Shakespeare and the Greek tragedies as Mr. Collins has done. The trouble is that he has not attempted to frame, and has failed to recognise the difficulties in the way of framing, any code as to legitimate and illegitimate inferences from literary parallels. Often he shows himself alive to the risks of false induction. Observing that

" we must *not* admit as evidence any parallels in
sentiment and reflection which, as they express
commonplaces, are likely to be mere coincidences,"
he fills several pages with interesting cases in point,
and yet thereafter stresses other parallels which are
no less constituted from commonplaces.   Thus he
writes that such parallels as the following may
point to no more than coincidence :

> To you your father should be as a god (M.S.N.D. i, 1).
>
> νόμιζε σαυτῷ τοὺς γονεῖς εἶναι θεούς.
>
> (Consider that thy parents are gods to thee.)
>
> (Menander, SENTEN. SINGULAR. in Stobaeus.)

Thus conscience doth make cowards of us all (HAMLET, iii, 1).

> ὁ συνιστορῶν αὐτῷ τι, κἂν ᾖ θρασύτατος,
> ἡ σύνεσις αὐτὸν δειλότατον εἶναι ποιεῖ.

(He who is conscious of aught, e'en though he be the
boldest of men, conscience makes him the most cowardly.—
Menander quoted in Stobaeus, SERM. xxiv.)

Yet he continues as follows :

But, "fat paunches have lean pates" (L.L.L. i, 1) is
undoubtedly from the anonymous Greek proverb :

> παχεῖα γαστὴρ λεπτὸν οὐ τίκτει νόον
>
> (Fine wit is never the offspring of a fat paunch) ;

and the line in 3 HENRY VI, i, 2, "For a kingdom any oath
may be broken," *as certainly* a reminiscence of Euripides,
PHOENISSAE, 524-5 :

> εἴπερ γὰρ ἀδικεῖν χρή, τυραννίδος πέρι
> κάλλιστον ἀδικεῖν.

(If indeed one must do injustice, injustice done for
sovereignty's sake is honorablest.)

Though this *may* have come through Seneca :

Imperio pretio quolibet constant bene.

PHOENISSAE, 664.

Now, the obvious comment here is that all the passages are alike of the nature of commonplaces, maxims, or pseudo-maxims, and that not " coincidence " but common currency is the explanation. To say that fat paunches have lean wits is to deal in proverbial wisdom no less than in saying "to you your father should be as a god." Such sayings are the common money of ancient literature, and as such were made current in Europe through the whole period of the Renaissance. The Interlude of CALISTO AND MELEBEA, dating from about 1530, and based upon the copious Spanish dramatic novel CELESTINA, begins by citing " Franciscus Petrarcus the poet lawreate " and " Eraclito the wyse clerk " to the effect that strife gives birth to and runs through all things, and that there is nothing under the firmament equivalent in all points with any other. There is no saying how many ancient sentences thus became current. The lost " tragic comedy of Celestina " is entered in the Stationers' Register in 1598 as a work " wherein are discoursed in most pleasant style many philosophical sentences and advertisements very necessary for young

gentlemen " ;[1] and other lost plays doubtless
drew much on Seneca and other classics for
reflections.   It is indeed conceivable that the
passage cited from 3 HENRY VI, i, 2, *may* be
a· reminiscence from Euripides or Seneca: the
spavined English line cries aloud its non-Shakespearean paternity ;   and the " university hack "
who wrote it may have read Euripides.   Peele,
we know, had.   But it is far more probable that
the tag was already current in the English form.
Oath-breaking and injustice are different concepts ;
but sayings of this sort on either theme could easily
be new-minted among the moderns without reminiscence of anything in Greek.   The odd thing
is that Mr. Collins did not bethink him of turning
on the one hand to the version of the PHOENISSAE
published in 1573 by Gascoigne, under the title of
JOCASTA, where the passage in question is translated :[2]

> If law of right may any way be broke
> Desire of rule within a climbing breast
> To break a vow may bear the buckler best,

and on the other hand to the works of the
English dramatists who preceded Shakespeare.   In

---

[1] See the pref. to the Malone Society's rep. of *Calisto and
Melebea*, 1909.

[2] Cunliffe's ed. of Gascoigne's Works, i, 272.

Greene's Selimus may be found no fewer than six variants of the sentiment in question :

> Bare faith, pure virtue, poor integrity,
> Are ornaments fit for a private man :
> Beseems a prince for to do all he can.
>
> (ll. 1400-2.)
>
> For nothing is more hurtful to a prince
> Than to be scrupulous and religious.
>
> (ll. 1731-2.)
>
> For th' only things that wrought our empery
> Were open wrongs, and hidden treachery.
>
> (ll. 1736-7.)
>
> I count it sacrilege for to be holy.
>
> (l. 249.)
>
> Make thou a passage for thy gushing flood
> By slaughter, treason, or what else thou can.
>
> (ll. 253-4.)
>
> I reck not of their foolish ceremonies
> But mean to take my fortune as I find.
>
> (ll. 272-3.)

To say nothing of the high probability that the passage in 3 Henry VI is actually from Greene's hand, such data clearly forbid the resort to the classics for the immediate source of any tag in a Shakespearean play.

Mr. Collins proceeds to cite as a probable case of reminiscence the passage :

> All places that the eye of heaven visits
> Are to a wise man ports and happy havens,
>
> (Richard II, i, 3.)

putting without comment the parallel :

> ἅπασα δὲ χθὼν ἀνδρὶ γενναίῳ πατρίς.
> (To a noble man every land is his fatherland.)
>   (Euripides, FRAG. EX INCERT. TRAG., xxxviii.)

Now, this particular maxim, as it happens, had been made current in Latin by Cicero ;[1] and it is found not only in Lyly's EUPHUES in the form : "he noted that every place was a country to a wise man,"[2] but in a whole series of other Elizabethan writers before Shakespeare. In the DAMON AND PITHIAS of Richard Edwards (1571) occurs the line :

> *Omne solum forti patria* : a wyse man may live every wheare.

It is used both by Greene and Peele :

> Tully said every country is a wise man's home.[3]
> And every climate virtue's tabernacle.[4]

And it appears in SOLIMAN AND PERSEDA [5] in the form :

> And where a man lives well, that is his country.

It is surely clear that in the face of such data no inference can be led from the bare fact of a parallel

---

[1] *Tusc. Disp.* v, 37, § 108 : "Patria est ubicumque est bene." This is cited from some lost tragedy. Aristophanes burlesques it (*Plutus*, 1151) and Euripides puts the idea twice.

[2] *Euphues : the Anatomy of Wit.* Arber's rep. p. 187. Cp. p. 189.

[3] Greene, *Mourning Garment.* Works, ed. Grosart, xi, 132.

[4] Peele, *Farewell*, 49.   [5] IV, ii, 7.

between a classic phrase and one in a Shakespearean play, disputed or undisputed. And the application of such texts as have been indicated, it will be found, serves to break down the majority of Mr. Collins's classic parallels. Many are non-significant ; many are phrases current in Elizabethan literature ; many more bear upon plays which a multitude of critics recognise to contain more or less of non-Shakespearean matter.

And as regards one of the parallels on which Mr. Collins laid most stress, that between a passage in TROILUS and one in Plato's FIRST ALCIBIADES—a parallel which is the more likely to impress the ordinary reader because it had been already drawn by the late Richard Grant White—it will be shown in the following treatise, where the TROILUS passage is dealt with, that the resort to Plato for its source is an error, there being others, lying to Shakespeare's hand in English, which more exactly meet the case. Yet other plausible and interesting parallels similarly dissolve under analysis. The referring of three lines in HENRY V (i, ii, 180–83), for instance, to a passage from Cicero's DE REPUBLICA, quoted by Augustine,[1] proceeds on the assumption that since there was no current translation of Augustine's

[1] *De Civitate Dei*, ii, 21.

book or of the fragments of the REPUBLIC, Shakespeare cannot reasonably be supposed to have met
with the passage save in the Latin.   Now, supposing the passage *had* reached him as a Latin
quotation, the power to give a free rendering of
it would be very far from justifying the inference
that he read much in the Latin classics ; and Mr.
Collins, as it happens, offers no further reason for
supposing that he had read the DE CIVITATE DEI.
To what then are we led ?   What can be more
unlikely than that such a passage should in Elizabethan England have been left for a dramatist to
put in currency?   In so common a book as Sir
Thomas Elyot's GOVERNOUR (1531) the central
idea is expounded in the opening chapter ; in De
Mornay's treatise on the Christian religion (translated in 1589) the thesis of the general harmony
of nature is reiterated in several chapters ; and it
lay open to every divine to comment it with the
sentence of Cicero out of Augustine.

Turning from such eminently unconvincing
instances of Shakespeare's study of Latin literature,
we find ourselves challenged by a series of parallels
of phrase such as those between "the lazy foot of
time" and Euripides' δαρὸν χρόνου πόδα (BACCH.
889) ; "the belly-pinched wolf" (LEAR, iii, 1) and
the κοιλογάστορες λύκοι of Aeschylus (SEPTEM C.

THEB. 1037–8); "blossoms of your love" and
ἔρωτος ἄνθος ; and so forth. "Such similarities of
expression are cumulatively very remarkable,"
says Mr. Collins.[1] Interesting they certainly are,
but surely not significant of anything save the
quite spontaneous duplication of many forms of
phrase in different lands and times, and the passage
of others from age to age in the common stream
of literature. The lean-waisted form of the wolf,
surely, is equally notable to all who know him ;
and "blossoms of love" is a natural trope wherever tropes are turned. After pronouncing such
things cumulatively remarkable, Mr. Collins
admits :[2] "All these may be of course, and *most
of them almost certainly are*, mere coincidences."

When, again, we are led for firmer footing to
instances of positive "Greekisms" in the plays,
that is, actual impositions of Greek idiom upon
English speech, we are left asking whether the
classical thesis has not by this time destroyed
itself. Mr. Collins's main contention, as we saw,
is that Shakespeare read Latin fluently, but resorted
to Latin translations for his knowledge of the
Greek classics. Now he has insensibly reached
the position that Shakespeare was so steeped
in Greek as to think in Greek idiom when

[1] *Studies*, p. 51.   [2] *Id.* p. 52.

writing dramatic English.   The argument is in
the air.

Leaving the special question of Shakespeare's
learning for further separate discussion, let us now
ask, How shall we ascertain or prove an *influence*
upon Shakespeare's thinking from what he read?
That he had read this book or that is a matter
of interest for all his students ; but the weighty
question is, What part did any book or books
play in developing his mind?   On this problem
Mr. Collins had little to say.   In concluding his
examination of my own essay, he admitted that
Montaigne's Essays, which were certainly known
to Shakespeare, "could hardly have failed to
attract and interest him greatly" ; [1] and again :
"It may have been that, with a genius stimulated,
and even enriched, by the author of the APOLOGY
OF RAIMOND SEBONDE, he went on with the
creation of Hamlet, and of Vincentio, or at all
events made them the mouthpieces of his own
meditative fancies.   But we must guard against
the old fallacy of *post hoc, ergo propter hoc*." [2]   And
he concludes thus : "The true nature of Shakespeare's indebtedness to Montaigne may be fairly
estimated if we say what, we believe, may be said
with truth, that had the Essays never appeared

[1] *Studies*, p. 294.   [2] *Id.* p. 295.

there is nothing to warrant the assumption that what he has in common with Montaigne would not have been equally conspicuous."

Does the same formula hold, then, for the alleged saturation of Shakespeare with the classics? How, to come to the point, is a literary influence to be proved or disproved? Mr. Collins, after proffering his classical parallels, candidly indicates a consciousness that he has raised more problems than he claims to have solved :

"But, it may be urged, if Shakespeare was acquainted with the Greek dramas he would have left unequivocal indications of that acquaintance with them by reproducing their form, by drawing with unmistakable directness on their *dramatis personae* for archetypes, by borrowing incidents, situations and scenes from them, or at least by directly and habitually referring to them. The answer to this is obvious. Of all playwrights that have ever lived Shakespeare appears to have been *the most practical and the most conventional.* The poet of all ages was pre-eminently the child of his own age. He belonged to a guild who spoke a common language, who derived their material from common sources, who cast that material in common moulds, and who appealed to a common audience. The Elizabethan drama was no exotic, but drew its vitality and nutriment from its native soil. The differences which separate Attic tragedy from Elizabethan are radical and essential. Had Shakespeare known the Greek plays by heart he could not have taken them for his models, or transferred, without recasting and reconstructing, a single scene from them. He had also to consider what appealed to his audience. The works of the Attic masters were as yet familiar only to scholars. Allusions to the legends of the houses of Atreus

2

and of Labdacus would not have been popularly intelligible ; and it is quite clear that Shakespeare, whatever concessions he may have made to it in his earlier works, abhorred pedantry. That he should, therefore, have given us in HAMLET so close an analogy to the story of the CHOËPHOROE and of the ELECTRA without either recalling or even referring to Orestes ; that he should have pictured Lear and Cordelia without any allusion to Oedipus and Antigone, is not at all surprising. There is the same absence of reference to the Attic Tragedies both in Ben Jonson and in Chapman, but of the acquaintance of both these scholars with them there can be no doubt."

The infirmity of the argument here is note-worthy. Shakespeare is called "the most conventional" of dramatists inasmuch as he paid no homage to the great source of dramatic convention ; and the most practical because, while constantly studying Greek drama, he made no such use of it as he did of Renaissance fiction. Shall we also be told that, being steeped in Greek drama, he took the best course open to him in his presentment of Athenian life in the MIDSUMMER NIGHT'S DREAM, where Theseus is a feudal Duke ?

All along the line the argument miscarries. Shakespeare, we are told, handled themes which expressly recalled the plots of the Attic tragedies, yet did not mention them ; even as the learned Jonson and Chapman abstained from such allusions in their plays. But did Jonson and Chapman, then, handle themes which expressly recalled the

Attic tragedies? If they did not, the analogy collapses. Shakespeare, we are further told, abhorred pedantry. But TITUS ANDRONICUS abounds in pedantry ; and there we do have references to two Attic tragedies. Mr. Collins, who insists that Shakespeare wrote TITUS, has failed to unify his case. If Shakespeare referred to the AJAX of Sophocles and the HECUBA of Euripides in one early tragedy, why should he not refer to the CHOËPHORI and the ELECTRA in HAMLET, or to the AGAMEMNON in MACBETH, or to the OEDIPUS and the ANTIGONE in LEAR, supposing these Attic tragedies to be familiar to him ? " In LEAR throughout," says Mr. Collins, "Shakespeare seems to be haunted with reminiscences of the ORESTES and PHOENISSAE : how closely, for example, the scene where Cordelia is watching over the sleeping Lear recalls ORESTES 135-240, and both Lear and Gloucester with Edgar and Cordelia, the Oedipus and Antigone of the end of the PHOENISSAE." [1] That is to say, a dramatist so steeped in Attic tragedy as to reproduce from it maxims, tags, and idioms, can be seen to be haunted by scenes to which he makes no allusion.

Concerning Shakespeare's HAMLET, again, Mr.

[1] *Studies,* p. 75.

Collins explains that " He approached his subject
from a totally different point of view, proceeding
in his treatment of it on diametrically opposite
lines, so that in his characters, in his incident, and
in his ethical purpose he is never, in any particular,
in touch with the Greek." [1]   Quite so.   And
when Mr. Collins does seek to show an intellectual
influence operating from the Greek tragedies upon
Shakespeare, the outcome is decisively inadequate
to his thesis :

" In passing to Shakespeare's parallels in metaphysical
speculation and generalised reflection on life, to use the term
in its most comprehensive sense, we may first notice the
possible influence exercised on him by Jocasta's magnificent
ῥῆσις in the PHOENISSAE, 582-5.   We trace in it Ulysses' great
speech in the second scene of the first act of TROILUS AND
CRESSIDA, which borrows its sentiments and even its imagery,
and catching its very cadence and rhythm, might have been
modelled on it ; in Henry V's noble soliloquy in the first
scene of the fourth act of the play ; and though we need not
emphasise as significant the parallel between Wolsey's

> Cromwell, I charge thee, fling away ambition :
> By that sin fell the angels, etc.,

and Jocasta's

> τί τῆς κακίστης δαιμόνων ἐφίεσαι
> φιλοτιμίας, παῖ; μὴ σύ γ᾽· ἄδικος ἡ θεός·

(Why art thou bent on ambition, the worst of deities ?
I pray thee forbear ; a goddess she who knows no justice),

it is perhaps worth noticing.   Nor would it be any exaggera-
tion to say that every article in Shakespeare's political creed,
a creed so elaborately preached and illustrated in his

---

[1] *Studies*, p. 79.

Historical Plays, is summed up in the first speech of Menelaus in the AJAX (1052-90) and Creon's speech to Haemon in the ANTIGONE (665-80).

"A sentiment peculiarly characteristic of the Greeks was their superstitious reverence for what was popularly accepted and become custom. This continually finds emphatic expression in the Greek dramas, and is indeed woven into the very fabric of their ethics. We need go no further than a line in Sophocles, as it is typical of innumerable other passages : τό τοι νομισθὲν τῆς ἀληθείας κρατεῖ (what custom establishes outmasters truth), FRAG. 84, and Euripides' BACCHAE, 894, where τὸ ἐν χρόνῳ μακρῷ νόμιμον δαιμόνιον (what has long been custom is divine). This is exactly Shakespeare's philosophy. 'What custom wills in all things should we do it' (COR. ii, 3). 'Our virtues lie in the interpretation of the time' (*Id.* iv, 7). But illustrations would be endless.

"And in his general reflections on life and death we see how much he has in common, and very strikingly in common, with the Greek dramatists. Is it too much to say that Hamlet's famous soliloquy and the Duke's speech in MEASURE FOR MEASURE are little more than superbly embellished adaptations of the following lines of Euripides (Fragments of PHOENIX quoted by Stobaeus, cxxi, 12) :

> ὦ φιλόζωοι βροτοί,
> οἳ τὴν ἐπιστείχουσαν ἡμέραν ἰδεῖν
> ποθεῖτ᾽ ἔχοντες μυρίων ἄχθος κακῶν.
> οὕτως ἔρως βροτοῖσιν ἔγκειται βίου.
> τὸ ζῆν γὰρ ἴσμεν· τοῦ θανεῖν δ᾽ ἀπειρίᾳ
> πᾶς τις φοβεῖται φῶς λιπεῖν τόδ᾽ ἡλίου.

(O life-loving mortals, who yearn to see the approaching day, burdened though ye be with countless ills, so urgent on all is the love of life ; for life we know, of death we know nothing, and therefore it is that every one of us is afraid to quit this life of the sun) ;

and of the Chorus (1211-48) in the OEDIPUS COLONEUS.

"And as is life such is man. To the Greek dramatists,

'breath and shadow only' (πνεῦμα καὶ σκιὰ μόνον), 'an apparition' (εἴδωλον), 'a thing of a day' (ἰσαμέριός τις), 'a mere nothing' (ἴσος καὶ τὸ μηδέν), 'a creature like a dream' (εἰκελόνειρος) ; to Shakespeare, 'such stuff as dreams are made of,' 'a walking shadow,' 'a poor player that struts and frets his hour upon the stage, and then is heard no more,' 'the quintessence of dust,'—all that is implied in the reflections of Hamlet, of Jacques, of Prospero. But it is not so much in the reflections themselves as in their tone and colour, in the absence of any flavour of cynicism, in the intense sincerity of 'the sense of tears in human things' from which they so obviously spring, that we recognise Shakespeare's kinship with his Greek predecessors. I lay, of course, no stress on these parallels themselves ; all that I wish to emphasise is, that the accentuation of what they express, as well as its note, differentiates the dramas of Shakespeare from those of his contemporaries and allies them with the Greek."

Here we arrive at the propositions (1) that in two great speeches in Shakespearean plays we may "trace" the influence of four lines in the PHOENISSAE; (2) that his references to the force of custom are in exact accord with a line of Sophocles and a fragment of Euripides; (3) that the Duke's speech on death in MEASURE FOR MEASURE and Hamlet's soliloquy are "little more than superbly embellished adaptations" of another Euripidean fragment; and (4) that the way in which Shakespeare speaks of the dream-like shadowiness of life "differentiates" his dramas "from those of his contemporaries and allies them with the Greek."

That is to say, the admittedly learned Jonson and Chapman show no differentiating effect of classical reading, but Shakespeare's writing does. Now, it so happens that all of the matter which Mr. Collins here takes as typically Greek is to be found many times over in Montaigne, to whose Essays he will finally allow no formative influence over Shakespeare, though we *know* that Shakespeare read in them. From this point the argument becomes more and more irrelevant. Admitting that "the development of the author of the plays preceding the second edition of HAMLET into the author of the plays succeeding it . . . is at least difficult to explain as merely the natural result of maturer powers," Mr. Collins goes on : "*If this was the case*, we must assume that instinct led Shakespeare to the Greek conception of the scope and functions of tragedy, and that by a certain natural affinity he caught also the accent and tone as well as some of the most striking characteristics of Greek tragedy."[1] Now, Mr. Collins had already admitted that, rich and plastic as was the genius of Shakespeare, "*its creative energy was never self-evolved.*"[2] He has thus finally failed to face his problem, and we are left with mere generalities which leave the problem untouched.

[1] *Studies,* pp. 86-87.   [2] *Id.* p. 71.

Nothing is made out by arguing, " It is surely
not too much to say that MACBETH, metaphysi-
cally considered, simply *unfolds* what is latent in "
a passage of the AGAMEMNON (210-16) telling
how Agamemnon "when he had put on the yoke-
band of Necessity . . . changed to all - daring
recklessness." Had Shakespeare ever referred to
the AGAMEMNON, the proposition might have had
some significance, however ill it could be supported ;
but as the case stands it has none. And the
further theorem as to an affinity between the
"simplicity and concentration" of Attic tragedy
and the "comprehensiveness and discursiveness" of
Shakespeare's has neither a bearing on the thesis
of "influence," nor any purport save one which
countervails that thesis.

We return yet again, then, to our primary
problem. Can "influence" be no better proved
in regard to Shakespeare's reading of Montaigne
than in regard to his alleged study of the classics ?
To establish the affirmative is the aim of the main
part of this volume ; and as against Mr. Collins's
negative position, which consists so ill with the
method of his exposition concerning the classics,
I will here submit what seem to me to be the
main conditions of a valid proof.

   1. Perusal of one writer by another, later in

time, is in the absence of external evidence to be
established primarily by significant *verbal* coincidences.   When Mr. Collins denies [1] that there is
any real resemblance between Edmund's speech
in LEAR, i, 2, 'This is the excellent foppery of the
world,' etc., and the passage in the essay OF JUDG-
ING OF OTHERS' DEATH, cited by me,[2] he commits
one of several textual oversights, by omitting an
essential part of the passage.   The sentences
textually given by me follow, as I have stated,
upon one in which Montaigne through Florio
speaks of the "common foppery" as to the sun
mourning Cæsar's death for a year ; and this Mr.
Collins does not mention.   But the verbal coincidence is a main part of the clue.

2. A significant verbal coincidence, concurring
with a coincidence of idea, tells of "influence" in
the way of setting up a train of thought.   This
is claimed to occur, for instance, in the passage
last referred to.

3. A series of coincidences, verbal and material,
running through a play or series of plays,
strengthens the proof of influence.

4. Where the influenced author can be shown
—as Mr. Collins virtually admits to be the case
in the development of Shakespeare from HAMLET

[1] *Studies*, pp. 282-83.   [2] Below, p. 108.

onwards — to exhibit a new and important movement of thought and *habit of reflection*, congruous with much that is characteristic in the author exercising the influence proved as aforesaid, we are entitled to count it as important, and to doubt whether such a habit of reflection would have been overtly developed to anything like the same extent in the absence of the influence in question.

If my essay substantially makes out a case of this kind for the influence of Montaigne upon Shakespeare, it is so far justified. If I have failed to show more than that Shakespeare in a number of passages has parallels with Montaigne which might or might not be chance coincidences, the main thesis has broken down. I would merely beg the reader to note that the possibility of chance coincidence is repeatedly recognised by me in regard to passages which would singly count for little, but are noted for the sake of completeness of survey.

I

THE GENERAL SHAKESPEARE PROBLEM

MANY reasonable judgments convey less edification than is unwittingly set up by one of another order, put forth by the late Mr. Halliwell Phillipps in 1850. Later in his life, the same industrious student did good service in commentating Shakespeare ; but it required probably the confidence of youth as well as the pre-evolutionary habit of thought to make possible the utterance in question. "An opinion has been gaining ground," wrote Mr. Halliwell Phillipps, "and has been encouraged by writers whose judgment is entitled to respectful consideration, that almost if not all the commentary on the works of Shakespeare of a necessary and desirable kind has already been given to the world." [1] No critic, it may be presumed, would venture such a deliverance to-day. In an age in which all lore,

[1] Preface to Eng. trans. of Simrock on *The Plots of Shakspere's Plays*, 1850.

down to the pre-suppositions of physics, is being
sceptically reconsidered, it will not be suggested
that the last word has been said on Shakespeare.
Rather may it be said that the body of work
labelled with his name is presenting itself to
critical eyes more and more as a series of problems
calling for a thoroughness of investigation never
yet attained by his most zealous students. The
extent and source of the non-Shakespearean matter
long seen or suspected in many of the plays, their
chronology, the evolution of their style, the
intellectual influences undergone by the poet, his
psychic and ethical cast—all these issues, to say
nothing of the irrepressible Baconian controversy,
and the problem of the sonnets, are more and
more coming to the front in Shakespeare study,
popular and academic. The most searching and
persuasive æsthetic criticism of the great tragedies
yet produced is the fruit of the early years of the
present century ; [1] and if other sides of the study
have been less successfully prosecuted there is
the more need to attend to them.

One of the main difficulties in regard to all
of the problems named is their interdependence.
The nature of Shakespeare's culture-preparation
and moral bias cannot be put with precision

[1] I allude, of course, to Professor Bradley's work.

and comprehensiveness until we settle what is and what is not genuine in the plays ascribed to him ; and in so far as points of chronology turn on points of style, it is necessary to make sure whose style we are reading at any point in the series. Nor, until that be settled, can there be certainty of judgment all along the line as to the ethical content of the dramas. Yet, thus far, the interdependence of the problems in question has hardly been realised. Questions as to Shakespeare's moral idiosyncrasy have been put and answered by critics who have not even noticed the question, *What* is Shakespeare ; and students who work at the problem of culture-influences have either settled with unwarrantable confidence or entirely overlooked the primary problem of discrimination between genuine and spurious matter. Thus Dr. H. R. D. Anders has usefully though imperfectly collected the data as to the literary influences of every kind undergone by the author of the plays ; but has never considered the difficulty of ascribing all the plays to one author. Others have made the same omission in the course of similar undertakings ; and emphatic pronounce-ments upon the poet's mental evolution proceed upon data of the most unequal solidity as to what the poet wrote, and when he wrote it.

If progress is to be made, however, it can hardly be by a simultaneous seizure of all the problems involved. We can but hope to keep the existence of the others in view in the attempt to solve any one. And it is with a full theoretic recognition, at least, of the complexity of the general problem that the present attempt is made to reach critical conclusions upon a special problem which was long ago raised for students of Shakespeare, and which is found to implicate other issues—the problem, namely, of the influence which the plays show their author to have undergone from the Essays of Montaigne.

II

THE THEORY OF MONTAIGNE'S INFLUENCE

As to the bare fact of the influence, there can be little question. That Shakespeare in one scene in the TEMPEST versifies a passage from the prose of Florio's translation of Montaigne's chapter OF THE CANNIBALS has been recognised by all the commentators since Capell (1767), who detected the transcript from a reading of the French only, not having compared the translation. The first thought of students was to connect the passage with Ben Jonson's allusion in VOLPONE[1] to frequent "stealings from Montaigne" by contemporary writers; and though VOLPONE dates from 1605, and the TEMPEST from 1610-1613, there has been no systematic attempt to apply the clue chronologically. Still, it has been recognised or

---

[1] *Lady Politick Would-be.* All our English writers,
I mean such as are happy in the Italian,
Will deign to steal out of this author [*Pastor Fido*] mainly
Almost as much as from Montaignie :
He has so modern and facile a vein,
Fitting the time, and catching the court ear.

Act III, Sc. 2.

surmised by a series of writers that the influence
of the essayist on the dramatist went further than
the passage in question. John Sterling, writing
on Montaigne in 1838 (when Sir Frederick
Madden's pamphlet on the autograph of Shakespeare in a copy of Florio[1] had called special
attention to the Essays), remarked that " on the
whole, the celebrated soliloquy in HAMLET presents
a more characteristic and expressive resemblance
to much of Montaigne's writings than any other
portion of the plays of the great dramatist which
we at present remember " ; and further threw
out the germ of a thesis which has since been
disastrously developed, to the effect that " the
Prince of Denmark is very nearly a Montaigne,
lifted to a higher eminence, and agitated by more
striking circumstances and a severer destiny, and
altogether a somewhat more passionate structure
of man." [2] In 1846, again, Philarète Chasles, an
acute and original critic, citing the passage in the
TEMPEST, went on to declare that " once on the

[1] This is now generally held to be a forgery ; but Mr. W.
Carew Hazlitt (*Shakespear*, 1902, p. 73) argues that the presumption
is still in its favour. It is to be feared that presumption has not
been strengthened by the publication of Mr. Francis P. Gervais,
Shakespeare not Bacon (4to, 1901), in which it is argued that not only
the autograph but the annotations on the volume are Shakespeare's.
They consist mainly of Latin maxims, mostly in a neat Italic
hand.

[2] *London and Westminster Review*, July 1838, p. 321.

track of the studies and tastes of Shakespeare, we find Montaigne at every corner, in HAMLET, in OTHELLO, in CORIOLANUS. Even the composite style of Shakespeare, so animated, so vivid, so new, so incisive, so coloured, so hardy, offers a multitude of striking analogies to the admirable and free manner of Montaigne."[1] The suggestion as to the "To be or not to be" soliloquy has been taken up by some critics, but rejected by others ; and the propositions of M. Chasles, so far as I am aware, have never been supported by evidence. Nevertheless, the general fact of a frequent reproduction or manipulation of Montaigne's ideas in some of Shakespeare's later plays has, I think, since been established.

In 1884 I incidentally cited, in an essay on the composition of HAMLET, some dozen of the Essays of Montaigne from which Shakespeare had apparently received suggestions, and instanced one or two cases in which actual peculiarities of phrase in Florio's translation of the Essays are adopted by him, in addition to a peculiar coincidence which has been independently pointed out by Mr. Jacob Feis in his work entitled SHAKSPERE AND MONTAIGNE ; and since then the late Mr.

---

[1] Article in *Journal des Débats*, November 7, 1846, reprinted in *L'Angleterre au seizième siècle*, ed. 1879, p. 136.

Henry Morley, in his edition of the Florio translation, has pointed to a still more remarkable
coincidence of phrase, in a passage of HAMLET
which I had traced to Montaigne without noticing
the decisive verbal agreement in question. Yet,
so far as I have seen, the matter has passed for
little more than a literary curiosity, arousing no
new ideas as to Shakespeare's mental development.
The notable suggestion of Chasles on that head
has been ignored more completely than the theory
of Mr. Feis, which in comparison is merely
fantastic. Either, then, there is an unwillingness
in England to conceive of Shakespeare as owing
much to foreign influences, or as a case of
intelligible mental growth ; or else the whole critical
problem which Shakespeare represents—and he may
be regarded as the greatest of critical problems—
comes within the general disregard for serious
criticism, noticeable among us of late years. And
the work of Mr. Feis, unfortunately, is as a whole
so extravagant that it could hardly fail to bring a
special suspicion on every form of the theory of
an intellectual tie between Shakespeare and Montaigne. Not only does he undertake to show in
dead earnest what Sterling had vaguely suggested
as conceivable, that Shakespeare meant Hamlet to
represent Montaigne, but he strenuously argues

that the poet framed the play in order to discredit Montaigne's opinions—a thesis which almost makes the Bacon theory specious by comparison. Naturally it has made no converts, even in Germany, where, as it happens, it had been anticipated.

In France, however, the neglect of the special problem of Montaigne's influence on Shakespeare is less easily to be explained, seeing how much intelligent study has been given of late by French critics to both Shakespeare and Montaigne. The influence is recognised ; but here again it is only cursorily traced. An able study of Montaigne has been produced by M. Paul Stapfer, a vigilant critic, whose services to Shakespeare-study have been recognised in both countries. But all that M. Stapfer claims for the influence of the French essayist on the English dramatist is thus put :

"Montaigne is perhaps too purely French to have exercised much influence abroad. Nevertheless his influence on England is not to be disdained. Shakspere appreciated him (*le goûtait*) ; he has inserted in the TEMPEST a passage of the chapter DES CANNIBALES ; and the strong expressions of the Essays on man, the inconstant, irresolute being, contrary to himself, marvellously vain, various and changeful, were perhaps not unconnected with (*peut-être pas étrangères à*) the conception of HAMLET. The author of the scene of the grave-diggers must have felt the savour and retained the impression of this thought, humid and cold as the grave : 'The heart and the life of a great and triumphant emperor are but the repast of a little worm.' The translation of Plutarch, or rather of Amyot, by Thomas North, and that of Montaigne by Florio, had together a great and long vogue in the English society of the seventeenth century." [1]

So modest a claim, coming from the French side, can hardly be blamed on the score of that very modesty. It is the fact, however, that, though M. Stapfer has in another work [2] compared· Shakespeare with a French classic critically enough, he has here understated his case. He was led to such an attitude in his earlier study of Shakespeare by the slightness of the evidence offered for the claim of M. Chasles, of which he wrote that it is " a gratuitous supposition, quite unjustified by the few traces in his writings of his having read the Essays." [3] But that verdict was passed without due scrutiny. The influence of Montaigne on Shakespeare was both wider and deeper than M. Stapfer has suggested ; and it is perhaps more fitting, after all, that the proof should be undertaken by some of us who, speaking Shakespeare's tongue, cannot well be suspected of seeking to belittle him when we trace the sources for his thought, whether in his life or in his culture. There is still, indeed, a tendency among the more primitively patriotic to look jealously at such

---

[1] *Montaigne* (Série des *Grands Écrivains Français*), 1895, p. 105.

[2] *Molière et Shakspere.*

[3] *Shakspere and Classical Antiquity*, Eng. tr. p. 297.

inquiries, as tending to diminish the glory of the worshipped name ; but for any one who is capable of appreciating Shakespeare's greatness, there can be no question of iconoclasm in the matter. Shakespeare ignorantly adored is a mere dubious mystery ; Shakespeare followed up and comprehended, step by step, albeit never wholly revealed, becomes more remarkable, more profoundly interesting, as he becomes more intelligible. We are embarked, not on a quest for plagiarisms, but on a study of the growth of a wonderful mind. And in the idea that much of the growth is traceable to the fertilising contact of a foreign intelligence there can be nothing but interest and attraction for those who have mastered the primary sociological truth that contacts of cultures are the very life of civilisation.

III

THE first requirement in the study, obviously, is an exact statement of the coincidences of phrase and thought in Shakespeare and Montaigne. Not that such coincidences are the main or the only results to be looked for : rather we may reasonably expect to find Shakespeare's thought often diverging at a tangent from that of the writer he is reading, or even directly gainsaying it. But there can be no solid argument as to such indirect influence until we have fully established the direct influence, and this can be done only by exhibiting a considerable number of coincidences. M. Chasles, while avowing that " the comparison of texts is indispensable—we must undergo this fatigue in order to know to what extent Shakespeare, between 1603 and 1615, became familiar with Montaigne "—strangely enough made no comparison of texts whatever beyond reproducing the familiar paraphrase in the TEMPEST, from the essay OF THE CANNIBALS ; and left absolutely unsupported his assertion as to HAMLET, OTHELLO, and CORIOLANUS. It is necessary to produce proofs, and to look narrowly to dates. Florio's translation, though licensed in 1601, was not published till 1603, the year of the piratical publication of the First Quarto of HAMLET, in which the play lacks much of its present matter, and shows in many parts so little trace of Shakespeare's spirit and versification that, even if we hold the text to have been imperfectly taken down in shorthand, as it no doubt was, we cannot suppose him to have at this stage completed his refashioning of the older play, which is undoubtedly the substratum of his.[1] We must therefore keep closely in view the divergences between this text and that of the Second Quarto, printed in 1604, in which the transmuting touch of Shakespeare is broadly evident. It is quite possible, and indeed probable, that Shakespeare saw parts of Florio's translation before 1603, or heard passages from it read. It may indeed have appeared in 1603 before his first revision of the old play which admittedly underlies his HAMLET. In any case, he belonged to the circle of Florio,

---

[1] See this point discussed in the *Free Review* of July 1895 ; and cp. the prize essays of Messrs. Herford and Widgery on *The First Quarto of "Hamlet,"* 1880 ; and the important essay of Mr. John Corbin, on *The Elizabethan Hamlet* (Elkin Matthews, 1895).

who was the friend of Ben Jonson and under the patronage of Lord Southampton ; and in that age the circulation of manuscripts was common. In point of fact we have the testimony of Sir William Cornwallis, published in 1600,[1] that he had seen several of Montaigne's essays in a MS. translation which he praises,—evidently that of Florio, who in turn tells us in his preface that it had passed through various hands. Seeing, too, that the book was licensed for the second time [2] two years before it was actually published, there is a fair presumption that the printing was going on during that period, and that Florio's friends were helping him to read his proofs. It is not certain, further, though it is very likely, that Shakespeare was unable to read Montaigne in the original ; but as it is from Florio that he is seen to have copied in the passages where his copying is beyond dispute, it is on Florio's translation that we must proceed.

I. In order to keep all the evidence in view, we may first of all collate once more the passage in the TEMPEST with that in the Essays which it unquestionably follows. In Florio's translation, Montaigne's words run :

---

[1] *Essays*, by Sir William Cornwalays, 1600, Essay 12.

[2] See Mr. W. C. Hazlitt's *Shakespear*, 1902, pp. 155-6, for an explanation of the two registrations.

" All things (saith Plato) are produced either by nature, by fortune, or by art. The greatest and fairest by one or other of the two first, the least and imperfect by the last. . . . Meseemeth that what in those nations we see by experience doth not only exceed all the pictures wherewith licentious Poesy hath proudly embellished the golden age, and all her quaint inventions to feign a happy condition of man, but also the conception and desire of philosophy.

" They [Lycurgus and Plato] could not imagine a genuity so pure and simple, as we see it by experience, nor ever believe our society might be maintained with so little art and human combination. It is a nation (would I answer Plato) that hath *no kind of traffic, no knowledge of letters,* no intelligence of numbers, *no name of magistrate, nor of politic superiority ; no use of service, of riches, or of poverty ; no contracts, no successions, no dividences, no occupations, but idle ;* no respect of kindred, but common ; no apparel, but natural ; no manuring of lands, *no use of wine, corn, or metal.* The very words that import lying, falsehood, treason, dissimulation, covetousness, envy, detraction, and passion, were never heard of amongst them. How dissonant would he find his imaginary commonwealth from this perfection ? " (Morley's ed. of Florio, p. 94).

Compare the speech in which the kind old Gonzalo seeks to divert the troubled mind of the shipwrecked King Alonso :

> " I' the commonwealth I would by contraries
> Execute all things : for no kind of traffic
> Would I admit ; no name of magistrate ;
> Letters should not be known ; no use of service,
> Of riches, or of poverty ; no contracts,
> Succession ; bound of land, tilth, vineyard, none :
> No use of metal, corn, or wine, or oil :
> No occupation, all men idle, all ;
> And women too : but innocent and pure :
> No sovereignty. . . ."

There can be no dispute as to the direct transcription here, where the dramatist is but incidentally playing with Montaigne's idea, going on to put some gibes at it in the mouths of Gonzalo's rascally comrades ; and it follows that Gonzalo's further phrase, " to excel the golden age," proceeds from Montaigne's previous words : " exceed all the pictures wherewith licentious poesy hath proudly embellished the golden age." The play was in all probability written in or before 1610. It remains to show that on his first reading of Florio's Montaigne, in 1603-4, Shakespeare was more deeply and widely influenced, though the specific proofs are in the nature of the case less palpable.

II. Let us take first the more decisive coincidences of phrase. Correspondences of thought which in themselves do not establish their direct connection, have a new significance when it is seen that other coincidences amount to manifest reproduction. And such a coincidence we have, to begin with, in the familiar lines :

> " There's a divinity that shapes our ends,
> Rough-hew them how we will." [1]

I pointed out in 1884 that this expression, which does not occur in the First Quarto HAMLET,

[1] *Hamlet*, Act V, Sc. 2.

corresponds very closely with the theme of Montaigne's essay, THAT FORTUNE IS OFTENTIMES MET WITHALL IN PURSUIT OF REASON,[1] in which occurs the phrase, "Fortune has more judgment[2] than we," a translation from Menander. But Professor Morley, having had his attention called to the subject by the work of Mr. Feis, who had suggested another passage as the source of Shakespeare's, made a more perfect identification. Reading the proofs of the Florio translation for his reprint, he found, what I had not observed in my occasional access to the old folio, not then reprinted, that the very metaphor of "rough-hewing" occurs in Florio's rendering of a passage in the Essays :[3] "My consultation doth somewhat roughly hew the matter, and by its first shew lightly consider the same : the main and chief point of the work I am wont to resign to Heaven." This is a much more exact coincidence than is presented in the passage cited by Mr. Feis from the essay OF PHYSIOGNOMY :[4] "Therefore do our designs so often miscarry. . . . The heavens are angry, and I may say envious of the extension and large privilege we ascribe to human wisdom, to the prejudice of theirs, and abridge them so

[1] B. I, Ch. 33. [2] *Advice* in Florio.
[3] B. III, Ch. 8. *Of the Art of Conferring.* [4] B. III, Ch. 12.

much more unto us by so much more we endeavour
to amplify them." If there were no closer parallel
than that in Montaigne, we should be bound to
take it as an expansion of a phrase in Seneca's
AGAMEMNON,[1] which was likely to have become
proverbial. I may add that the thought is often
repeated in the Essays,[2] and that in several passages it compares notably with Shakespeare's lines.
These begin :

> " Rashly,
> —And praised be rashness for it—Let us know
> Our indiscretion sometimes serves us well
> When our deep plots do pall ; and that should learn us
> There's a divinity," etc.

Compare the following extracts from Florio's
translation :

" The *Daemon* of Socrates were peradventure a certain
impulsion or will which without the advice of his discourse
presented itself unto him. In a mind so well purified, and
by continual exercise of wisdom and virtue so well prepared
as his was, it is likely his inclinations (though rash and
inconsiderate) were ever of great moment, and worthy to be
followed. Every man feeleth in himself some image of such
agitations, of a prompt, vehement, and casual opinion. It is
in me to give them some authority, that afford so little to our
wisdom. And I have had some (equally weak in reason and
violent in persuasion and dissuasion, which was more ordinary
to Socrates) by which I have so happily and so profitably

---

[1] " Ubi animus errat, optimum est casum sequi."
                              Actus II, Sc. 1, 144.
[2] It is as old as Cæsar. See Plutarch, *Sulla*, c. 6.

suffered myself to be transported, as they might perhaps be thought to contain some matter of divine inspiration." [1]

"Where I seek myself, I find not myself; and I find myself more by chance than by the search of mine own judgment." [2]

"Even in our counsels and deliberations, some chance or good luck must needs be joined to them ; for whatsoever our wisdom can effect is no great matter " [3] (Morley's ed. p. 52).

"When I consider the most glorious exploits of war, methinks I see that those who have had the conduct of them employ neither counsel nor deliberation about them, but for fashion sake, and leave the best part of the enterprise to fortune ; and on the confidence they have in her aid, they still go beyond the limits of all discourse. Casual rejoicings and strange furies ensue among their deliberations," [4] etc.

Compare finally Florio's translation of the lines of Manilius cited by Montaigne at the end of the forty-seventh essay of the First Book :

> " 'Tis best for ill-advis'd, wisdom may fail, [5]
> Fortune proves not the cause that should prevail,
> But here and there without respect doth sail :
> A higher power forsooth us overdraws,
> And mortal states guides with immortal laws."

It is to be remembered, indeed, that the idea expressed in Hamlet's words to Horatio is partly anticipated in the rhymed speech of the Player-

---

[1] B. I, Ch. 11, *end.*   [2] B. I, Ch. 10, *end.*
[3] B. I, Ch. 23.   [4] B. I, Ch. 23.
[5] Some slip of the pen seems to have occurred in this confused line. The original—*Et male consultis pretium est ; prudentia fallax* —is sufficiently close to Shakespeare's phrase.

King in the play-scene in Act III, which occurs in the First Quarto.   There we have :

> " Our wills, our fates do so contrary run
>   That our devices still are overthrown ;
>   Our thoughts are ours, their ends none of our own."

Such a passage, reiterating a familiar common-place, might seem at first sight to tell against the view that Hamlet's later speech to Horatio is an echo of Montaigne.   But that view being found justified by the evidence, and the idea in that passage being exactly coincident with Montaigne's, while the above lines are only partially parallel in meaning, we are led to admit that Shakespeare may have been influenced by Montaigne even where a partial precedent might be found in his own or other English work.

III. The phrase " discourse of reason," which is spoken by Hamlet in his first soliloquy,[1] and which first appears in the Second Quarto, is not used by Shakespeare in any play before HAMLET ; unless we so reckon TROILUS AND CRESSIDA,[2] which was probably rewritten later ; while " discourse of thought " appears in OTHELLO ;[3] and " discourse," in the sense of reasoning faculty, is used in Hamlet's last soliloquy.[4]   In English

---

[1] " O heaven ! a beast that wants discourse of reason."

Act I, Sc. 2.

[2] Act II, Sc. 2.   [3] Act IV, Sc. 2.   [4] Act IV, Sc. 4.

literature the use of the phrase in drama seems to be new in Shakespeare's period,[1] and it has been noted by an admirer as a finely Shakespearean expression. But the expression "discourse of reason" occurs at least four times in Montaigne's Essays, and in Florio's translation of them : in the essay [2] THAT TO PHILOSOPHISE IS TO LEARN HOW TO DIE ; again at the close of the essay [3] *À demain les affaires* (TO-MORROW IS A NEW DAY in Florio) ; again in the first paragraph of the APOLOGY OF RAIMOND SEBONDE ; [4] and yet again in the essay on THE HISTORY OF SPURINA ; [5] and though it seems to be scholastic in origin, and occurs before 1600 in English books, it is difficult to doubt that, like the other phrase above cited, it came to Shakespeare through Florio's Montaigne. The word

[1] See Furniss's Variorum edition of *Hamlet, in loc.* Between the Variorum editions and the *New Dictionary* (which alike overlook Florio) I find only the four following works before 1600 cited as containing the phrase : *The Pilgrimage of the Sowle* (Caxton, 1483), Eden's *Treatise of the Newe India* (1553), Saville's translation of the *Agricola* of Tacitus (1591), and Davys's *Reports* (?). I have myself found it, however, in Geffray Fenton's translation of Guicciardini, 1579, pp. 6, 143, etc. Bacon uses the phrase in 1599 (putative pamphlet on Squire's conspiracy : *Letters and Life*, ii, 116) and in 1605, in the *Advancement of Learning* (B. I, Routledge's ed. of *Works*, 1905, p. 54). Afterwards it is found current in philosophy, *e.g.* Hobbes's phrase "mental discourse" (*Leviathan*, B. I, cc. 3, 7).

[2] B. I, Ch. 19 ; Ed. Firmin-Didot, vol. i, p. 68 (Morley, p. 33).

[3] B. II, Ch. 4 ; Fr. ed. cited, i, 382.

[4] B. II, Ch. 12 ; Fr. ed. cited, i, 459.

[5] B. II, Ch. 33 (Morley, p. 373).

discours is a hundred times used singly by Montaigne, as by Shakespeare in the phrase "of such large discourse," for the process of ratiocination.

IV. Then again there is the clue of Shakespeare's use of the word "consummation" in the revised form of the "To be" soliloquy. This, as Mr. Feis pointed out,[1] is the word used by Florio as a rendering of *anéantissement* in the speech of Socrates as given by Montaigne in the essay [2] OF PHYSIOGNOMY. Shakespeare makes Hamlet speak of annihilation as "a consummation devoutly to be wished." Florio has : "If it (death) be a consummation of one's being, it is also an amendment and entrance into a long and quiet night. We find nothing so sweet in life as a quiet and gentle sleep, and without dreams." Here not only do the words coincide in a peculiar way, but the idea in the two phrases is the same ; the theme of sleep and dreams being further common to the two writings.

Beyond these, I have not noted any correspondences of phrase so precise as to prove reminiscence beyond possibility of dispute ; but it is not difficult to trace striking correspondences which, though falling short of explicit reproduction, inevitably suggest a relation ; and these it

[1] *Shakspere and Montaigne*, 1884, p. 88.   [2] B. III, Ch. 12.

now behoves us to consider. The remarkable
thing is, as regards HAMLET, that they almost all
occur in passages not present in the First Quarto.

V. When we compare part of the speech of
Rosencrantz on sedition[1] with a passage in Montaigne's essay, OF CUSTOM,[2] we find a somewhat
close coincidence. In the play Rosencrantz
says :

> " The cease of *Majesty*,
> Dies not alone ; but like a gulf doth draw
> What's near with it : it is a massy wheel
> Fix'd on the summit of the highest mount,
> To whose huge spokes ten thousand lesser things
> Are mortised and adjoined ; which, when it falls,
> Each small annexment, petty consequence,
> Attends the boisterous ruin."

Florio has :

> "Those who attempt to shake an Estate are commonly
> the first overthrown by the fall of it. . . . The contexture
> and combining of this monarchy and great building having
> been dismissed and dissolved by it, namely, in her old years,
> giveth as much overture and entrance as a man will to like
> injuries. Royal *majesty* doth more hardly fall from the top
> to the middle, than it tumbleth down from the middle to the
> bottom" (Morley's Florio, p. 48.)

The verbal correspondence here is only less
decisive — as regards the use of the word
" majesty " — than in the passages collated by
Mr. Morley ; while the thought corresponds as
closely.

[1] Act III, Sc. 3.   [2] B. I, Ch. 22.

4

VI. The speech of Hamlet,[1] " There is nothing either good or bad but thinking makes it so " ; and Iago's " 'Tis in ourselves that we are thus or thus," [2] are expressions of a favourite thesis of Montaigne's, to which he devotes an entire essay.[3] The Shakespearean phrases echo closely such sentences as :

"If that which we call evil and torment be neither torment nor evil, but that our fancy only gives it that quality, it is in us to change it. . . . That which we term evil is not so of itself." . . . "Every man is either well or ill according as he finds himself."

And in the essay [4] OF DEMOCRITUS AND HERACLI-TUS there is another close parallel :

"Therefore let us take no more excuses from external qualities of things. To us it belongeth to give ourselves account of it. Our good and our evil hath no dependency but from ourselves."

Here, of course, we are in touch with proverbial wisdom ; and the mere phrase " it is the disposition of the thought that altereth the nature of the thing," lay to hand in EUPHUES,[5] which alone might have served to give it English currency. Spenser, too, has the line :

---

[1] Act II, Sc. 2. [2] *Othello,* Act II, Sc. 3.
[3] B. I, Ch. 40, "That the taste of goods or evils doth greatly depend on the opinion we have of them."
[4] B. I, Ch. 50. [5] Arber's rep. p. 43.

"It is the mind that maketh good or ill." [1]

Shakespeare might have met with the thought, indeed, in Dolman's translation of Cicero's Tusculans.[2]   But in HAMLET we find the formula *felt* ; and this in the midst of matter pointing independently to Montaigne for its stimulus.   In EUPHUES it is put as the wayward utterance of the young Euphues justifying his waywardness against an old man's chiding.   Iago and Hamlet speak in a deeper sense ; and it is by Montaigne that such formulas are best vitalised.   Of any moral influence from Spenser, Shakespeare shows no trace.

VII. Hamlet's apostrophe to his mother on the power of custom—a passage which, like the others above cited, first appears in the Second Quarto—is similarly an echo of a favourite proposition of Montaigne, who devotes to it the essay [3] OF CUSTOM, AND HOW A RECEIVED LAW SHOULD NOT EASILY BE CHANGED.   In that there occur the typical passages :

"Custom doth so blear us that we cannot distinguish the usage of things. . . . Certes, chastity is an excellent virtue, the commodity whereof is very well known ; but to use it, and according to nature to prevail with it, is as hard as it is easy to endear it and to prevail with it according to custom, to laws and precepts."   "The laws of conscience, which we say are born of nature, are born of custom" (Morley, pp. 45-46).

---

[1] *Faerie Queene*, B. VI, c. ix, st. 30.
[2] *Tusc. Disp*. iii, 11 ; iv, 7.   [3] B. I, Ch. 22.

Again, in the essay OF CONTROLLING ONE'S WILL [1]
we have : "Custom is a second nature, and not
less potent." [2]

Hamlet's words are :

> "That monster, custom, who all sense doth eat
> Of habits devil, is angel yet in this
> That to the use of actions fair and good
> He likewise gives a frock or livery
> That aptly is put on . . .
> For use can almost change the stamp of nature."

No doubt the idea is a classic commonplace ; and
in Shakespeare's early comedy TWO GENTLEMEN OF
VERONA [3] [adapted, I think, from one by Greene [4]]
we actually have the line, " How use doth breed
a habit in a man " ; but here again there seems
reason to regard Montaigne as having suggested
Shakespeare's vivid and many-coloured wording
of the idea in the tragedy.   Indeed, even the line
cited from the early comedy may have been one
of the poet's many later additions to his text.

VIII. A less close but still a noteworthy
resemblance is that between the passage in which
Hamlet expresses to Rosencrantz and Guildenstern

---

[1] B. III, Ch. 10.

[2] In the essay OF GLORY (B. II, Ch. 16, *end*) we have a citation
from Cicero (*De Fin.* ii.) : "that alone is called honest which is
glorious by popular report" ; and there are many other allusions to
the theme in the Essays ; but in these the application is different.

[3] Act V, Sc. 4.

[4] Cp. Anders, *The Books of Shakespeare*, 1904, pp. 145-6.

the veering of his mood from joy in things to disgust with them, and the paragraph in the Apology of Raimond Sebonde in which Montaigne sets against each other the splendour of the universe and the littleness of man. Here the thought diverges, Shakespeare making it his own as he always does, and altering its aim ; but the language is curiously similar. Hamlet says :

" It goes so heavily with my disposition that this goodly frame, the earth, seems to me a sterile promontory : this most excellent canopy, the air, look you, this brave o'erhanging firmament, this majestical roof, fretted with golden fire, why it appears no other thing to me than a foul and pestilent congregation of vapours. What a piece of work is man ! How noble in reason ! how infinite in faculties ! in form and moving, how express and admirable ! in action, how like an angel ! in apprehension, how like a God ! the beauty of the world ! the paragon of animals ! And yet to me what is this quintessence of dust ? Man delights not me."

Montaigne, as translated by Florio, has :

" Let us see what hold-fast or free-hold he [man] hath in this gorgeous and goodly equipage. . . . Who hath persuaded him, that this admirable moving of heaven's vaults, that the eternal light of these lamps so fiercely rolling over his head . . . were established . . . for his commodity and service ? Is it possible to imagine anything so ridiculous as this miserable and wretched creature, which is not so much as master of himself, exposed and subject to offences of all things, and yet dareth call himself Master and Emperor of this universe ? . . . [To consider . . . the power and domination these [celestial] bodies have, not only upon our lives and conditions of our fortune . . . but also over our dispositions and inclinations, our discourses and wills, which they rule, provoke, and move at the pleasure of their influences.] . . . Of all creatures man is the most miserable and frail, and therewithal the proudest and disdainfullest. Who perceiveth himself placed here, amidst the filth and mire of the world . . . and yet dareth imaginarily place himself above the circle of the Moon, and reduce heaven under his feet. It is through the vanity of the same imagination that he dare equal himself to God."

The passage in brackets is left here in its place, not as suggesting anything in Hamlet's speech, but as paralleling a line in MEASURE FOR MEASURE, to be dealt with later. But it will be seen that the rest of the passage, though turned to quite another purpose than Hamlet's, brings together in the same way a set of contrasted ideas of human greatness and smallness, and of the splendour of the midnight firmament.[1] And though a partly similar train of thought occurs in Cicero's

[1] On reverting to Mr. Feis's book I find that in 1884 he had noted this and others of the above parallels, which I had not observed when writing on the subject in that year. In view of some other parallels and clues drawn by him, our agreements leave me a little uneasy. He decides, for instance (p. 93), that Hamlet's phrase "foul as Vulcan's stithy" is a "sly thrust at Florio" who in his preface calls himself "Montaigne's Vulcan"; that the Queen's phrase "thunders in the index" is a reference to "the Index of the Holy See and its thunders"; and that Hamlet's lines "Why let the stricken deer go weep" are clearly a satire against Montaigne, "who fights shy of action." Mr. Feis's book contains so many propositions of this order that it is difficult to feel sure that he is ever judicious. Still, I find myself in agreement with him on some four or five points of textual coincidence in the two authors.

Tusculans,[1] of which there was already an English translation, and which Shakespeare elsewhere seems to have possibly read, the antithetic element is there lacking.

IX. The nervous protest of Hamlet to Horatio on the point of the national vice of drunkenness,[2] of which all save the beginning is added in the Second Quarto just before the entrance of the Ghost, has several curious points of coincidence with Montaigne's essay[3] on THE HISTORY OF SPURINA, which discusses at great length a matter of special interest to Shakespeare—the character of Julius Cæsar. In the course of the examination Montaigne takes trouble to show that Cato's use of the epithet "drunkard" to Cæsar could not have been meant literally ; that the same Cato admitted Cæsar's sobriety in the matter of drinking. It is after making light of Cæsar's faults in other matters of personal conduct that the essayist comes to this decision :

"But all these noble inclinations, rich gifts, worthy qualities, were altered, smothered, and eclipsed by this furious passion of ambition. . . . To conclude, this only vice (in mine opinion) lost and overthrew in him the fairest natura and richest ingenuity that ever was, and hath made his memory abominable to all honest minds."

---

[1] *Tusc. Disp.* i, 28.   [2] Act I, Sc. 4.
[3] B. II, Ch. 33.

Compare the exquisitely high-strung lines, so congruous in their excited rapidity with Hamlet's intensity of expectation, which follow on his notable outburst on the subject of drunkenness :

> " So oft it chances in particular men,
>   That for some vicious mode of nature in them,
>   As in their birth (wherein they are not guilty,
>   Since nature cannot choose its origin),
>   By the o'ergrowth of some complexion,
>   Oft breaking down the pales and forts of reason ;
>   Or by some habit that too much o'er-leavens
>   The form of plausive manners ; that these men,—
>   Carrying, I say, the stamp of one defect ;
>   Being nature's livery, or fortune's star,—
>   Their virtues else (be they as pure as grace,
>   As infinite as man may undergo)
>   Shall in the general censure take corruption
>   From that particular fault. . . ."

Even the idea that "nature cannot choose its origin" is suggested by the context in Montaigne.[1]

---

[1] It is further relevant to note that in the essay *Of Drunkenness* (ii, 2) Montaigne observes that "drunkenness amongst others appeareth to me a gross and brutish vice," that "the worst estate of man is where he loseth the knowledge and government of himself," and that "the grossest and rudest nation that liveth amongst us at this day, is only that which keepeth it in credit." The reference is to Germany ; but Shakespeare in *Othello* (Act II, Sc. 3) makes Iago pronounce the English harder drinkers than either the Danes or the Hollanders ; and the lines :

> " This heavy-headed revel, east and west,
>   Makes us traduced and taxed of other nations ;
>   They clepe us drunkards, and with swinish phrase,
>   Soil our addition,"

might also be reminiscent of Montaigne, though of course there is nothing peculiar in such a coincidence.

Shakespeare's estimate of Cæsar, of course, diverged from that of the essay.

X. I find a certain singularity of coincidence between the words of King Claudius on kingship :

> " There's such divinity doth hedge a king,
>   That treason can but peep to what it would,
>   Acts little of his will,"

and a passage in the essay [1] OF THE INCOMMODITY OF GREATNESS :

> " To be a king, is a matter of that consequence, that only by it he is so. That strange glimmering and eye-dazzling light, which round about environeth, overcasteth and hideth from us : our weak sight is thereby bleared and dissipated, as being filled and obscured by that greater and further-spreading brightness."

The working out of the metaphor here gives at once to Shakespeare's terms " divinity " and " can but peep " a point not otherwise easily seen ; but the idea of a dazzling light seems to be really what was meant in the play ; and one is inclined to pronounce the passage a reminiscence of Montaigne. And seeing that in the First Quarto we have the lines :

> " There's such divinity doth wall a king
>   That treason *dares not look on*,"

we are again moved to surmise that Shakespeare

[1] B. III, Ch. 7.

had seen or heard the passage in Montaigne before the publication of Florio's folio.

XI. In Hamlet's soliloquy on the march of the army of Fortinbras—one of the many passages added in the Second Quarto—there is a strong general resemblance to a passage in the essay OF DIVERSION.[1]   Hamlet first remarks to the Captain :

> " Two thousand souls and twenty thousand ducats
>   Will not debate the question of this straw :
>   This is the imposthume of much wealth and peace " ;

and afterwards soliloquises :

> " Examples gross as earth exhort me :
> Witness, this army of such mass and charge,
> Led by a delicate and tender prince,
> Whose spirit, by divine ambition puff'd,
> Makes mouths at the invisible event ;
> Exposing what is mortal and unsure
> To all that fortune, death, and danger dare,
> Even for an egg-shell.   Rightly to be great,
> Is not to stir without great argument,
> But greatly to find quarrel in a straw.
> When honour is at stake . . .
>   . . . to my shame I see
> The imminent death of twenty thousand men,
> That for a fantasy and trick of fame,
> Go to their graves like beds ; fight for a plot
> Whereon the numbers cannot try the cause. . . ."

Montaigne has the same general idea in the essay OF DIVERSION :

---

[1] B. III, Ch. 4.

"If one demand that fellow, what interest he hath in such a siege : The interest of example (he will say) and common obedience of the Prince : I nor look nor pretend any benefit thereby . . . I have neither passion nor quarrel in the matter. Yet the next day you will see him all changed, and chafing, boiling and blushing with rage, in his rank of battle, ready for the assault. It is the glaring reflecting of so much steel, the flashing thundering of the cannon, the clang of trumpets, and the rattling of drums, that have infused this new fury and rancour in his swelling veins. A frivolous cause, will you say? How a cause? There needeth none to excite our mind. A doting humour without body, without substance, overswayeth it up and down."

The thought recurs in the essay OF CONTROLLING ONE'S WILL.[1]

"Our greatest agitations have strange springs and ridiculous causes. What ruin did our last Duke of Burgundy run into, for the quarrel of a cart-load of sheep-skins? . . . See why that man doth hazard both his honour and life on the fortune of his rapier and dagger ; let him tell you whence the cause of that confusion ariseth, he cannot without blushing ; so vain and frivolous is the occasion " ;

and again in the essay OF BAD MEANS EMPLOYED TO A GOOD END,[2] where he notes how we are

"daily accustomed to see in our wars many thousands, of foreign nations, for a very small sum of money, to engage both their blood and life in quarrels wherein they are nothing interested."

And the idea in Hamlet's lines "rightly to be

---

[1] B. III, Ch. 10.   [2] B. II, Ch. 23, *end.*

great," etc., is suggested in the essay OF RE-
PENTING,[1] where we have :

> "The nearest way to come unto glory were to do that for
> conscience which we do for glory. . . . The worth of the
> mind consisteth not in going high, but in going orderly. Her
> greatness is not exercised in greatness ; in mediocrity it is."

In the essay OF EXPERIENCE[2] there is a sentence partially expressing the same thought, which
is cited by Mr. Feis as a reproduction :

> "The greatness of the mind is not so much to draw up,
> and hale forward, as to know how to range, direct, and circum-
> scribe itself. It holdeth for great what is sufficient, and
> sheweth her height in loving mean things better than eminent."

Here, certainly, as in the previous citation, the
idea is not identical with that expressed by Hamlet.
But the elements he combines are there ; and
again, in the essay OF SOLITARINESS[3] we have the
picture of the soldier fighting furiously for the
quarrel of his careless king, with the question :
"Who doth not willingly chop and counter-change
his health, his ease, yea his life, for glory and
reputation, the most unprofitable, vain, and counter-
feit coin that is in use with us ? "

And yet again the thought presents itself in
the APOLOGY OF RAIMOND SEBONDE :

> "This horror-causing array of so many thousands of armed
> men, so great fury, earnest fervour, and undaunted courage,

---

[1] B. III, Ch. 2.   [2] B. III, Ch. 13.   [3] B. I, Ch. 38.

it would make one laugh to see on how many vain occasions it is raised and set on fire. . . . The hatred of one man, a spite, a pleasure . . . causes which ought not to move two scolding fishwives to catch one another, is the soul and motive of all this hurly-burly."

XII. Yet one more of Hamlet's sayings peculiar to the revised form of the play seems to be an echo of a thought of Montaigne's. At the outset of the soliloquy last quoted from, Hamlet says :

> "What is a man
> If his chief good and market of his time,
> Be but to sleep and feed ?   A beast ; no more.
> Sure He that made us with such large discourse,
> Looking before and after, gave us not
> That capability and godlike reason
> To fust in us unused."

The bearing of the thought in the soliloquy, where Hamlet spasmodically applies it to the stimulation of his vengeance, is certainly never given to it by Montaigne, who has left on record[1] his small approbation of revenge ; but the thought itself is there, in the essay[2] ON GOODS AND EVILS.

" Shall we employ the intelligence Heaven hath bestowed upon us for our greatest good, to our ruin, repugning nature's design and the universal order and vicissitude of things, which implieth that every man should use his instrument and means for his own commodity ? "

Again, there is a passage in the essay OF THE AFFECTION OF FATHERS TO THEIR CHILDREN,[3]

[1] B. III, Ch. 4.   [2] B. I, Ch. 40.   [3] B. II, Ch. 8.

where there occurs a specific coincidence of phrase, the special use of the term " discourse," which we have already traced from Shakespeare to Montaigne; and where at the same time the contrast between man and beast is drawn, though not to the same purpose as in the speech of Hamlet :

> "Since it hath pleased God to endow us with some capacity of discourse, that as beasts we should not servilely be subjected to common laws, but rather with judgment and voluntary liberty apply ourselves unto them, we ought somewhat to yield unto the simple authority of Nature, but not suffer her tyrannically to carry us away ; only reason ought to have the conduct of our inclinations."

Finally we have a third parallel, with a slight coincidence of terms, in the essay [1] OF GIVING THE LIE :

> "Nature hath endowed us with a large faculty to entertain ourselves apart, and often calleth us unto it, to teach us that partly we owe ourselves unto society, but in the better part unto ourselves."

It may be argued that these, like one or two of the other sayings above cited as echoed by Shakespeare from Montaigne, are of the nature of general religious or ethical maxims, traceable to no one source ; and if we only found one or two such parallels, their resemblance of course would have no evidential value, save as regards coincidence of terms.   For this very passage, for

[1] B. II, Ch. 18.

instance, there is a classic original, or at least a
familiar source, in Cicero,[1] where the commonplace of the contrast between man and beast is
drawn in terms that come in a general way pretty
close to Hamlet's. This treatise of Cicero was
available to Shakespeare in several English translations ;[2] and only the fact that we find no general
trace of Cicero in the play entitles us to suggest a
connection in this special case with Montaigne, of
whom we do find so many other traces. It is
easy besides to push the theory of any influence
too far ; and when, for instance, we find Hamlet
saying he fares " Of the chameleon's dish : I eat
the air, promise-crammed," it would be as idle to
assume a reminiscence of a passage of Montaigne
on the chameleon[3] as it would be to derive
Hamlet's phrase " A king of shreds and patches "
from Florio's rendering in the essay[4] OF THE
INCONSTANCY OF OUR ACTIONS :

"We are all framed of flaps and patches, and of so shape-
less and diverse a contexture, that every ˙piece and every
moment playeth his part."

---

[1] *De Officiis*, i, 4 : cp. 30.

[2] 1534, 1558, 1583, 1600. See also the compilation entitled *A
Treatise of Morall Philosophie*, by W. Baudwin, 4th enlargement by
T. Paulfreyman, 1600, pp. 44-46, where there is a closely parallel
passage from Zeno as well as that of Cicero.

[3] Mr. Feis makes this attribution.

[4] B. II, Ch. 1.

In the latter case we have a mere coincidence of idiom ; in the former a proverbial allusion.[1] An uncritical pursuit of such mere accidents of resemblance has led Mr. Feis to such enormities as the assertion that Shakespeare's contemporaries knew Hamlet's use of his tablets to be a parody of the "much-scribbling Montaigne," who had avowed that he made much use of his ; the assertion that Ophelia's "Come, my coach !" has reference to Montaigne's remark that he has known ladies who would rather lend their honour than their coach ; and a dozen other propositions, if possible still more amazing. But when, with no foregone conclusion as to any polemic purpose on Shakespeare's part, we restrict ourselves to real parallels of thought and expression ; when we find that a certain number of these are actually textual ; when we find further that in a single soliloquy in

---

[1] This may fairly be argued, perhaps, even of the somewhat close parallel, noted by Mr. Feis, between Laertes' lines (i, 3) :

> "For nature, crescent, does not grow alone
> In thews and bulk, but as this temple waxes
> The inward service of the mind and soul
> Grows wide withal,"

and Florio's rendering of an extract from Lucretius in the *Apology* :

> "The mind is with the body bred, we do behold :
> It jointly grows with it, it waxeth old."

Only the slight coincidence of the use of the (then familiar) verb "wax" in both passages could suggest imitation in the case of such a well-worn commonplace.

the play there are several reproductions of ideas in the essays, some of them frequently recurring in Montaigne; and when finally it is found that, with only one exception, all the passages in question have been added to the play in the Second Quarto, after the publication of Florio's translation, it seems hardly possible to doubt that the translation influenced the dramatist in his work.

Needless to say, the influence is from the very start of that high sort in which he that takes becomes co-thinker with him that gives, Shakespeare's absorption of Montaigne being as vital as Montaigne's own assimilation of the thought of his classics. The process is one not of surface reflection, but of kindling by contact; and we seem to see even the vibration of the style passing from one intelligence to the other; the nervous and copious speech of Montaigne awakening Shakespeare to a new sense of power over rhythm and poignant phrase, at the same time that the stimulus of the thought gives him a new confidence in the validity of his own reflection. Some cause there must have been for this marked development in the dramatist at that particular time; and if we find pervading signs of one remarkable new influence, with no countervailing evidence of another adequate to the effect, the inference is about as reasonable as many which pass for valid in astronomy.   For it will be found, on the one hand, that there is no sign worth considering of a Montaigne influence on Shakespeare before HAMLET; and, on the other hand, that the influence to some extent continues beyond that play.   Indeed, there are still further minute signs of it there, which should be noted before we pass on.

XIII. Among parallelisms of thought of a less direct kind, one may be traced between an utterance of Hamlet's and a number of Montaigne's sayings on the power of imagination and the possible equivalence of dream life and waking life.   In his first dialogue with Rosencrantz and Guildenstern, where we have already noted an echo of Montaigne, Hamlet cries :

"O God ! I could be bounded in a nutshell, and count myself a king of infinite space ; were it not that I have bad dreams " ;

and Guildenstern answers :

"Which dreams, indeed, are ambition ; for the very substance of the ambitious is merely the shadow of a dream."

The first sentence may be compared with a

number in Montaigne,[1] of which the following [2] is a type :

"Man clean contrary [to the Gods] possesseth goods in imagination and evils essentially. We have had reason to make the powers of our imagination to be of force, for all our felicities are but in conceit, and as it were in a dream ";

while the reply of Guildenstern further recalls several of the passages already cited.

XIV. Another apparent parallel of no great importance, but of more verbal closeness, is that between Hamlet's jeering phrase : [3] "Your worm is your only emperor for diet," and a sentence in the APOLOGY : "The heart and the life of a great and triumphant emperor are the dinner of a little worm," which M. Stapfer compares further with the talk of Hamlet in the gravediggers' scene. Here, doubtless, we are near the level of proverbial sayings, current in all countries.

XV. As regards HAMLET, I can find no further parallelisms so direct as any of the foregoing, except some to be considered later, in connection with the "To be" soliloquy. I do not think it can be made out that, as M. Chasles affirmed, Hamlet's words on his friendship for Horatio can be traced directly to any of Montaigne's passages on that theme. "It would be easy," says M.

[1] See some cited at the close of this essay in another connection.
[2] B. II, Ch. 12. [3] Act IV, Sc. 3.

Chasles, "to show in Shakespeare the *branloire perenne*[1] of Montaigne, and the whole magnificent passage on friendship, which is found reproduced (*se trouve reporté*) in HAMLET." The idea of the world as a perpetual mutation is certainly prevalent in Shakespeare's work; but I can find no exact correspondence of phrase between Montaigne's pages on his love for his dead friend Étienne de la Boëtie and the lines in which Hamlet speaks of his love for Horatio:

> "Since my dear soul was mistress of her choice
> And could of men distinguish, her election
> Hath sealed thee for herself."

In the succeeding lines he rather gives his reasons for his love than describes the nature and completeness of it in Montaigne's way.

The description of Horatio raises another issue:

> "Thou hast been
> As one, in suffering all, that suffers nothing;
> A man that fortune's buffets and rewards
> Hast ta'en with equal thanks; and blest are those
> Whose blood and judgment are so well commingled
> That they are not a pipe for fortune's finger
> To sound what stop she please. Give me that man
> That is not passion's slave, and I will wear him
> In my heart's core, ay, in my heart of heart,
> As I do thee."

---

[1] "*Le monde est un branloire perenne*" (B. III, Ch. 2). Florio translates that particular sentence: "The world runs all on wheels"—a bad rendering.

Such a speech might proceed from many literary precedents. It could have been independently suggested by, for instance, such a treatise as Seneca's DE CONSTANTIA SAPIENTIS, which is a monody on the theme with which it closes : *esse aliquem invictum, esse aliquem in quem nihil fortuna possit*—" to be something unconquered, something against which fortune is powerless." In the fifth section the idea is worded in a fashion that could have motived Shake'speare's utterance of it ; and he might easily have met with some citation of the kind. But, on the other hand, this note of passionate friendship is not only new in Shakespeare but new in HAMLET, in respect of the First Quarto, where the main part of the speech to Horatio does not occur, and in view of the singular fact that in the first Act of the play as it stands Hamlet greets Horatio as a mere acquaintance. It is further to be noted that the description of Horatio is broadly suggested by the quotation from Horace in Montaigne's essay OF THE INEQUALITY THAT IS BETWEEN US : [1]

> " Sapiens, sibique imperiosus,
> Quem neque pauperies, neque mors, neque vincula terrent,
> Responsare cupidinibus, contemnere honores
> Fortis, et in se ipso totus teres atque rotundus,

---

[1] B. I, Ch. 42.

Externi ne quid valeat per leve morari
In quem manca ruit semper fortuna "

(SAT. II, vii, 83),

which Florio thus translates :

" A wise man, of himself commander high,
Whom want, nor death, nor bands can terrify,
Resolved t'affront desires, honours to scorn,
All in himself, close, round, and neatly-borne
As nothing outward on his smooth can stay,
'Gainst whom still fortune makes a lame assay."

" Such a man," adds Montaigne, " is five hundred degrees beyond kingdoms and principalities : himself is a kingdom unto himself." Here, certainly, is a cue for the speech of Hamlet. It is in part given, too, in an earlier passage in the nineteenth essay (which, as we have already seen, impressed Shakespeare), and by various other sayings in the Essays. After the quotation from Horace (*Non vultus instantis tyranni*), in the nineteenth essay, Florio's translation runs :

" She [the soul] is made mistress of her passions and concupiscences, lady of indigence, of shame, of poverty, and of all fortune's injuries. Let him that can, attain to this advantage. Herein consists the true and sovereign liberty, that affords us means wherewith to jest and make a scorn of force and injustice, and to deride imprisonment, gyves, or fetters."

Again, in the essay OF THREE COMMERCES OR SOCIETIES,[1] we have this :

---

[1] B. III, Ch. 3.

"We must not cleave so fast unto our humours and dispositions. Our chiefest sufficiency is to supply ourselves to diverse fashions. It is a being, but not a life, to be tied and bound by necessity to one only course. The goodliest minds are those that have most variety and pliableness in them. . . . Life is a motion unequal, irregular, and multiform. . . .

". . . My fortune having inured and allured me, even from my infancy, to one sole, singular, and perfect amity, hath verily in some sort distasted me from others. . . . So that it is naturally a pain unto me to communicate myself by halves, and with modification. . . .

"I should commend a high-raised mind that could both bend and discharge itself; that wherever her fortune might transport her, she might continue constant. . . . I envy those which can be familiar with the meanest of their followers, and vouchsafe to contract friendship and frame discourse with their own servants."

Again, La Boëtie is panegyrised by Montaigne for his rare poise of character;[1] in the essay in which Montaigne with his boundless frankness avows his own changeableness and perturbability :

"Of a great man in general, and that hath so many excellent parts together, or but one in such a degree of excellence as he may thereby be admired, or but compared to those of former ages whom we honour, my fortune hath not permitted me to see one. And the greatest I ever knew living (I mean of natural parts of the mind, and the best borne) was Estienne de la Boëtie. Verily it was a complete

---

[1] B. II, Ch. 17. Elsewhere (B. II, Ch. 11) Montaigne names Socrates as his ideal man, and this on the score of his absolute and invariable self-possession ; and in naming La Boëtie as the one modern whom he has met fit to be tested by the ancient standard he ascribes to him a similar type of personality.

mind, and who set a good face and showed a fair countenance upon all matters ; a mind after the old stamp . . ." (Florio, p. 358).

Seeing then that also in the essay OF THREE COMMERCES Montaigne has brought the ideal of the imperturbable man into connection with his ideal of friendship, it could well be—though we cannot hold the point as proved — that in this as in other matters the strong general impression that Montaigne was so well fitted to make on Shakespeare's mind was the source of such a change in the conception and exposition of Hamlet's relation to Horatio as is set up by Hamlet's protestation of his long-standing admiration and love for his friend. Shakespeare's own relations with the friend of the Sonnets might make him specially alive to such suggestion.

XVI. We now come to the suggested resemblance between the " To be or not to be " soliloquy and the general tone of Montaigne on the subject of death. On this resemblance I am less disposed to lay stress now than I was on a first consideration of the subject, many years ago. While I find new coincidences of detail on a more systematic search, I am less impressed by the alleged general resemblance of tone. In point of fact, the general drift of Hamlet's soliloquy is rather alien to the general tone of Montaigne on the same theme. That tone, as we shall see, harmonises much more nearly with the speech of the Duke to Claudio, on the same theme, in MEASURE FOR MEASURE. What really seems to subsist in the "To be" soliloquy, after a careful scrutiny, is a series of echoes of single thoughts.

First, there is the striking coincidence of the word "consummation" (which first appears in the Second Quarto), with Florio's translation of *anéantissement* in the essay OF PHYSIOGNOMY, as above noted. Secondly, there is a curious resemblance between the phrase "take arms against a sea of troubles" and a passage in Florio's version of the same essay, which has somehow been overlooked in the disputes over Shakespeare's line. It runs :

"I sometimes suffer myself by starts to be surprised with the pinchings of these unpleasant conceits, which, whilst I arm myself to expel or wrestle against them, assail and beat me. Lo here another huddle or tide of mischief, that on the neck of the former came rushing upon me."

There arises here the difficulty that Shakespeare's line had been satisfactorily traced to Aelian's[1] story of the Celtic practice of rushing into the sea to resist a high tide with weapons ;

[1] *Varia Historia*, XII, 23.

and the matter must, I think, be left open, on the ground that such a story would pass from mouth to mouth, and so may easily have been heard by Shakespeare, even if he had not met with it in any translation or citation.[1]

Again, the phrase " Conscience doth make cowards of us all " is very like the echo of two passages in the essay [2] OF CONSCIENCE : " Of such marvellous working power is the sting of conscience ; which often induceth us to bewray, to accuse, and to combat ourselves " ; " which as it doth fill us with fear and doubt, so doth it store us with assurance and trust " ; and the lines about " the dread of something after death " might point to the passage in the fortieth essay in which Montaigne cites the saying of Augustine that " Nothing but what follows death, makes death to be evil " (*malam mortem non facit, nisi quod sequitur mortem*) cited by Montaigne in order to dispute it. The same thought, too, is dealt with in the essay [3] on A CUSTOM OF THE ISLE OF CEA, which contains a passage suggestive of Hamlet's earlier soliloquy on self-slaughter.   But,

---

[1] The story certainly had a wide vogue, being found in Aristotle, *Eudemian Ethics*, iii 1, and in Nicolas of Damascus ; while Strabo (VII, ii, § 1) gives it further currency by contradicting it as regards the Cimbri.

[2] B. II, Ch. 5.   [3] B. II, Ch. 3.

for one thing, Hamlet's soliloquies are contrary in drift to Montaigne's argument ; and, for another, the phrase " Conscience makes cowards of us all " existed in the soliloquy as it stood in the First Quarto, while the gist of the idea is actually found twice in a previous play, where it has a proverbial ring.[1] And " the *hope* of something after death " figures in the First Quarto also, where it may be one of the many errors of the piratical reporter.

Finally, there are other sources than Montaigne for parts of the soliloquy, sources nearer, too, than those which have been pointed to in the Senecan tragedies. There is, indeed, as Dr. Cunliffe has pointed out,[2] a broad correspondence between the whole soliloquy and the chorus of women at the end of the second Act of the TROADES, where the question of a life beyond is pointedly put :

> " Verum est ? an timidos fabula decepit,
>   Umbras corporibus vivere conditis ? "

It is true that the choristers in Seneca pronounce definitely against the future life :

> " Post mortem nihil est, ipsaque mors nihil . . .
>   Rumores vacui verbaque inania,
>   Et par sollicito fabula somnio."

---

[1] *Richard III*, I, 4 ; V, 3.
[2] *The Influence of Seneca on Elizabethan Tragedy*, 1893, pp. 80-85.

But wherever in Christendom the pagan's words were discussed, the Christian hypothesis would be pitted against his unbelief, with the effect of making one thought overlay the other ; and in this fused form the discussion may easily have reached Shakespeare's eye and ear. So it would be with the echo of two Senecan passages noted by Mr. Munro in the verses on " the undiscovered country from whose bourn no traveller returns." In the HERCULES FURENS [1] we have :

> "Nemo ad id sero venit, unde nunquam
> Quum semel venit potuit reverti " ;

and in the HERCULES OETAEUS [2] there is the same thought :

> " regnum canis inquieti
> Unde non unquam remeavit ullus."

But here, as elsewhere, Seneca himself was employing a standing sentiment, for in the best known poem of Catullus we have :

> " Qui nunc it per iter tenebricosum
> Illuc, unde negant redire quemquam." [3]

And though there was in Shakespeare's day no English translation of Catullus, the commentators

---

[1] Actus III, 865-866.   [2] Actus IV, 1526-7.
[3] This in turn is an echo from the Greek.   See note in Doering's edition.

long ago noted that in Sandford's translation of Cornelius Agrippa[1] (? 1569), there occurs the phrase, "The countrie of the dead is irremeable, that they cannot return," a fuller parallel to the passage in the soliloquy than anything cited from the classics.

Finally, in Marlowe's EDWARD II,[2] written before 1593, we have :

> " Weep not for Mortimer,
> That scorns the world, and, as a traveller,
> Goes to discover countries yet unknown." [3]

So that, without going to the Latin, we have obvious English sources of suggestion for notable parts of the soliloquy.

Thus though, as we saw, Shakespeare may well (1) have seen part of the Florio translation, or separate translations of some of the essays, before the issue of the First Quarto ; or may (2) have heard that very point discussed by Florio, who was the friend of his friend Jonson, or by those who had read the original ; or may even

---

[1] Described by Steevens as "once a book of uncommon popularity."

[2] Yet again, in Marston's *Insatiate Countess*, the commentators have noticed the same sentiment :
> " Death,
> From whose stern cave none tracks a backward path."

It was in fact a poetic commonplace.

[3] Act V, Sc. 6.

(3) himself have read in the original ; and though further it seems quite certain that his " consummation devoutly to be wished " was an echo of Florio's translation of Montaigne's version of the Apology of Socrates ; on the other hand we are not entitled to trace the soliloquy as a whole to Montaigne's stimulation of Shakespeare's thought. That Shakespeare read Montaigne in the original once seemed probable to me, as to others ; but, on closer study, I consider it unlikely, were it only because the Montaigne influence in his work apparently begins, as aforesaid, in HAMLET. Of all the apparent coincidences I have noticed between Shakespeare's unquestionably previous plays and the essays, none has any evidential value.

XVII. In examining this question, it must be remembered that priority of assigned date for a given play does not carry the consequence that every passage in it is of the date given, even if that be correct. Unquestionably most of the earlier plays were revised by Shakespeare after 1600. We shall see later that an important passage in HENRY V must be post-dated ; and the same process may be found necessary in regard to other passages which raise the question of Montaigne's influence. Professor Collins, in his criticism of the first edition of this work, contended that

"a far more remarkable parallel than any there cited is afforded by a passage in ALL's WELL THAT ENDS WELL (ii, 3):

"'They say that miracles are past : and we have our philosophical persons to make modern and familiar, things supernatural and causeless. Hence is it that we make trifles of errors, ensconcing ourselves into seeming knowledge, when we should submit ourselves to an unknown fear.'

" And Montaigne :

"Nothing is so firmly believed as that which a man knoweth least, nor are there people more assured in their reports than such as tell us fables, such as Alchemists, Prognosticators, *et id genus omne.* To which, if I durst, I would join a rabble of men that are ordinary interpreters and controllers of God's secret designs, presuming to find out the causes of every accident, and to pry into the secrets of God's Divine will, the incomprehensible motives of his works.'" [1]

It is not to be denied that the ideas here coincide ; and the passage from Montaigne had actually been cited by me with a parallel from LEAR.[2] But even in that connection, where the parallel is considerably closer, allowance must be made for the general currency of the thought. It was a common sentiment in Shakespeare's age, as in many centuries before, and in the modern world down till the other day. Shakespeare may indeed have had it freshly suggested to him by Montaigne, but he must also have heard from his elders just

[1] Bk. I, Ch. 31. Morley's Florio, p. 107.
[2] See below, p. 107.

such head-wagging philosophy, a hundred times over.   Bacon's rejoinders[1] show that divines vended it on all hands, then as later.   It was precisely as spontaneous, and it was produced in the same spirit, and in as abundant a quantity, in the age of Shakespeare as in that of Euripides, to one of whose fragments Professor Collins refers as bearing a "still closer resemblance" to the words of Lafeu than they bear to those of Montaigne.[2] If we may not trace it to the book which we know to have stimulated Shakespeare, it is idle to turn for it to Euripides.   Since, however, it was in Montaigne's way to give a new vibration of actuality to commonplaces, he may have played that part for Shakespeare in this as in other instances.   But it does not follow that the contact occurred before the issue of Florio's translation.

The date of ALL'S WELL is still unsettled. Malone and Chalmers put it in 1606 ; Drake and Delius in 1598 ; Dr. Furnivall in 1601-2 ; Mr. Fleay, who takes it to be a recast of LOVE'S LABOUR WON (mentioned by Meres), in 1604, "as near to MEASURE FOR MEASURE as possible." While agreeing with Mr. Fleay as to the date, I have long suspected that the plot was originally

[1] *Novum Organum*, B. I, Aph. 65, 89, etc. ; *Valerius Terminus*, pars. 7 and 8 ; *Filum Labyrinthi* (Eng.), 7, etc.
[2] *Studies*, pp. 57-8, 284.

Greene's, being very much in his taste ; and that there are still in it some remains of his diction. In any case, if the play as it stands is to be dated 1604, the question of a pre-Florio study of Montaigne does not arise ; and if we put it before 1603 there still remains the likelihood of a later revision. Unquestionably the diction of Lafeu's speech is in the manner and spirit of the prose in LEAR, and neither in the manner nor in the spirit of the prose of the earlier plays. And the same may be said of the speech of the first Lord in Act IV, Sc. 3, of ALL'S WELL :

" The web of our life is of a mingled yarn, good and ill together : our virtues would be proud if our faults whipped them not ; and our crimes would despair if they were not cherished by our virtues " ;

to which there are notable parallels in Montaigne's essay OF VANITY : [1]

" No man is so exquisitely honest or upright in living but brings all his actions and thoughts within compass and danger of the laws, and that ten times in his life might not lawfully be hanged "

(which recalls also Hamlet's " Give every man his deserts and who shall 'scape whipping ? "), and again in the essay WE TASTE NOTHING PURELY : [2]

" When I religiously confess myself unto myself, I find

---

[1] B. III, Ch. 9.   Florio, p. 507.
[2] B. II, Ch. 20.   Florio, p. 345.

the best good I have hath some vicious taint. . . . Man is
all but a botching and parti-coloured work.   The very laws
of justice cannot subsist without some commixture of
injustice."

Here again, of course, in the absence of a
verbal coincidence, we cannot assert with confidence any literary contact : such thoughts could
occur to Englishmen as to Frenchmen.   But the
fact remains that they do not occur in Shakespeare
in plays or parts of plays known to have been
written before 1603 ; and here they suggest, if
any Montaigne influence, one occurring from the
perusal of Florio's translation.

For proofs of an influence before 1603, then,
we must turn to plays which may without
hesitation be assigned in whole to that period ;
and the only semblances of parallel that I have
noted in such plays give us small foothold.

(1) The lines on the music of the spheres in
the MERCHANT OF VENICE[1] recall the passage on
the subject in Montaigne's essay OF CUSTOM ; [2]
but then the original source is Cicero, IN SOMNIUM

[1] Act V, Sc. 1.

[2] Bk. I, Ch. 22.   Dr. R. Beyersdorff, who says of Shakespeare's
knowledge of Montaigne, " aber auch das französische Original muss
er schon früher gekannt haben " (Art. on " Giordano Bruno und
Shakespeare " in *Shakespeare Jahrbuch* for 1891), on the strength
of the passage under notice, has overlooked the existence of the
translation of the *Somnium*.

Scipionis, which had been translated into English in 1577; and the idea is alluded to at the end of Sidney's Apologie for Poetrie, which, written about 1581, must have circulated in manuscript before being printed in 1595.

(2) Falstaff's rhapsody on the virtues of sherris[1] recalls a passage in the essay Of Drunkenness,[2] but then Montaigne avows that what he says is the common doctrine of wine-drinkers.

(3) Montaigne cites[3] a variant[4] of the old saying of Petronius, *Totus mundus agit histrionem*, which occurs in the form "all the world's a stage," in As You Like It; but the Shakespearean phrase was already current in England, being found in Thomas Newton's stanzas "to the reader in the behalfe of this book," prefixed in 1587 to John Higgins's expanded edition of the Mirrour of Magistrates :

> "Certes this worlde a Stage may well be calde
> Whereon is playde the parte of ev'ry wight."

Indeed, even apart from such vernacular adaptations, the phrase of Petronius, being preserved by John of Salisbury, would be known to many in England, and is actually found in some modification in several pre-Shakespearean plays. It is in

---

[1] 2 *Henry IV*, iv, 3.   [2] B. II, Ch. 2.   [3] B. II, Ch. 10.
[4] "Mundus universus exercet histrioniam."

fact recorded to have been the motto of the
Globe Theatre.

(4) In the essay of Mr. Francis P. Gervais,
SHAKESPEARE NOT BACON,[1] perhaps the least far-
fetched parallel put forward is that between a
passage in As You LIKE IT and one in the essay
OF CRUELTY,[2] on stag-hunting, where the " poor
silly and innocent beast" who "doth bequeath
himself unto us," "with tears suing to us for
mercy," certainly recalls Shakespeare's " poor
sequestered stag," with the tears running down
" his innocent nose," who according to Jaques
"makes a testament."[3]   The idea in the lines
as to the "testament," it must be confessed, is
quite different from Montaigne's.   If, however,
we stretch a point and pronounce the verbal connection sufficient to prove contact, we do but find
that, since As You LIKE IT cannot be dated before
the latter half of 1599,[4] Shakespeare could have
seen the translation of the essay in manuscript,
as Cornwallis had seen others in or before 1600.
Thus, while we are the more strongly convinced
of a Montaigne influence beginning with HAMLET,

[1] "At the Unicorn, 7 Cecil Court, St. Martin's Lane," 1901.
4to.

[2] B. II, Ch. 11 (Mr. Gervais gave a wrong reference).

[3] *As You Like It*, Act II, Sc. 1.

[4] See Fleay's *Life of Shakespeare*, pp. 208-9.   Dr. Furnivall
dates the play 1600.

we are bound to concede the relative doubtfulness
of any apparent influence before 1603. At most
we may say that both of Hamlet's soliloquies
which touch on suicide probably owe something to
the discussions set up by Montaigne's essays.
We cannot reasonably suppose that Shakespeare
owed to Montaigne the thought put in the lines

> " Or that the everlasting had not fixed
>   His canon 'gainst self-slaughter."

Commentators have naïvely wondered to what
" canon " Hamlet alludes. It is presumably the
pagan doctrine that the deity forbids men's departure from life without leave, as the soldier is
forbidden to leave his post. This is cited by
Montaigne in the essay on A CUSTOM OF THE ISLE
OF CEA, as an opinion held by many. But Shakespeare could have found the passage in Cicero's
TUSCULANS [1] translated in Dolman's version of
1561 :

" For that God that ruleth within us, forbiddeth us to
depart hence without his leave " ;

and he might well have read the similar passage in
the SOMNIUM SCIPIONIS,[2] in the translation of

[1] " Vetat enim dominans ille in nobis deus injussu hinc nos suo
demigrare."—*Tusc. Disp.* i, 30 (74).

[2] " Nec injussu ejus a quo ille est vobis datus, ex hominum vita
migrandum est ; ne munus humanum assignatum a Deo, defugisse
videamini." Cap. iii.

1577, or that in the DE SENECTUTE,[1] of which there
were at least two current translations.   But he need
not even have gone for it to translations from the
classics, for he could have found it in Spenser,[2]
who doubtless got it from Cicero.   Indeed, he may
even have found it in the original HAMLET ; since
Kyd, in his translation of the CORNÉLIE of Garnier
(1594), reproduces [3] that dramatist's adaptation of
the maxim of Cicero, that the soul is as a garrison
placed by heaven in a fort, which it must not
desert without leave.   The vogue of the sentiment
in Elizabethan literature, in short, is one more
warning against the ascription of classical knowledge to Shakespeare in respect of every classical
commonplace he may happen to cite.

XVIII. In the case of the Duke's exhortation
to Claudio in MEASURE FOR MEASURE, on the
contrary, the whole speech may be said to be a
synthesis of favourite propositions of Montaigne.
The pervading thought in itself, of course, is not
new or out-of-the-way ; much of it is to be found
suggested in the Greek and Latin classics ; [4] it is

---

[1] "Vetat Pythagoras injussu imperatoris, id est Dei, de praesidio
et statione vitae decedere."   Cap. xx.

[2] *Faerie Queene*, B. I, c. ix, st. 41.

[3] *Cornelia*, Act III, ll. 326-337, ed. Boas.

[4] Says Cicero : "Alcidamas quidem, rhetor antiquus in primis
nobilis, scripsit etiam laudationem mortis, quae constat ex enumera-
tione humanorum malorum."—*Tusc. Disp*. i, 48 (§ 116).

in part put forth by Augustine,[1] and the suggestion as to death and sleep, which is of the nature
of a commonplace, had been made universally
familiar by the dying speech of Socrates ; but in
the light of what is certain for us as to Shakespeare's study of Montaigne, and of the special
resemblances noted below, it is difficult to doubt
that Montaigne is for Shakespeare the source of
stimulus. Let us take a number of passages from
Florio's translation of the nineteenth essay, to
begin with :

"The end of our career is death : it is the necessary
object of our aim ; if it affright us, how is it possible
we should step one foot further without an ague ?"

"What hath an aged man left him of his youth's vigour,
and of his forepast life ? . . . When youth fails in us, we
feel, nay we perceive, no shaking or transchange at all in
ourselves : which in essence and verity is a harder death
than that of a languishing and irksome life, or that of age.
Forasmuch as the leap from an ill being into a not being is
not so dangerous or steepy as it is from a delightful and
flourishing being into a painful and sorrowful condition. A
weak bending and faint stopping body hath less strength to
bear and undergo a heavy burden : So hath our soul."

"Our religion hath no surer human foundation than the
contempt of life. Discourse of reason doth not only call
and summon us unto it. For why should we fear to lose a
thing, which being lost, cannot be moaned ? But also, since
we are threatened by so many kinds of death, there is no

---

[1] *De Civ. Dei*, xiii, 9-11.

more inconvenience to fear them all than to endure one : what matter it when it cometh, since it is unavoidable ? . . . Death is a part of yourselves ; you fly from yourselves. The being you enjoy is equally shared between life and death. The first day of your birth doth as well address you to die as to live. . . . The continual work of your life is to contrive death ; you are in death during the time you continue in life . . . during life you are still dying."

" A thousand men, a thousand beasts, and a thousand other creatures die in the very instant that you die . . .

" Had you not had death, you would then uncessantly curse and cry out against me [Nature] that I had deprived you of it."

The same line of expostulation occurs in other essays. In the fortieth we have :

" Now death, which some of all horrible things call the most horrible, who knows not how others call it the only haven of this life's torments ? the sovereign good of nature ? the only stay of our liberty ? and the ready and common receipt of our evils ? . . .

". . . Death is but felt by discourse, because it is the emotion of an instant. A thousand beasts, a thousand men, are sooner dead than threatened."

Then take a passage occurring near the end of the APOLOGY OF RAIMOND SEBONDE :

" We do foolishly fear a kind of death, whereas we have already passed and daily pass so many others. . . . The flower of age dieth, fadeth, and fleeteth, when age comes upon us, and youth endeth in the flower of a full-grown man's age, childhood in youth, and the first age dieth in infancy ; and yesterday endeth in this day, and to-day shall die in to-morrow."

Turn again to the last essay of all, OF EXPERI-
ENCE, which runs so much to commentary on
disease and death :

" Look on an aged man, who sueth unto God to maintain
him in perfect, full, and vigorous health. . . . Is it not
folly ? The gout, the stone, the gravel and indigestion are
symptoms or effects of long-continued years." . . . " Consider his [disease's] slowness in coming : he only incom-
modeth that state and incumbereth that season of thy life
which . . . is now become barren and lost. . . . Thou art
seen to sweat with labour, to grow pale and wan, to wax red,
to quake and tremble, to cast and vomit blood, to endure
strange contractions, to brook convulsions. . . . Thou diest
not because thou art sick ; thou diest because thou art
living. . . . The cholic is oftener no less long-lived than
you. . . . If thou embrace not death, at least thou takest her
by the hand once a month." " Even now I lost one of my
teeth. . . . That part of my being, with divers others, are
already dead. . . . Death intermeddleth and everywhere
confounds itself with our life."

Now compare textually the Duke's speech :

" Be absolute for death : either death or life
    Shall thereby be the sweeter. Reason thus with life :—
If I do lose thee, I do lose a thing
That none but fools would keep : a breath thou art
(Servile to all the skiey influences)
That dost this habitation, where thou keep'st,
Hourly afflict : merely, thou art death's fool ;
For him thou labour'st by thy flight to shun,
And yet run'st towards him still : Thou art not noble ;
For all the accommodations that thou bear'st
Are nursed by baseness : Thou art by no means valiant,
For thou dost fear the soft and tender fork

Of a poor worm : Thy best of rest is sleep,
And that thou oft provok'st ; yet grossly fear'st
Thy death, which is no more.   Thou art not thyself ;
For thou exist'st on many thousand grains
Which issue out of dust : Happy thou art not ;
For what thou hast not, still thou striv'st to get,
And what thou hast forget'st : Thou art not certain,
For thy complexion shifts to strange effects,
After the moon : If thou art rich, thou art poor ;
For, like an ass whose back with ingots bows,
Thou bear'st thy heavy riches but a journey,
And death unloads thee : Friend hast thou none ;
For thine own bowels, which do call thee sire,
Do curse the gout, serpigo, and the rheum,
For ending thee no sooner : Thou hast no youth nor age,
But, as it were, an after-dinner's sleep,
Dreaming on both : for all thy blessed youth
Becomes as aged, and doth beg the alms
Of palsied eld ; and when thou art old and rich,
Thou hast neither heat, affection, limbs, nor beauty,
To make thy riches pleasant.   What's yet in this,
That bears the name of life ?   Yet in this life
Lie hid more thousand deaths : yet death we fear,
That makes these odds all even." [1]

Then collate yet further some more passages from
the Essays :

"They perceived her [the soul] to be capable of diverse
passions, and agitated by many languishing and painful
motions . . . subject to her infirmities, diseases, and offences,

---

[1] When this is compared with the shorter speech of similar drift
in the anonymous play of *Edward III* (" To die is all as common
as to live," etc., Act IV, Sc. 4) it will be seen that the querying form
as well as the elaboration constitutes a special resemblance between
the speech in Shakespeare and the passages in Montaigne.

even as the stomach or the foot . . . dazzled and troubled by the force of wine ; removed from her seat by the vapours of a burning fever. . . . She was seen to dismay and confound all her faculties by the only biting of a sick dog, and to contain no great constancy of discourse, no virtue, no philosophical resolution, no contention of her forces, that might exempt her from the subjection of these accidents. . . ." [1]

" It is not without reason we are taught to take notice of our sleep, for the resemblance it hath with death. How easily we pass from waking to sleeping ; with how little interest we lose the knowledge of light, and of ourselves. . . ." [2]

" Wherefore as we from that instant take a title of being, which is but a twinkling in the infinite course of an eternal night, and so short an interruption of our perpetual and natural condition, death possessing whatever is before and behind this moment, and also a good part of this moment." [3]

" Every human nature is ever in the middle between being born and dying, giving nothing of itself but an obscure appearance and shadow, and an uncertain and weak opinion." [4]

Compare finally the line " Thy best of rest is sleep " (where the word " rest " seems a printer's error) with the passage " We find nothing so sweet in life as a quiet and gentle sleep," already cited in connection with our fourth parallel.

XIX. The theme, in fine, is one of Montaigne's favourites. And the view that Shakespeare had been impressed by it seems to be decisively cor-

---

[1] *Apology of Raimond Sebonde.* Morley's ed. of Florio, p. 280.
[2] Bk. II, Ch. 6, *Of Exercise or Practice.*
[3] *Apology*, Morley's Florio, p. 267. [4] *Ibid.* p. 309.

roborated by the fact that the speech of Claudio
to Isabella, expressing those fears of death which
the Duke seeks to calm, is likewise an echo of a
whole series of passages in Montaigne. Shakespeare's lines run :

> " Ay, but to die, and go we know not where,
>   To lie in cold obstruction and to rot :
>   This sensible warm motion to become
>   A kneaded clod ; and the delighted spirit
>   To bathe in fiery floods or to reside
>   In thrilling regions of thick-ribbèd ice ;
>   To be imprisoned in the viewless winds,
>   And blown with restless violence round about
>   The pendent world ; or to be worse than worst
>   Of those, that lawless and incertain thoughts
>   Imagine howling !—'tis too horrible ! . . ."

So far as I know, the only ideas in this passage
which belong to the current English superstition
of Shakespeare's day, apart from the natural
notion of death as a mere rotting of the body,
are that of the purgatorial fire and that as to the
souls of criminals (as of unbaptised children)
being blown about until the day of judgment.
The notion may be traced back to the account
given by Empedocles, as cited in Plutarch,[1] of
the punishment of the offending daemons, who
were whirled between earth and air and sun and

[1] *On Isis and Osiris,* c. 26.

sea ; and from paganism it had passed into popular Christianity. For Chaucer's day,

> " brekers of the lawë, soth to seyne,
> And lecherous folk, after that they be dede,
> Shal alwey whirle aboutë therthe in peyne " ; [1]

and doubtless the belief subsisted popularly in Shakespeare's.[2] Dante's INFERNO, with its pictures of carnal sinners tossed about by the winds in the dark air of the second circle,[3] and of traitors punished by freezing in the ninth,[4] was probably not known to the dramatist ; nor does Dante's vision coincide with Claudio's, in which the souls are blown " about the pendent world." Shakespeare may indeed have heard some of the old tales of a hot and cold purgatory, such as that of Drihthelm, given by Bede,[5] whence (rather than from Dante) Milton drew his idea of an alternate torture.[6] But there again, the correspondence is only partial ; whereas in Montaigne's APOLOGY

---

[1] Chaucer, *The Parlement of Foules*, 78-80.

[2] It does not figure in Spenser, however (cp. *Faerie Queene*, B. I, c. II, xix, 9, with B. II, c. VIII, xlv, 8-9), though he makes a paynim soul wander on the shores of Styx (I, IV, xlviii, 9).

[3] Canto v.   [4] Canto xxxii.

[5] It would seem to be from those early monkish legends that the mediæval Inferno was built up. The torture of cold was the northern contribution to the scheme. Compare Warton, *History of English Poetry*, sec. 49 ; Farmer's *Essay on the Learning of Shakespeare*, ed. 1767, p. 24 ; and Wright's *Saint Patrick's Purgatory*, 1844, p. 18.

[6] *Paradise Lost*, B. II, 587-603.

OF RAIMOND SEBONDE we find, poetry apart, nearly every notion that enters into Claudio's speech :

"The most universal and received fantasy, and which endureth to this day, hath been that whereof Pythagoras is made author . . . which is that souls at their departure from us did but pass and roll from one to another body, from a lion to a horse, from a horse to a king, incessantly wandering up and down, from house to mansion. . . . Some added more, that the same souls do sometimes ascend up to heaven, and come down again. . . . Origen waked them eternally, to go and come from a good to a bad estate. The opinion that Varro reporteth is, that in the revolutions of four hundred and forty years they reconjoin themselves unto their first bodies. . . . Behold her [the soul's] progress elsewhere : He that hath lived well reconjoineth himself unto that star or planet to which he is assigned ; who evil, passeth into a woman. And if then he amend not himself, he transchangeth himself into a beast, of condition agreeing to his vicious customs, and shall never see an end of his punishments until . . . by virtue of reason he have deprived himself of those gross, stupid, and elementary qualities that were in him. . . . They [the Epicureans] demand, what order there should be if the throng of the dying should be greater than that of such as be born . . . and demand besides, what they should pass their time about, whilst they should stay, until any other mansion were made ready for them. . . . Others have stayed the soul in the deceased bodies, wherewith to animate serpents, worms, and other beasts, which are said to engender from the corruption of our members, yea, and from our ashes. . . . Others make it immortal without any science or knowledge. Nay, there are some of ours who have deemed that of condemned men's souls devils were made. . . ."[1]

---

[1] Edit. Firmin-Didot, i, 597-598 ; Florio, pp. 283-4.

It is at a short distance from this passage that we find the suggestion of a frozen purgatory :

"Amongst them [barbarous nations] was also found the belief of purgatory, but after a new form, for what we ascribe unto fire they impute unto cold, and imagine that souls are both purged and punished by the rigor of an extreme coldness." [1]

XX. Over and above this peculiar correspondence between the Essays and the two speeches on death, we may note how some of the lines of the Duke in the opening scene connect with two of the passages above cited in connection with Hamlet's last soliloquy, expressing the idea that nature or deity confers gifts in order that they should be used. The Duke's lines are among Shakespeare's best :

> "Thyself and thy belongings
> Are not thine own so proper as to waste
> Thyself upon thy virtues, them on thee.
> Heaven doth with us as we with torches do,
> Not light them for themselves : for if our virtues
> Did not go forth of us, 'twere all alike
> As if we had them not.   Spirits are not finely touched
> But to fine issues : nor nature never lends
> The smallest scruple of her excellence
> But, like a thrifty goddess, she determines
> Herself the glory of a creditor,
> Both thanks and use. . . ."

Here we have once more a characteristically

[1] Edit. Firmin-Didot, i, 621 ; Florio, p. 294.

Shakespearean transmutation and development of the idea rather than a reproduction ; and the same appears when we compare the admirable lines of the poet with a homiletic sentence from the Apology of Raimond Sebonde :

> " It is not enough for us to serve God in spirit and soul ; we owe him besides and we yield unto him a corporal worshipping : we apply our limbs, our motions, and all external things to honour him."

But granting the philosophic as well as the poetic heightening, we are still led to infer a stimulation of the poet's thought by the Essays—a stimulation not limited to one play, but affecting other plays written about the same time. Another point of connection between Hamlet and Measure for Measure is seen when we compare the above passage, " Spirits are not finely touched but to fine issues," with Laertes' lines : [1]

> " Nature is fine in love, and when 'tis fine
> It sends some precious instance of itself
> After the thing it loves."

And though such data are of course not conclusive as to the time of composition of the plays, there is so much of identity between the thought in the Duke's speech, just quoted, and a notable passage in Troilus and Cressida, as to strengthen

[1] Act IV, Sc. 5.

greatly the surmise that the latter play was also written, or rather worked-over, by Shakespeare about 1604. The phrase :

> "if our virtues
> Did not go forth or us, 'twere all the same
> As if we had them not,"

is developed in the speech of Ulysses to Achilles [1] in Troilus :

> " A strange fellow here
> Writes me that man—how dearly ever parted
> How much in having, or without, or in—
> Cannot make boast to have that which he hath,
> Nor feels not what he knows, but by reflection ;
> As when his virtues shining upon others
> Heat them, and they retort their heat again
> To the first giver."

It is of some importance to trace the origins of this passage, since there is involved the old issue as to Shakespeare's direct knowledge of the classics. The late Mr. Churton Collins, in an essay entitled "Did Shakespeare read the Greek Tragedies ?" [2] undertook to prove that he read Latin with ease, and knew the Greek classics in Latin versions ; and part of his attempted proof consists in tracing the passage before us to Plato. Mr. Collins devoted so much learning and zeal to the serious study of Shakespeare that one is

---

[1] Act III, Sc. 3.
[2] Reprinted in his *Studies in Shakespeare*, 1904.

reluctant to discard his results ; but in this case
they are clearly fallacious. Beginning his quotation
from Troilus and Cressida with the phrase,
"A strange fellow here writes me," he oddly
elides the essential speech of Ulysses,[1] and proceeds
to cite as completing the passage the lines of
Achilles in reply :

> "The beauty that is borne here in the face
>   The bearer knows not, but commends itself
>   To others' eyes ; nor doth the eye itself,
>   That most pure spirit of sense, behold itself,
>   Not going from itself, but eye to eye opposed
>   Salutes each other with each other's form ;
>   For speculation turns not to itself
>   Till it hath travell'd, and is mirror'd there
>   Where it may see itself."

Then Mr. Collins advances[2] the proposition
that the "strange fellow" of Ulysses' speech is
clearly Socrates, because in the Platonic dialogue
First Alcibiades Socrates is made to say :

---

[1] Mr. Collins carried his oversight here to the point of completely
misstating my argument. He represented me (p. 33, *note*) as suggesting that "the passage" was borrowed from Seneca ; going on to
declare that "there is not the smallest parallel in the passages cited
from Seneca." The parallel I indicated is avowedly drawn with the
passage *elided by Mr. Collins from his quotation.* There, it is his
own parallel that breaks down, as does the next drawn by him.

[2] The suggestion was made before him by Richard Grant White,
Art. "Glossaries and Lexicons" (1869 ?) reprinted in his *Studies in
Shakespeare*, 1885, p. 299. Mr. Collins was unaware of this when
he wrote his essay. The fact that White and he independently saw
the parallel is of course in favour of their argument.

"You have observed then that the face of him who looks into the eye of another appears visible to himself in the eye of the person opposite to him. . . . An eye, therefore, beholding an eye and looking into that in the eye which is most perfect, and which is the instrument of vision, would thus see itself? . . . Then if the eye is to see itself, it must look at the eye and at that part of the eye in which the virtue of the eye resides, and which is like herself. . . . Nor should we know that we were the persons to whom anything belonged, if we did not know ourselves."

Further, Mr. Collins puts it as beyond question that the further lines of Ulysses :

> "'No man is the lord of anything
> Though in and of him there be much consisting
> Till he communicates his parts to others,'

"*are derived* from an earlier paragraph in the dialogue : 'When a person is able to impart his knowledge to another, that surely proves his own understanding of any matter.'"

Obviously, the last derivation is astray. The two propositions are fundamentally different, that of Ulysses being a restatement of that cited by him from "a strange fellow," whereas this second citation from Plato is a familiar commonplace with another purport. But this is not all. Putting aside for the moment the fact that Mr. Collins has so handled the passage as to make "a strange fellow here" father not what Ulysses quotes but what Achilles says in comment, we have to note that even the proposition of Achilles was sub-

stantially a literary commonplace in the England
of Shakespeare's day, and is *not* the special proposition cited from Plato. Shakespeare had
previously used the idea in JULIUS CÆSAR :

> " the eye sees not itself
> But by reflection, by some other things " ; [1]

and on that passage the commentators long ago
cited two parallels from Sir John Davies' poem
NOSCE TEIPSUM [2] (1599) besides a later one from
Marston's PARASITASTER (1606).   And even apart
from these instances, which could probably be
multiplied on search, the main thought lay to
Shakespeare's hand in a much more accessible
classic than the Latin translation of Plato, to wit,
in Dolman's English translation [3] of Cicero's
TUSCULANS, where the passage :

> " Non valet tantum animus, ut se ipse videat ; at ut
> oculus sic animus se non videns alia cernit.   Non videt
> autem, quod minimum est, formam suam " [4]

---

[1] Act I, Sc. 2.

[2] See Davies' *Complete Poems*, Grosart's ed. 1876, i, 20, 25. The
same ascription has recently been made by Mr. Charles Crawford
(*Collectanea*, ii, 95-97) ; and there is one special ground, not noted
by Mr. Crawford or the commentators, for looking to Davies'
poem as a source for the passage in *Troilus*. Davies in the same
poem twice uses the expression "spirits of sense" (ed. cited, pp. 71,
73) ; and in the speech of Achilles "spirit of sense" is used in the
same application. It occurs also in Act I, Sc. 1.

[3] *Those fyve Questions which M. Tullye Cicero disputed in his
manor of Tusculum* . . . englished by J. Dolman, 1561.

[4] *Tusc. Disp*. i, 28.

is thus paraphrased :

> "The soul is not able in this body to see himself. No more is the eye, which, although he seeth all other things, yet (that which is one of the least) cannot discern his own shape."

But it is surely plain, further, that the proposition of Achilles is not that of Ulysses, and that Shakespeare presents the former as missing the idea of the latter while professing to assent to it. And this idea, which is the purport of Ulysses' whole argument, is not at all involved in the passage cited from the Platonic dialogue, while on the other hand it frequently occurs in Montaigne.[1] In the essay OF COACHES [2] we have :

> "For, taking the matter exactly as it is, a king hath nothing that is properly his own : he oweth even himself to others. . . . A superior is never created for his own profit ; but rather for the benefit of the inferior ; and a physician is instituted for the sick, not for himself. All magistracy, even as each art, rejecteth her end out of herself. *Nulla ars in se versatur*.[3] 'No art is all in itself.'"

Here we have a close parallel to the passage in MEASURE FOR MEASURE, and at the same time the gist of that in TROILUS AND CRESSIDA. But again, in the essay OF VANITY,[4] we have :

> "I am of this opinion, that the honorablest vocation is

---

[1] In the first edition of this essay these passages were overlooked.
[2] B. III, Ch. 6.   [3] Cicero, *De finibus*, v, 6.
[4] B. III, Ch. 9.

to serve the commonwealth, and be profitable to many : ' *Fructus enim ingenii et virtutis, omnisque praestantiae, tum maximus accipitur, quum in proximum quemque confertur* ' : 'For then is most fruit reaped, both of our wit and virtue and all other excellency, when it is bestowed on our neighbours.' "

The quotation here is from Cicero ;[1] and later in the same essay [2] there is a return to the theme, this time with a quotation from Seneca :[3]

"With me no pleasure is fully delightsome without communication, and no delight absolute except imparted. I do not so much as apprehend one rare conceit, or conceive one excellent good thought in my mind, but methinks I am much grieved and grievously perplexed to have produced the same alone, and that I have no sympathising companion to impart it unto. ' *Si cum hac exceptione detur sapientia, ut illam inclusam teneam, nec enuntiem, reiiciam* ' : 'If wisdom should be offered, with the exception that I should keep it concealed and not utter it, I would refuse it.' "

Here the most direct parallel, apart from Montaigne's own words, is that from Cicero ON FRIENDSHIP ; and looking to the context in TROILUS AND CRESSIDA, where Ulysses admits the idea to be " familiar," we are bound to admit that Shakespeare may well have met with it elsewhere than in Montaigne. The adage *Frustra habet qui non utitur* is given in one of the earliest sections of the ADAGIA of Erasmus ; and it is one likely to have been frequently commented, though it is

---

[1] *De Amicitia*, c. 19.
[2] Edit. cited, p. 438 (Morley's Florio, p. 505).   [3] Epist. vi.

not included by Taverner in his little English anthology from the main collection (1539, 1552, and 1570). Nay, it might well have been a commonplace among Shakespeare's more scholarly friends, who must often have talked of books over their wine at the Mermaid Tavern. On the other hand, however, he may have met with it in one of the translations of the period, reading the DE AMICITIA either in the Earl of Worcester's version (1530 ?), where the passage before us is rendered :

"The grettest fruyte of naturall Vertue and all excellence ys thenne taken whan yt is geven and departed to theym that be next in frendshyppe and good wyll " ;[1]

or in Harrington's version of 1550, where it is rendered :

"For thence chiefly is the fruite of ones witte vertue and all honestie taken, when it is bestowed on him that is nearest alied."[2]

Either of these versions, in turn, may have set some of Cicero's sayings in circulation. And still the list of possible sources—every one more probable than the Latin translation of Plato, who yields a different thought—is not exhausted. For Seneca in his treatise DE BENEFICIIS[3] throws out

[1] *Tullius de amicicia in Englysh*, fol. xiii.
[2] *The booke of freendeship of Marcus Tullie Cicero*, 1550, p. 47.
[3] B. V, cc. 8, 9, 10. Cp. VI, 2, 3.

the germ of the ideas as to Nature demanding back her gifts, and as to virtue being nothing if not reflected ; and even suggests the principle of "thanks and use." [1] This treatise, too, lay to Shakespeare's hand in Golding's translation of 1578, where the passages : "Rerum natura nihil dicitur perdere, quia quidquid illi avellitur, ad illam redit ; nec perire quidquam potest, quod quo excidat non habet, sed eodem evolvitur unde discedit" ; and "quaedam quum sint honesta, pulcherrima summae virtutis, nisi cum altero non habent locum," are rendered :

"The nature of the thing cannot be said to have foregone aught, because that whatsoever is plucked from it returneth to it again ; neither can anything be lost which hath not whereout of to pass, but windeth back again unto whence it came" ;

and

"Some things though they be honest, very goodly and right excellently vertuous, yet have they not their effect but in a co-partner."

In face of all this it is an extravagance to claim, as does Mr. Collins, that in the passage under discussion "the reference is to a passage in the FIRST ALCIBIADES" which the poet must have read in the Latin version.

[1] B. V, cc. 22-25.

Whether Shakespeare's reading of Montaigne sent him to Cicero, or to Seneca, to whom Montaigne[1] avows so much indebtedness, we of course cannot tell; but it is enough for the purpose of our argument to say that we have here another point or stage in a line of analytical thought on which Shakespeare was embarked about 1603, and of which the starting-point or initial stimulus was the perusal of Florio's Montaigne. We have the point of contact with Montaigne in HAMLET, where the saying that reason is implanted in us to be used, is seen to be one of the many correspondences of thought between the play and the Essays. The idea is more subtly and deeply developed in MEASURE FOR MEASURE, and still more subtly and philosophically in TROILUS AND CRESSIDA. The fact of the process of development is all that is here affirmed, over and above the actual phenomena of reproduction before set forth.

As to these, the proposition is that in sum they constitute such an amount of reproduction of Montaigne as explains Jonson's phrase about habitual "stealings." There is no justification for applying that to the passage in the TEMPEST, since not only is that play not known to have existed in

[1] B. II, Ch. 32.

its present form in 1605,[1] when VOLPONE was
produced, but the phrase plainly alleges not one
but many borrowings. Of course, Jonson may
have been thinking of Marston, whom Mr.
Charles Crawford shows to have echoed Montaigne
repeatedly in plays published in 1605-6.[2] But his
words in *Volpone* tell of more writers than one ;
and here, at all events, in two plays of Shakespeare,
then fresh in memory—the Second Quarto having
been published in 1604 and MEASURE FOR MEASURE
produced in the same year—were echoes enough
from Montaigne to be noted by Jonson, whom we
know to have owned, as presumably did Shakespeare, the Florio folio, and to have been Florio's
warm admirer. And there seems to be a con-
firmation of our thesis in the fact that, while we
find detached passages savouring of Montaigne
in some later plays of the same period, as in
one of the concluding period, the TEMPEST, we

[1] The arguments of Dr. Karl Elze, in his *Essays on Shakespeare*
(Eng. tr. p. 15), to show that the *Tempest* was written about 1604,
seem to me to possess no weight. He goes so far as to assume that
the speech of Prospero in which Shakespeare transmutes four lines
of the Earl of Stirling's *Darius* must have been written immediately
after the publication of that work. The argument is (1) that
Shakespeare must have seen *Darius* when it came out, and (2) that
he would imitate the passage then or never.

[2] See in Mr. Crawford's valuable *Collectanea*, second series (1907),
the paper on "Montaigne, Webster, and Marston : Doune and
Webster." Webster's echoes of Montaigne are later than 1605.

do not again find in any one play such a cluster of reminiscences as we have seen in HAMLET and MEASURE FOR MEASURE, though the spirit of Montaigne's thought, turned to a deepening pessimism, may be said to tinge all the later tragedies.

XXI. In OTHELLO (? 1604) we have Iago's " 'Tis in ourselves that we are thus or thus," already considered, to say nothing of Othello's phrase :

> " I saw it not, thought it not, it harmed not me. . . .
>   He that is robb'd, not wanting what is stolen,
>   Let him not know it, and he's not robb'd at all "

—a philosophical commonplace which compares with various passages in the fortieth essay.

XXII. In LEAR (1606) we have such a touch as the king's lines : [1]

> "And take upon's the mystery of things
>   As if we were God's spies " ;

which recalls the vigorous protest of the essay, THAT A MAN OUGHT SOBERLY TO MEDDLE WITH JUDGING OF THE DIVINE LAWS,[2] where Montaigne avows that if he dared he would put in the category of impostors the

" interpreters and controllers of God's secret designs, presuming to find out the causes of every accident, and to pry into the secrets of God's divine will, the incomprehensible motives of his works."

---

[1] Act V, Sc. 3.   [2] B. I, Ch. 31.

As has been remarked above, it is impossible to be sure that such a common theological sentiment was specially suggested to Shakespeare by Montaigne. We can but note that it is a recurrent note with him ; and that much of the argument of the APOLOGY is typified in the sentence :

" What greater vanity can there be than to go about by our proportions and conjectures to guess at God ? "

XXIII. But there is a more striking coincidence between a passage in the essay [1] OF JUDGING OF OTHERS' DEATH and the speech of Edmund [2] on the subject of stellar influences. In the essay Montaigne sharply derides the habit of ascribing human occurrences to the interference of the stars —which very superstition he had supported by his own authority in the APOLOGY, as we have seen above, in the passage on the "power and domination" of the celestial bodies. The passage in the thirteenth essay of the Second Book is the more notable in itself, being likewise a protest against human self-sufficiency, though the bearing of the illustration is directly reversed. Here he derides man's conceit : " We entertain and carry all with us : whence it followeth that we deem our death to be some great matter, and which passeth not so easily, nor without a solemn consultation of

[1] B. II, Ch. 13.   [2] Act I, Sc. 2.

the stars." Then follow references to Cæsar's sayings as to his star, and the "*common foppery*" as to the sun mourning his death a year :

"And a thousand such, wherewith the world suffers itself to be so easily cony-catched, deeming that our own interests disturb heaven, and his infinity is moved at our least actions. 'There is no such society between heaven and us that by our destiny the shining of the stars should be as mortal as we are.'"

There seems to be an unmistakable reminiscence of this passage in Edmund's speech, where the word "foppery" is a special clue :

"This is the excellent foppery of the world ! that when we are sick in fortune (often the surfeit of our own behaviour), we make guilty of our disasters the sun, the moon, and the stars : as if we were villains by necessity ; fools by heavenly compulsion ; knaves, thieves, and traitors by spherical pre-dominance ; drunkards, liars, and adulterers by an enforced obedience of planetary influence ; and all that we are evil in, by divine thrusting on. . . ."

XXIV. Two passages in Montaigne recall Kent's cry :

"As flies to wanton boys are we to the Gods :
They kill us for their sport."

In the discursive essay UPON SOME VERSES OF VIRGIL [1] occurs the sentence :

"I believe that which Plato says to be true, that man was made by the Gods for them to toy and play withal ;"

---

[1] B. III, Ch. 5 (Morley's Florio, p. 446).

and again in the essay OF VANITY [1] we have :

"The gods play at hand-ball with us, and toss us up and down on their hands. '*Enimvero dii nos homines quasi pilas habent.*' [2] 'The gods perdie do reckon and racket us men as their tennis balls.'"

And both essays have something of the atmosphere of the ethical thought in LEAR, though they have not its intensity of pessimism.

XXV. Again, in MACBETH (1606), the words of Malcolm to Macduff : [3]

"Give sorrow words : the grief that does not speak,
  Whispers the o'erfraught heart and bids it break"

—an idea which also underlies Macbeth's "this perilous stuff, which weighs upon the heart"—recalls the essay [4] OF SADNESS, in which Montaigne remarks on the

"mournful silent stupidity which so doth pierce us when accidents surpassing our strength overwhelm us," and on the way in which "the soul, bursting afterwards forth into tears and complaints . . . seemeth to clear and dilate itself"; going on to tell how the German Lord Raisciac looked on his dead son "till the vehemency of his sad sorrow, having suppressed and choked his vital spirits, felled him stark dead to the ground."

The parallel here, such as it is, is at least much more vivid than that drawn between Shakespeare's lines and that often-quoted one of Seneca : "Curae

[1] B. III, Ch. 9.
[2] Plautus, *Captivi*, prol.   [3] Act IV, Sc. 3.   [4] B. I, Ch. 2.

leves loquuntur : ingentes stupent "[1] : "Light troubles speak : the great ones are dumb."

Certainly no one of these latter passages, which are of the nature of commonplaces,[2] would singly suffice to prove that Shakespeare had read Montaigne, though the peculiar coincidence of one word in Edgar's speech with a word in Florio, above noted, would alone raise the question. And nothing can be made, I think, of one or two coincidences of proverbial sayings in the Essays and in ANTONY AND CLEOPATRA. The maxim uttered by Enobarbus :[3]

> "I see men's judgments are
> A parcel of their fortunes,"

may be often matched in Montaigne ; but such parallels count for little ; and when Mr. Gervais notes the verbal correspondence of Antony's[4]

---

[1] *Hippolytus*, 615 (607). The line, as it happens, is quoted by Montaigne in the same essay.

[2] Spenser puts the thought in the lines :
> " He oft finds med'cine who his griefe imparts,
> But double griefs afflict concealing hearts,
> As raging flames who striveth to suppress."
>
> (*Faerie Queene*, B. II, c. ii, st. 34.)

In *The Spanish Tragedy* (I, iii, 9) we have :
> "For deepest cares break never into tears " ;

and in *Titus Andronicus* (ii, 5), probably from the hand of Greene, who (following Lyly) often uses the same tag, we have :
> " Sorrow concealèd, like an oven stopp'd,
> Doth burn the heart to cinders where it is."

Cp. *Did Shakespeare write " Titus Andronicus" ?* pp. 104-5, 156.

[3] Act III, Sc. 13.   [4] Act IV, Sc. 4.

> " Yea, very force
> Entangles itself with strength,"

he shows, by citing fuller expressions of the same
idea from RICHARD II as well as HAMLET and
HENRY VIII, that, though Shakespeare may
have echoed the " entangles " in Montaigne's essay,
the idea was familiar to him. It is expressed in
Sonnet xxiii more finely than ever in Montaigne.

XXVI. Professor Alois Brandl, disputing, in
his notice[1] of the first edition of this essay, the
conclusion that there are no clear traces of
Montaigne in Shakespeare before Hamlet, maintained in rebuttal that " the monologue of Henry
V at the lonely watch-fire on the night before
Agincourt on the responsibility and the burden of
kingship . . . is to be found almost step for step
in Montaigne's essay OF THE INCOMMODITY OF
GREATNESS." Professor Brandl had forgotten
that though HENRY V was produced before 1600
the soliloquy in question was not, being entirely
absent from the 1600 Quarto. Thus, as the style
belongs to the MEASURE FOR MEASURE period,
any Montaigne influence in it is to be traced to
Florio's translation. At the outset, however,
Professor Brandl's thesis as he puts it must be set
aside. There is no "step for step" parallelism
between the speech and the essay in question.

[1] *Shakespeare Jahrbuch* for 1899, p. 314.

Beyond the general and familiar idea that a king's life is very burdensome, the soliloquy and the essay have hardly a proposition in common ; and it is inconceivable that the general idea should have been new to Shakespeare even at twenty. In the very essay cited, Montaigne notes that he " was not long since reading of two Scottish books striving upon this subject. The popular makes the king to be of worse condition than a carter ; and he that extolleth monarchy placeth him both in power and sovereignty many steps above the gods." The two books in question were presumably Buchanan's DE JURE REGNI (1580) and (either) one of the books produced by Scottish exiles during the period of Catholic ascendancy[1] or one of the books published in reply to Buchanan by Catholic Scots abroad.[2] When such topics were discussed in Scotland, they cannot have been unfamiliar in England.[3]

Professor Brandl, however, might much more plausibly have pointed for a parallel between Henry's soliloquy and Montaigne to the essay OF

[1] Cp. Hallam, *Lit. of Europe*, ed. 1872, ii, 136.

[2] Hallam cites one of these, published in 1600 by William Barclay, *De Regno et regali potestate adversus Buchananum*. But there were presumably earlier replies.

[3] See Hallam, as cited, p. 136 sq., concerning the work of Poynet or Pounet, *A Short Treatise of Politique Power*, 1558.

THE INEQUALITY THAT IS BETWEEN US.[1]   Here
there are many more points of coincidence.   Compare, for instance, the lines :

> " Thinkst thou the fiery fever will go out
>   With titles blown from adulation ?
>   Will it give place to flexure and low bending ? "

with the sentences :

"Doth the ague, the megrim, or the gout, spare him [the
king] more than us ?   If he chance to be jealous or capricious,
will our lowting curtzies, or putting off of hats, bring him in
tune again ? "[2]

the subsequent quotation from Lucretius (ii, 34) :

"Nec calidae citius decedunt corpore febres," etc.,

which Florio translates :

> " Fevers no sooner from thy body fly
>   If thou on arras or red scarlet lie," etc. ;

and the sentence :

"The first fit of an ague, or the first gird that the gout
gave him, what avails his goodly titles of Majesty ? "

Compare again the lines :

> "What infinite hearts-ease
> Must kings neglect, that private men enjoy ?
> And what have kings, that privates have not too,
> Save ceremony, save general ceremony ? "

with the passage :

"We see it is a delight for princes, and a recreation for
them, sometimes to disguise themselves, and to take upon
them a base and popular kind of life " (p. 131) ;

---

[1] B. I, Ch. 42.   [2] Florio, p. 130.

the accompanying quotation from Horace (ODES,
III, xxix, 13) :

> " Plerumque gratae principibus vices,
> Mundaeque parvo sub lare pauperum
> Caenae sine aulaeis et ostro,
> Sollicitam explicuere frontem "

which Florio clumsily translates :

" Princes do commonly like interchange
And cleanly meals where poor men poorly house
Without all tapestry or carpets strange,
Unwrinkled have their care-knit, thought-bent brows " ; [1]

and the further passages :

" . . . being so barred that he [the king] cannot at his
liberty travel to go where he pleaseth, being as it were a
prisoner within the limits of his country" (p. 132) ;

" Princely advantages are in a manner but imaginary
pre-ëminences " ;

" He [the king] perceiveth himself deprived of all mutual
friendship, reciprocal society, and familiar conversation,
wherein consisteth the most perfect and sweetest fruit of
human life" (p. 132) ;

" All the true commodities that princes have are common
unto them with men of mean fortune " (p. 133).

Yet again, compare :

> " Art thou aught else but place, degree, and form
> Creating awe and fear in other men ?
> Wherein thou art less happy, being feared,
> Than they in fearing,"

---

[1] Apropos of Florio's translations, it is impossible to forget that
in rendering this essay he makes the most amusing of his " howlers,"
rendering "*les enfants de chœur*"—that is, choir-boys—by "high-
minded men," and making the passage meaningless.

with the sentence :

"Touching commanding of others, which in shew seemeth to be so sweet . . . I am confidently of this opinion, that it is much more easie and plausible to follow than to guide" (p. 131) ;

and the lines concerning the king's sleeplessness and the toiler's rest with the passage :

"In truly enjoying of carnal sensualities they are of much worse condition than *private men* ; forasmuch as ease and facility depriveth them of that sour-sweet tickling which we find in them" (p. 131).

Here, indeed, we might claim to find the soliloquy "step for step" in Montaigne ; and the very fact that this soliloquy, with its Montaignesque flavour, was added to the play in a period in which Shakespeare received so many stimuli from the Essays, goes far to prove the point. There are, indeed, countervailing considerations, in particular this, that several of the passages above cited are avowedly transcriptions from "Hieron in Xenophon." In point of fact, the main drift of the soliloquy is so fully present in Xenophon's dialogue that it is hard to understand how the passage has failed to be cited as a proof of Shakespeare's familiarity with the classics. But here, once more, there is a reasonable presumption that the near source rather than the remote was that which stimulated Shakespeare.

We have now, at least, seen enough of
Montaigne matter in the plays to account for
Jonson's gibe in VOLPONE.   That gibe, indeed,
even if it were meant for Shakespeare and no other,
is not really so ill-natured as the term "steal"
is apt to make it sound for our ears, especially
if we are prepossessed—as even Mr. Fleay seems
to have been—by the old commentators' notion of
a deep ill-will on Jonson's part towards Shakespeare.   There was probably no such ill-will in
the matter, the burly scholar's habit of robust
banter being enough to account for the form of
his remark.   As a matter of fact, his own plays
are strewn with classic transcriptions ; and though
he evidently plumed himself on his power of
"invention"[1] in the matter of plots—a faculty
which he knew Shakespeare to lack—he cannot
conceivably have meant to charge his rival with
having committed any discreditable plagiarism
in drawing upon Montaigne.   At most he
would mean to convey that borrowing from
the English translation of Montaigne was an
easy game as compared with his own scholarlike practice of translating from the Greek
and Latin.

[1] See the Prologue to *Every Man in His Humour*, first ed., preserved by Gifford.

However that might be, the fact stands that Shakespeare did about 1604 reproduce Montaigne as we have seen ; and it remains to consider what the reproduction signifies, as regards Shakespeare's mental development.

IV

SHAKESPEARE AND THE CLASSICS

BUT first the question must be asked whether the Montaigne influence is unique or exceptional. Of the many literary influences which an Elizabethan dramatist might undergo, was Montaigne's the only one which wrought deeply upon Shakespeare's spirit, apart from those of his contemporary dramatists and the pre-existing plays, which were then models and points of departure? It is clear that Shakespeare must have thought much and critically of the methods and the utterance of his co-rivals in literary art, as he did of the methods of his fellow-actors. The author of the advice to the players in HAMLET was hardly less a critic than a poet; and the sonnet [1] which speaks of its author as

"Desiring this man's art and that man's scope,"

is one of the least uncertain revelations that those enigmatic poems yield us. We may pretty confi-

[1] The twenty-ninth.

dently decide, too, with Professor Minto,[1] that
the eighty-sixth Sonnet, beginning   :

"Was it the full, proud sail of his great verse ?"

has reference to Chapman, in whom Shakespeare
might well see one of his most formidable competitors in poetry.   But we are here concerned
with influences of thought, as distinct from influences of artistic example ; and the question is :
Do the plays show any other culture-contact
comparable to that which we have been led to
recognise in the case of Montaigne's Essays ?

The matter cannot be said to have been
very fully investigated when even the Montaigne
influence has been thus far left so much in the
vague.   As regards the plots, there has been
exhaustive and instructive research during two
centuries ; and of collations of parallel passages,
apart from Montaigne, there has been no lack ;
but the deeper problem of the dramatist's mental
history can hardly be said to have arisen till the
last generation.   As regards many of the parallel
passages, the ground has been pretty well cleared
by the dispassionate scholarship brought to bear
on them from Farmer onwards ; though the
idolatry of the Coleridgean school, as represented

[1] See his *Characteristics of English Poets*, 2nd ed. p. 222.

by Knight, did much to retard scientific conclusions on this as on other points. Farmer's ESSAY ON THE LEARNING OF SHAKESPEARE (1767) proved for all open-minded readers that much of Shakespeare's supposed classical knowledge was derived from translations alone ; [1] and further investigation does but establish his general view.[2] Such is the effect of M. Stapfer's chapter on Shakespeare's Classical Knowledge ; [3] and the pervading argument of that chapter will be found to hold good as against the view suggested, with judicious diffi-

[1] The most elaborate of the earlier attempts to prove Shakespeare classically learned is that made in the *Critical Observations on Shakespeare* (1746) of the Rev. John Upton, a man of great erudition and much random acuteness (shown particularly in bold attempts to excise interpolations from the Gospels), but devoid of the higher critical wisdom, by the admission of Mr. Churton Collins. To a reader of to-day, his arguments from Shakespeare's diction and syntax are peculiarly unconvincing.

[2] It may not be out of place here to say a word for Farmer in passing, as against the strictures of M. Stapfer, who, after recognising the general pertinence of his remarks, proceeds to say (*Shakespeare and Classical Antiquity*, Eng. trans. p. 83) that Farmer "fell into the egregious folly of speaking in a strain of impertinent conceit : it is as if the little man—for little he must assuredly have been— was eaten up with vanity." This is in its way as unjust as the abuse of Knight and Dr. Maginn. M. Stapfer has misunderstood Farmer's tone, which is one of banter against, not Shakespeare, but those critics who blunderingly ascribed to him a wide and close knowledge of the classics. Towards Shakespeare, Farmer was admiringly appreciative ; and in the preface to the second edition of his essay he wrote : " Shakespeare wanted not the stilts of languages to raise him above all other men."

[3] Ch. iv of vol. cited.

dence, by Dr. John W. Cunliffe, concerning the influence of Seneca's tragedies on Shakespeare's. Unquestionably the body of Senecan tragedy, as Dr. Cunliffe's valuable research has shown, did much to colour the style and thought of the Elizabethan drama, as well as to suggest its themes and shape its technique. But it is noteworthy that while there are in the plays, as we have seen, apparent echoes from the Senecan treatises, and while, as we have seen, Dr. Cunliffe suggests sources in the Senecan tragedies for some Shakespearean passages, he is doubtful as to whether they represent any direct study of Seneca by Shakespeare.

"Whether Shakespeare was directly indebted to Seneca," he writes, " is a question as difficult as it is interesting. As English tragedy advances, there grows up an accumulation of Senecan influence within the English drama, in addition to the original source, and it becomes increasingly difficult to distinguish between the direct and the indirect influence of Seneca. In no case is the difficulty greater than in that of Shakespeare. Or Marlowe, Jonson, Chapman, Marston, and Massinger, we can say with certainty that they read Seneca, and reproduced their readings in their tragedies ; of Middleton and Heywood we can say with almost equal certainty that they give no sign of direct indebtedness to Seneca ; and that they probably came only under the indirect influence, through the imitations of their predecessors and contemporaries. In the case of Shakespeare we cannot be absolutely certain either way. Professor Baynes thinks it is probable that Shakespeare read Seneca at school ; and even if he did not, we may be sure that at some period of his career he would turn to the generally accepted model of classical tragedy, either in the original or in the translation." [1]

This seems partially inconsistent ; and, so far as the evidence from particular parallels goes, we are not led to take with any confidence the view put in the last sentence. Long ago, Warton pronounced it "remarkable that Shakespeare has borrowed nothing from the English Seneca" ; [2] and that careful scholar's judgment will be found to stand the tests of any investigation. The above-noted parallels between Seneca's tragedies and Shakespeare's are but cases of citation of sentences likely to have grown proverbial ; and the most notable of the others that have been cited by Dr. Cunliffe is one which, as he notes, points to Aeschylus as well as to Seneca. The cry of Macbeth :

> "Will all great Neptune's ocean wash this blood
> Clean from my hand ?   No, this my hand will rather
> The multitudinous seas incarnadine,
> Making the green one red" :

certainly corresponds closely with that of Seneca's Hercules : [3]

---

[1] *The Influence of Seneca on Elizabethan Tragedy*, pp. 66-67.
[2] *History of English Poetry*, ed. 1781, iii, 393.
[3] *Hercules Furens*, ad fin. (1324-1329).

> " Quis Tanais, aut quis Nilus, aut quis persica
> Violentus unda Tigris, aut Rhenus ferox
> Tagusve ibera turbidus gaza fluens,
> Abluere dextram poterit ?   Arctoum licet
> Maeotis in me gelida transfundat mare,
> Et tota Tethys per meas currat manus,
> Haerebit altum facinus "

and that of Seneca's Hippolytus : [1]

> " Quis eluet me Tanais ?   Aut quae barbaris,
> Maeotis undis pontico incumbens mari ?
> Non ipso toto magnus Oceano pater
> Tantum expiarit sceleris."

But these declamations, deriving as they do, to begin with, from Aeschylus,[2] are seen from their very recurrence in Seneca to have become stock speeches for the ancient tragic drama ; and they were clearly well-fitted to become so for the medieval.   The phrases used were already classic when Catullus employed them before Seneca :

> " Suscipit, O Gelli, quantum non ultima Thetys,
> Non genitor Nympharum, abluit Oceanus." [3]

In the Renaissance we find the theme reproduced by Tasso ; [4] and it had doubtless been freely used by Shakespeare's English predecessors and contemporaries.   In LOCRINE [5] we have a declamation of the same sort :

---

[1] *Hippolytus*, Act II, 715-718 (723-726).

[2] *Choëphori*, 63-65.

[3] Carm. lxxxviii, *In Gellium*.   See the note in Doering's edition.

[4] *Gerusalemme*, xviii, 8.   [5] Act IV, Sc. 4.

> " O what Danubius now may quench my thirst ;
> What Euphrates, what light-foot Euripus,
> May now allay the fury of that heat
> Which raging in my entrails eats me up ? "

What Shakespeare did in MACBETH was but to set the familiar theme to a rhetoric whose superb sonority must have left theirs tame, as it leaves Seneca's stilted in comparison. Marston did his best with it, in a play which may have been written before, though published after, MACBETH : [1]

> " Although the waves of all the Northern sea
> Should flow for ever through those guilty hands,
> Yet the sanguinolent stain would extant be "

—a sad foil to Shakespeare's

> " The multitudinous seas incarnadine."

There is no trace of such sonority in the English translation of Seneca, published in 1581, where the passage in the HERCULES FURENS runs : [2]

> "What Tanais or what Nilus else, or with his Persian wave
> What Tygris violent of stream, or what fierce Rhenus flood,
> Or Tagus troublesome that flows with Iber's treasures
> good
> May my right hand now wash from guilt ? although Maeotis
> cold

---

[1] *The Insatiate Countess*, published in 1613.
[2] *Seneca, his Tenne Tragedies translated into Englysh*, 1581, p. 20.

The waves of all the Northern sea on me shed out now
    wolde,
And all the water thereof should now pass by my two
    hands,
Yet will the mischief deep remain."

It seems clear, then, that we are not here
entitled to suppose Shakespeare a reader of the
Senecan tragedies ; and even were it otherwise, the
passage in question is a figure of speech rather
than a reflection on life or a stimulus to such
reflection.   And the same holds good of the other
interesting but inconclusive parallels drawn by
Dr. Cunliffe.   Shakespeare's

> " Diseases desperate grown
> By desperate appliance are relieved,
> Or not at all," [1]

which he compares with Seneca's

> " Et ferrum et ignis saepe medicinae loco est.
> Extrema primo nemo tentavit loco," [2]

—a passage that may very well be the original for
the modern oracle about fire and iron—is really
much closer to the aphorism of Hippocrates, that
" Extreme remedies are proper for extreme
diseases," and cannot be said to be more than a
proverb.   It occurs in so well known a book as
the ANNALS of Tacitus : [3]

---

[1] *Hamlet*, Act IV, Sc. 3.   [2] *Agamemnon*, 152-153.
[3] *Ann.* iii, 54.

"Ne corporis quidem morbos veteres, et diu auctos, nisi per dura et aspera coërceas";

and the ANNALS had been translated by Richard Greenwey in 1598, the passage in question being rendered :

"We see that old inveterate diseases of the body cannot be cured but by sharp and rough remedies."[1]

Yet again, Richard Taverner, in his twice-reprinted anthology from the ADAGIA of Erasmus, has the phrases : "A strong disease requireth a strong medicine," as a parallel to the Latin *Malo nodo malus quaerendus cuneus* ;[2] and Lyly has : "A desperate disease is to be committed to a desperate doctor."[3]   In any case, it lay to Shakespeare's hand in Montaigne,[4] as translated by Florio :

"To extreme sicknesses, extreme remedies."

Equally inconclusive is the equally close parallel between Macbeth's

"Canst thou not minister to a mind diseased?"

and the sentence of Hercules :

---

[1] *The Annales of Tacitus, etc.* (trans. by R. Greenwey), 1598, p. 80.

[2] *Proverbes or Adagies gathered out of the Chiliades of Erasmus*, by Rycharde Tauerner, ed. 1570, fol. v.

[3] *Euphues, the Anatomy of Wit*, 1579, Arber's ed. p. 67.

[4] B. II, Ch. 3 (near beginning).

"Nemo polluto queat
Animo mederi." [1]

Such a reflection was sure to win a proverbial vogue, and in THE TWO NOBLE KINSMEN (in which Shakespeare indeed seems to have had a hand), we have the doctor protesting : " I think she has a perturbed mind, which I cannot minister to." [2]

And so, again, with the notable resemblance between Hercules' cry :

> " Cur animam in ista luce detineam amplius,
> Morerque, nihil est. Cuncta jam amisi bona,
> Mentem, arma, famam, conjugem, natos, manus,
> Etiam furorem " [3]

and Macbeth's :

> " I have lived long enough : my way of life
> Is fallen into the sear, the yellow leaf ;
> And that which should accompany old age,
> As honour, love, obedience, troops of friends,
> I must not look to have." [4]

Here there is indeed every appearance of imitation ; but, though the versification in Macbeth's speech is certainly Shakespeare's, such a

---

[1] *Hercules Furens*, Actus V, 1261-2.

[2] Act IV, Sc. 3.

[3] *Hercules Furens*, 1258-61. Compare *Agamemnon*, Actus II, Sc. i, 112 :

> " Periere mores, jus, decus, pietas, fides,
> Et qui redire, quam perit, nescit, pudor."

[4] *Macbeth*, Act V, Sc. 2.

lament had doubtless been made in other English plays, in direct reproduction of Seneca ; and Shakespeare, in all probability, was again only perfecting some previous declamation.

The same impression is set up even in the case of the remarkable parallel noted by Professor Brandl between Lady Macbeth's appeal to the spirits to unsex her and the first monologue of Medea, of which the Elizabethan translators give a very free rendering ; [1] in the absence of any verbal co-incidence we can but say that the general resemblance suggests intermediate forms of declamation.   In any case, the translation is distinctly nearer Lady Macbeth's soliloquy than the original.

There is a quite proverbial quality, finally, in such phrases as :

"Things at the worst will cease, or else climb upward
  To that they were before " ; [2]

and

"We but teach
Bloody instructions, which, being taught, return
To plague the inventor " ; [3]

which might be traced to other sources nearer Shakespeare's hand than Seneca.[4]   And beyond

[1] See it in Anders, *Shakespeare's Books*, p. 35.
[2] *Id.* Act IV, Sc. 2.   [3] *Id.* Act I, Sc. 7.
[4] The commentators note the idea in Bellenden's translation of

such sentences and such tropes as those above considered, there was really little or nothing in the tragedies of Seneca to catch Shakespeare's eye or ear ; nothing to generate in him a deep philosophy of life or to move him to the manifold play of reflection which gives his later tragedies their commanding intellectuality. Some such stimulus, as we have seen, he might indeed have drawn from one or two of Seneca's treatises, which do, in their desperately industrious manner, cover a good deal of intellectual ground, making some tolerable discoveries by the way. But by the tests alike of quantity and quality of reproduced matter, it is clear that the indirect influence of the Senecan tragedies and treatises on Shakespeare was slight compared with the direct influence of Montaigne's essays. Nor is it hard to see why, even as regards the treatises ; and even supposing Shakespeare to have had Seneca at hand in translation. Despite Montaigne's own leaning to Seneca, as compared with Cicero, we may often say of the former what Montaigne says of the latter, that " his manner of writing seemeth very tedious."

Hector Boece's account of Macbeth, and also in Holinshed. And Seneca's phrase :

> " Per scelera semper sceleribus tutum est iter "
>
> (*Agamemnon*, 115.)

is cited in the *Spanish Tragedy* (III, xiii, 6) with the translation,

> " For evils unto ills conductors be."

Over the DE BENEFICIIS and the DE IRA one is
sometimes moved to say, as the essayist does [1] over
Cicero, " I understand sufficiently what death and
voluptuousness are ; let not a man busy himself
to anatomise them." For the swift and penetrating flash of Montaigne, which either goes to the
heart of a matter once for all or opens up a far
vista of feeling and speculation, leaving us newly
related to our environment and even to our
experience, Seneca can but give us a conscientious
examination of the ground, foot by foot, with a
policeman's lantern, leaving us consciously footsore,
eyesore, and ready for bed. Under no stress of
satisfaction from his best finds can we be moved
to call him a man of genius, which is just what
we call Montaigne after a few pages. It is the
broad difference between industry and inspiration,
between fecundity and pregnancy, between Jonson
and Shakespeare. And, though a man of genius
is not necessarily dependent on other men of
genius for stimulus, we shall on scrutiny find
reason to believe that in Shakespeare's case the
nature of the stimulus counted for a great deal.

[1] B. II, Ch. 10.

V

SHAKESPEARE AND BRUNO

EVEN before that is made clear, however, there can be little hesitation about dismissing the only other outstanding theory of a special intellectual influence undergone by Shakespeare —the theory of Dr. Benno Tschischwitz, that he read and was impressed by the Italian writings of Giordano Bruno. In this case, the bases of the hypothesis are of the scantiest and the flimsiest. Bruno was in England from 1583 to 1586, before Shakespeare came to London. Among his patrons were Sidney and Leicester, but neither Southampton nor Pembroke. In all his writings only one passage has been cited which even faintly suggests a coincidence with any in Shakespeare ; and in that the suggestion is faint indeed. In Bruno's ill-famed comedy IL CANDELAJO, Octavio asks the pedant Manfurio, " Che è la materia di vostri versi ? " and the pedant replies, " Litterae, syllabae, dictio et oratio, partes propinquae et remotae," on which Octavio again asks, "Io dico, quale è il suggetto et il proposito?"[1]   So far as it goes, this is something of a parallel to Polonius's question to Hamlet as to what he reads, and Hamlet's answer, "Words, words." But the scene is obviously a stock situation ; and if there are any episodes in HAMLET which clearly belong to the pre-Shakespearean play, the fooling of Hamlet with Polonius is one of them. And beyond this, Dr. Tschischwitz's parallels are quite unconvincing ; indeed they promptly put themselves out of court. He admits that nothing else in Bruno's comedy recalls anything else in Shakespeare ;[2] but he goes on to find analogies between other passages in HAMLET and some of Bruno's philosophic doctrines. Quoting Bruno's theorem that all things are made up of indestructible atoms, and that death is but a transformation, Dr. Tschischwitz cites as a reproduction of it Hamlet's soliloquy :

"O, that this too, too solid flesh would melt ! "

It is difficult to be serious over such a contention ; and it is quite impossible for anybody out

[1] Tschischwitz, *Shakespeare-Forschungen*, i, 1868, p. 52.

[2] "Es ist übrigens nicht zu bedauern, dass Shakespeare Bruno's Komödie nicht durchweg zum Muster genommen, denn sie enthält so masslose Obscönitäten, dass Shakespeare an seinen stärksten Stellen daneben fast jungfräulich erscheint" (Work cited, p. 52).

of Germany or the Bacon-Shakespeare party to be
as serious over it as Dr. Tschischwitz, who finds
that Hamlet's figure of the melting of flesh into
dew is an illustration of Bruno's " atomic system,"
and goes on to find a further Brunonian significance in Hamlet's jeering answers to the king's
demand for the body of Polonius.   Of these
passages he finds the source or suggestion in one
which he translates from Bruno's CENA DE LE
CENERI :

> " For to this matter, of which our planet is formed, death
> and dissolution do not come ; and the annihilation of all
> nature is not possible ; but it attains from time to time, by a
> fixed law, to renew itself and to change all its parts, re-
> arranging and recombining them ; all this necessarily taking
> place in a determinate series, under which everything assumes
> the place of another." [1]

In the judgment of Dr. Tschischwitz, this
theorem, which anticipates so remarkably the
modern scientific conception of the universe,
"elucidates" Hamlet's talk about worms and
bodies, and his further sketch of the progress of
Alexander's dust to the plugging of a beer-barrel.
It seems unnecessary to argue that all this is the
idlest supererogation.   The passages cited from
HAMLET, all of them found in the First Quarto,

---

[1] Work cited, p. 57.   I follow Dr. Tschischwitz's translation, so
far as syntax permits.

might have been drafted by a much lesser man
than Shakespeare, and that without ever having
heard of Bruno or the theory of the indestructi-
bility of matter. There is nothing in the case
approaching to a reproduction of Bruno's far-
reaching thought;[1] while on the contrary the
"leave not a wrack behind," in the TEMPEST, is an
expression which sets aside, as if it were unknown,
the conception of an endless transmutation of
matter, in a context where the thought would
naturally suggest itself to one who had met with
it. Where Hamlet is merely sardonic in the
plane of popular or at least exoteric humour, Dr.
Tschischwitz credits him with pantheistic philosophy. Where, on the other hand, Hamlet
speaks feelingly and ethically of the serious side
of drunkenness,[2] Dr. Tschischwitz parallels the
speech with a sentence in the BESTIA TRIONFANTE,
which gives a merely Rabelaisian picture of
drunken practices.[3] Yet again, he puts Bruno's
large aphorism, "Sol et homo generant hominem,"
beside Hamlet's gibe about the sun breeding
maggots in a dead dog—a phrase possible to any

[1] A little more plausibly, Professor Churton Collins has traced
Ariel's "Nothing of him that doth change" to Lucretius ; but, as is
shown below (Art. on "The Learning of Shakespeare"), several
Lucretian passages conveying the idea lay to the poet's hand in
Montaigne.

[2] Act I, Sc. 4.   [3] Tschischwitz, p. 59.

euphuist of the period.   That the parallels amount
at best to little, Dr. Tschischwitz himself indirectly
admits, though he proceeds to a new extravagance
of affirmation :

> "We do not maintain that such expressions are philoso-
> phemes, or that Shakespeare otherwise went any deeper into
> Bruno's system than suited his purpose, but that such passages
> show Shakespeare, at the time of his writing of HAMLET, to
> have already reached the heights of the thought of the age
> (*Zeitbewusstsein*), and to have made himself familiar with
> the most abstract of the sciences.   Many hitherto almost
> unintelligible passages in HAMLET are now cleared up by the
> poet's acquaintance with the atomic philosophy and the
> writings of the Nolan."

All this belongs to the uncritical method of
the German Shakespeare-criticism of the days
before Rümelin.   It is quite possible that Shakespeare may have heard something of Bruno's
theories from his friends ; and we may be sure
that much of Bruno's teaching would have profoundly interested him.   If Bruno's lectures at
Oxford on the immortality of the soul included
the matter he published later on the subject, they
may have called English attention to the Pytha-
gorean lore concerning the fate of the soul after
death,[1] above cited from Montaigne.   We might
again, on Dr. Tschischwitz's lines, but with more
plausibility than he attains to, trace the verses on

[1] See Mrs. Frith's *Life of Giordano Bruno*, 1889, pp. 121-128.

the "shaping fantasies" of "the lunatic, the lover and the poet," in the MIDSUMMER NIGHT'S DREAM,[1] to such a passage in Bruno as this :

"The first and most capital painter is the vivacity of the phantasy ; the first and most capital poet is the inspiration that originally arises with the impulse of deep thought, or is set up by that, through the divine or akin-to-divine breath of which they feel themselves moved to the fit expression of their thoughts. For each it creates the other principle. Therefore are the philosophers in a certain sense painters ; the poets, painters and philosophers ; the painters, philosophers and poets : true poets, painters, and philosophers love and reciprocally admire each other. There is no philosopher who does not poetise and paint. Therefore is it said, not without reason : To understand is to perceive the figures of phantasy, and understanding is phantasy, or is nothing without it."[2]

But since Shakespeare does not recognisably echo a passage which he would have been extremely likely to produce in such a context had he known it, we are bound to infer that he had not even heard it more than partially cited, much less read it. And so with any other remote resemblances between his work and that of any author whom he may have read. In regard even to passages

[1] "Lovers and madmen have such seething brains,
　　Such shaping fantasies, that apprehend
　　More than cool reason ever comprehends.
　　The lunatic, the lover and the poet
　　Are of imagination all compact," etc.
　　　　　　　　　　Act V, Sc. i.

[2] Cited by Noack, Art. "Bruno," in *Philosophie-geschichtliches Lexikon*.

in Shakespeare which come much nearer their
originals than any of these above cited come to
Bruno, we are forced to suppose that Shakespeare
got his thought at second or third hand. Thus
the famous passage in HENRY V[1] in which the
Archbishop figures the State as a divinely framed
harmony of differing functions, is clearly traceable
to Plato's REPUBLIC and Cicero's DE REPUBLICA ;[2]
yet rational criticism must decide with M. Stapfer[3]
that Shakespeare knew neither the former treatise
nor Augustine's quotation from the latter, but got
his suggestion from some English translation or
citation.

In fine, we are constrained by all our knowledge concerning Shakespeare, as well as by the
abstract principles of proof, to regard him in
general as a reader of his own language only,
albeit not without a smattering of others ; and
among the books in his own language which
we know him to have read in, and can prove him
to have been influenced by, we come back to
Montaigne's Essays, as by far the most important and the most potential for suggestion and
provocation.

[1] Act I, Sc. 2.   [2] See above, Introd.
[3] Work cited, p. 90.

VI

SHAKESPEARE'S CULTURE-EVOLUTION

To have any clear idea, however, of what
Montaigne did or could do for Shakespeare, we
must revise our conception of the poet in the light
of the positive facts of his life and circumstances
—a thing made difficult for us in England
through the transcendental direction given to our
Shakespeare lore by those who first shaped it sym-
pathetically, to wit, Coleridge and the Germans.
An adoring idea of Shakespeare, as a mind of
unapproachable superiority, has thus become so
habitual with most of us that it is difficult to
reduce our notion to terms of normal individuality
of character and mind as we know them in life.
When we read Coleridge, Schlegel, and Gervinus,
or even the admirable essay of Charles Lamb, or
the eloquent appreciations of Mr. Swinburne, or
such eulogists as Hazlitt and Knight, we are in a
world of abstract æsthetics or of abstract ethics ;
we are not within sight of the man Shakespeare,

who became an actor for a livelihood in an age
when the best actors played in inn-yards. for rude
audiences, mostly illiterate and not a little brutal ;
then added to his craft of acting the craft of play-
patching and refashioning ; who had his partnership share of the pence and sixpences paid by the
mob of noisy London prentices and journeymen
and idlers that filled the booth theatre in which
his company performed ; who sued his debtors
rigorously when they did not settle-up ; worked
up old plays or took a hand in new, according as
the needs of his concern and his fellow-actors
dictated ; and finally went with his carefully
collected fortune to spend his last years in ease
and quiet in the country town in which he was
born.   Our sympathetic critics, even when, like
Dr. Furnivall, they know absolutely all the
archæological facts as to theatrical life in Shakespeare's time, do not seem to bring those facts
into vital touch with their æsthetic estimate of
his product : they remain under the spell of
Coleridge and Gervinus.[1]   Emerson, it is true,

[1] It would be unjust to omit to acknowledge that Dr. Furnivall
seeks to frame an inductive notion of Shakespeare, even when rejecting good evidence and proceeding on deductive lines ; that in
the works of Professor Dowden on Shakespeare there is always an
effort towards a judicial method, though he refuses to take some of
the most necessary steps ; and that Mr. Fleay and other English
critics have by the use of metrical tests made a most important

protested at the close of his essay that he "could not marry this fact," of Shakespeare's being a jovial actor and manager, "to his verse"; but that deliverance has served only as a text for those who have embraced the fantastic tenet that Shakespeare was but the theatrical agent and representative of Bacon; a delusion of which the vogue may be partly traced to the lack of psychological solidity in the ordinary presentment of Shake-

contribution to the scientific comprehension of Shakespeare. On the other hand, it may be said that the naturalistic conception of Shakespeare as an organism in an environment was first closely approached in the past century by French critics, as Guizot and Chasles (for Taine's picture of the Elizabethan theatre, adopted by Green, had been founded on a study by Chasles); that the naturalistic comprehension of *Hamlet*, as an incoherent whole resulting from the putting of new cloth into an old garment, was first reached by the German Rümelin (*Shakespeare Studien*); and that the structural anomalies of *Hamlet* as an acting play were first clearly put by the German Benedix (*Die Shakspereomanie*)—these two critics thus making amends for much vain discussion of *Hamlet* by their countrymen before and since; while the naturalistic conception of the man Shakespeare has latterly been best developed in America. The admirable work of Messrs. Clarke and Wright and Fleay in the analysis of the text and the revelation of its non-Shakespearean elements, seems to make little impression on English culture; while such a luminous manual as Mr. Barrett Wendell's *William Shakspere: a Study in Elizabethan Literature* (New York, 1894), with its freshness of outlook and appreciation, points to decided progress in rational Shakespeare-study in the States, though, like the *Shakespeare Primer* of Professor Dowden, it is not consistently scientific throughout.

[To this note, written in 1895, I cannot omit to add that the best work of æsthetic criticism on the tragedies, that of Professor A. C. Bradley, has appeared in England, in the twentieth century.]

speare by his admirers. The heresy, of course, merely leaps over the difficulty, into absolute irrelevance. Emerson was intellectually to blame in that, seeing as he did the hiatus between the poet's life and the prevailing conception of his verse, he did not try to conceive it all anew, but rather resigned himself to the solution that Shakespeare's mind was out of human ken. " A good reader can in a sort nestle into Plato's brain and think from thence," he said ; " but not into Shakespeare's ; we are still out of doors." We should indeed remain so for ever did we not set about patiently picking the locks where the transcendentalist has dreamily turned away.

It is imperative that we should recommence vigilantly with the concrete facts, ignoring all the merely æsthetic and metaphysic syntheses. Where Coleridge and Schlegel more or less ingeniously invite us to acknowledge a miraculous artistic perfection ; where Lamb more movingly gives forth the intense vibration aroused in his spirit by Shakespeare's ripest work, we must turn back to track down the youth from Stratford. We note him as the son of a burgess once prosperous, but destined to sink steadily in the world ; married at eighteen, under pressure of circumstances, with small prospect of income, to the woman of twenty-five; specially ill at ease in that position because of lack of means to maintain a rapidly growing family; and at length, having made friends with a travelling company of actors, come to London to earn a living in any tolerable way by means of his moderate education, his "small Latin and less Greek," his knack of fluent rhyming, and his turn for play-acting. To know him as he began we must measure him narrowly by his first performances. These are not to be looked for in even the earliest of his plays, not one of which can be taken to represent his young and unaided faculty, whether as regards construction or diction. Collaboration, the frequent resort of the modern dramatist, must have been in some form forced on him in those years by the nature of his situation; and after all that has been said by adorers of the quality of his wit and his verse in such early comedies as LOVE'S LABOUR'S LOST and THE TWO GENTLEMEN OF VERONA, the critical reader is apt to be left pretty evenly balanced between the two reflections that the wit and the versification have indeed at times a certain happy naturalness of their own, and that nevertheless, if they really be Shakespeare's throughout, the most remarkable thing in the matter is his later progress. But even apart from such disputable issues, we may safely say with Mr. Fleay that "there is not a play of his that can be referred even on the rashest conjecture to a date anterior to 1594, which does not bear the plainest internal evidence of having been refashioned at a later time." [1]   These plays, then, with all their evidences of immaturity, of what Mr. Bagehot called "clever young-mannishness," cannot serve us as safe measures of Shakespeare's mind at the beginning of his career.

But it happens that we have such a measure in performances which imply no technical arrangement, and are of a homogeneous literary substance. The tasks which the greatest of our poets set himself when near the age of thirty, and to which he presumably brought all the powers of which he was then conscious, were the uninspired and pitilessly prolix poems of Venus and Adonis and The Rape of Lucrece, the first consisting of some 1200 lines and the second of more than 1800 ; one a calculated picture of female concupiscence and the other a still more calculated picture of female chastity : the two alike abnormally fluent, yet external, unimpassioned, endlessly descriptive, elaborately unimpressive. Save for the sexual attraction of the subjects, on the current vogue of

[1] *Life and Work of Shakespeare*, 1886, p. 128.

which the poet had obviously reckoned in choosing them, these performances could have no unstudious readers in our day and few warm admirers in their own, so little sign do they give of any high poetic faculty save the two which singly occur so often without any determining superiority of mind—inexhaustible flow of words and endless observation of concrete detail. Of the countless thrilling felicities of phrase and feeling for which Shakespeare is renowned above all English poets, not one, I think, is to be found in those three thousand fluently-scanned and smoothly-worded lines : on the contrary, the fatiguing succession of stanzas, stretching the themes immeasurably beyond all natural fitness and all narrative interest, might seem to signalise such a lack of artistic judgment as must preclude all great performance ; while the apparent plan of producing an effect by mere multiplication of words, mere extension of description without intension of idea, might seem to prove a lack of capacity for any real depth of passion. Above all, by the admission of the most devoted of Shakespeareans, they are devoid of dramatic quality.[1] They were simply manufactured poems, consciously constructed for the market,

---

[1] Cp. Coleridge, *Biographia Literaria*, ch. xv, § 4 ; and Ten Brink, *Lectures on Shakespeare*, Eng. trans. 1895, p. 109 sq.

10

the first designed at the same time to secure the patronage of the Maecenas of the hour, Lord Southampton, to whom it was dedicated, and the second produced and similarly dedicated on the strength of the success of the first. The point here to be noted is that they gained the poet's ends. They succeeded as saleable literature, and they gained the Earl's favour.

And the rest of the poet's literary career, from this point forward, seems to have been no less prudently calculated. Having plenty of evidence that men could not make a living by poetry, even if they produced it with facility, and that they could as little count on living steadily by the sale of plays, he joined with his trade of actor the business not merely of play-wright but of part-sharer in the takings of the theatre. The presumption from all we know of the commercial side of the play-making of the times is that, for whatever pieces Shakespeare touched up, collaborated in, or composed for his company, he received a certain payment once for all;[1] since there was no reason why his partners should treat his plays differently in this regard from the plays

[1] Professor Dowden notes in his *Shakespeare Primer* (p. 12) that before 1600 the prices paid for plays by Henslowe, the theatrical lessee, vary from £4 to £8, and not till later did it rise as high as £20 for a play by a popular dramatist.

they bought of other men. Doubtless, when his reputation was made, the payments would be considerable. But the main source of his income, or rather of the accumulations with which he bought land and house and tithes at Stratford, must have been his share in the takings of the theatre—a share which would doubtless increase as the earlier partners disappeared. He must have speedily become the principal man in the firm, combining as he did the work of composer, reviser, and adapter of plays with that of actor and working partner. We are thus dealing with a temperament or mentality not at all obviously original or masterly, not at all conspicuous at the outset for intellectual depth or seriousness, not at all obtrusive of its "mission"; but exhibiting simply a gift for acting, an abundant faculty of rhythmical speech, and a power of minute observation, joined with a thoroughly practical or commercial handling of the problem of life, in a calling not usually adopted by commercially - minded men. What emerges for us thus far is the conception of a very plastic intelligence, a good deal led and swayed by immediate circumstances, but at bottom very sanely related to life, and so possessing a latent faculty for controlling its destinies; not much cultured, not profound, not deeply passionate ; not particularly reflective though copious in utterance ; a personality which of itself, if under no pressure of pecuniary need, would not be likely to give the world any serious sign of mental capacity whatever.

In order, then, that such a man as this should develop into the Shakespeare of the great tragedies and tragic comedies, there must concur two kinds of life-conditions with those already noted—the fresh conditions of deeply-moving experience and of deep intellectual stimulus. Without these, such a mind would no more arrive at the highest poetic and dramatic capacity than, lacking the spur of necessity or of some outside call, it would be moved to seek poetic and dramatic utterance for its own relief. There is no sign here of an innate burden of thought, bound to be delivered ; there is only the wonderful sensitive plate or responsive faculty, capable of giving back with peculiar vividness and spontaneity every sort of impression which may be made on it. The faculty, in short, which could produce those 3000 fluent lines on the bare data of the stories of Venus and Adonis and Tarquin and Lucrece, with only the intellectual material of a rakish Stratford lad's schooling and reading, and the culture coming of a few years' association with the primitive English stage and its hangers-on, was capable of broadening and deepening, with vital experience and vital culture, into the poet of LEAR and MACBETH. But the vital culture must come to it, like the experience : this was not a man who would go out of his way to seek the culture. A man so minded, a man who would bear hardship in order to win knowledge, would not have settled down so easily into the actor-manager with a good share in the company's profits. There is very little to show that the young Shakespeare read anything save current plays, tales, and poems. Such a notable book as North's PLUTARCH, published in 1579, does not seem to have affected his literary activity till about the year 1600 :[1] and even then the subject of JULIUS CÆSAR was presumably suggested to him by some other playmaker, as was the case with his chronicle histories.

In his contemporary, Ben Jonson, we do see the type of the young man bent on getting scholarship as the best thing possible to him. The

---

[1] Professor Brandl, in his notice of this essay in the *Shakespeare Jahrbuch* for 1899, objects that the Theseus of the *Midsummer Night's Dream* is "unleugbar aus dem ersten Kapitel des grossen Biographers [*Plutarch*] geschöpft." I can see small basis for this sweeping assertion. The play proceeds on the bare datum that Theseus wedded Hippolyta after overcoming her. Of the many other details in Plutarch's compilation it shows no knowledge. But in any case, Theseus is a mere *deus ex machina* for the play as a whole.

bricklayer's apprentice, unwillingly following the craft of his stepfather, sticking obstinately all the while to his Horace and his Homer, resolute to keep and to add to the humanities he had learned in the grammar school, stands out clearly alongside of the other, far less enthusiastic for knowledge and letters, but also far more plastically framed, and at the same time far more clearly alive, perforce, to the seriousness of the struggle for existence as a matter of securing the daily bread-and-butter.   It may well be, indeed, that but for that peculiarly early marriage, with its consequent family responsibilities, Shakespeare would have allowed himself a little more of youthful breathing-time : it may well be that it was the existence of Ann Hathaway and her three children that made him a seeker for pelf rather than a seeker for knowledge in the years between twenty and thirty, when the concern for pelf sits lightly on most intellectual men.   The thesis undertaken in Love's Labour's Lost—that the truly effective culture is that of life in the world rather than that of secluded study—perhaps expresses a process of inward and other debate in which the wish has become father to the thought.   Scowled upon by jealous collegians like Greene for presuming, actor as he was, to write dramas, he must have asked himself whether there was not something to be gained from such schooling as theirs.[1] But then he certainly made more than was needed to keep the Stratford household going ; and the clear shallow flood of Venus and Adonis and The Rape of Lucrece stands for ever to show how far from tragic consciousness was the young husband and father when close upon thirty years old. It was in 1596 that his little Hamnet died at Stratford ; and there is nothing to show, says Mr. Fleay,[2] that Shakespeare had ever been there in the interval between his departure in 1587 and the child's funeral.

But already, doubtless, some vital experience had come. Professor Ten Brink, recognising like so many other students the psychic transmutation wrought between the period of the comedies and the production of Hamlet, points[3] for the causation to the political episode (1601) of Essex's rebellion, in which Shakespeare's patron, Southampton, was so seriously implicated that he remained in prison till the end of Elizabeth's reign. And this episode is indeed likely to have stirred

[1] Compare the seventy-eighth Sonnet, which ends :

> " But thou art all my art, and dost advance
> As high as learning my rude ignorance."

[2] *Life of Shakespeare*, pp. 29, 128.

[3] *Lectures on Shakespeare*, Eng. trans. 1895, p. 84.

the young poet to a new gravity in his relation to life and to dramatic themes. But it is impossible to leave out of account in such an inquiry the sombre episode of faithless love so enigmatically sketched in the Sonnets. If, with Mr. Flèay,[1] we date these between 1594 and 1598, there had happened thus early in the dramatist's career enough to deepen and impassion the plastic personality of the rhymer of VENUS AND ADONIS ; to add a new string to the heretofore Mercurial lyre. All the while, too, he was undergoing the kind of culture and of psychological training involved in his craft of acting—a culture involving a good deal of contact with the imaginative literature of the Renaissance, so far as then translated, and a

---

[1] See his *Life of Shakespeare*, pp. 120-24. Mr. Fleay's theory of the Sonnets, though perhaps the best "documented" of all, has received less attention than Mr. Tyler's, which has the attraction of fuller detail. Whatever may be the true solution of the enigma of the Sonnets, it seems impossible to accept the chronology of Mr. Samuel Butler, who dates Sonnet 107 by the Armada (*Shakespeare's Sonnets*, 1899, ch. xi) and makes the main series run from 1585 to 1588. It cannot even be shown that by 1585 Shakespeare had come to London. But no chronology is yet substantiated. The crucial sonnet which Mr. Butler dates 1588 is by Mr. Fleay (p. 121) assigned to 1598, in connection with the Peace of Vervins ; by Mr. Tyler (*Shakespeare's Sonnets*, 1890, p. 266) to 1601, in connection with the rebellion of Essex ; and by Mr. Lee (*Life of Shakespeare*, pp. 87, 147, 149), following Massey and Minto, to 1603, in connection with the death of Elizabeth and the release of Southampton. The last assignment seems best to suit the purport. But certainty is thus far impossible ; and there has been an undue assumption of it in every theorist's treatment of the subject.

psychological training of great though little recognised importance to the dramatist. It seems obvious that the practice of acting, by a profoundly plastic and receptive temperament, capable of manifold appreciation, must have counted for much in developing the faculties at once of sympathy and expression. In this respect Shakespeare stood apart from his rivals, with their merely literary training. And in point of fact we do find in his earlier plays, year by year, a strengthening sense of the realities of human nature, despite their frequently idealistic method of portraiture, the verbalism and factitiousness of much of their wit, and their conventionality of plot.

Above all things, the man who drew so many fancifully delightful types of womanhood must have been intensely appreciative of the charm of sex ; and it is on that side that we are to look for his first contacts with the deeper forces of life. What marks off the Shakespeare of thirty-five, in fine, from all his rivals, is just his peculiarly true and new [1] expression of the living grace of woman-

---

[1] Only in Chaucer (*e.g. The Book of the Duchess*) do we find before his time the successful expression of the same perception ; and Chaucer counted for little in Elizabethan letters. [A slightly stronger assertion to this effect in the first edition Professor Brandl found "unbegreiflich." It would be difficult to convey by explicit statement how little of the Chaucerian spirit there is in Spenser, who of the Elizabethan poets most studied Chaucer. Shakespeare, in so many

hood, always, it is true, abstracted to the form of poetry and skilfully purified from the blemishes of the actual, but none the less convincing and stimulating.   We are here in presence at once of a rare receptive faculty and a rare expressive faculty : the plastic organism of the first poems touched through and through with a hundred vibrations of deeper experience ; the external and extensive method gradually ripening into an internal and intensive ; the innate facility of phrase and alertness of attention turned from the physical to the psychical. But still it is to the psychics of sex, for the most part, that we are limited.   Of the deeps of human nature, male nature, as apart from the love of woman, the playwright still shows no special perception, save in the vivid portrait of Shylock, the exasperated Jew.   The figures in which we can easily recognise his hand in the earlier historical plays are indeed marked by his prevailing sanity of perception ; always they show the play of the seeing eye, the ruling sense of reality which shaped his life ; it is this visible actuality that best marks them off from the non-Shakespearean figures around them.   And in the wonderful figures of Falstaff and his group we have a roundness of ways nearer him, shows few signs of knowing him. Sidney had certainly read him, but the *Arcadia* is of another world, even as is *Euphues.* On the drama Chaucer seems to have had small influence.]

comic reality to which nothing else in modern literature thus far could be compared. But still this, the most remarkable of all, remains comic reality ; and, what is more, it is a comic reality of which, as in the rest of his work, the substratum was pre-Shakespearean. For it is clear that the figure of Falstaff, as Oldcastle, had been popularly successful before Shakespeare took hold of it :[1] and what he did here, as elsewhere, with his uninventive mind, in which the faculty of imagination always rectified and expanded rather than originated types and actions, was doubtless to give the hues and tones of perfect life to the half-real inventions of others.

This must always be insisted on as the special psychological characteristic of Shakespeare. Excepting in the possible but doubtful case of LOVE's LABOUR'S LOST, he never invented a plot ; his male characters are almost always developments from an already sketched original ; it is in drawing his heroines, where he is most idealistic, that he seems to have been most independently creative, his originals here being doubtless the women who had charmed him, set living in ideal scenes to charm others. And it resulted from this specialty of structure that the greater reality of his earlier male

[1] See Fleay's *Life of Shakespeare*, pp. 130-131.

historic figures, as compared with those of most of
his rivals, is largely a matter of saner and more
felicitous declamation—the play of his great and
growing faculty of expression—since he had no
more special knowledge of the types in hand
than had his competitors. It is only when his
unequalled receptive faculty has been acted upon
by a peculiarly concentrated and readily assimilated
body of literature, the English version by Sir
Thomas North of Amyot's French translation of
Plutarch's LIVES, that we find Shakespeare incon-
testably superior to his contemporaries in the virile
treatment of virile problems no less than in the
sympathetic rendering of emotional charm and
tenderness and the pathos of passion. The tragedy
of ROMEO AND JULIET, with all its burning fervours
and swooning griefs, remains for us a presentment
of the luxury of woe : it is truly said of it that it
is not fundamentally unhappy. But in JULIUS
CÆSAR we have measured a further depth of sadness. For the moving tragedy of circumstance, of
lovers sundered by fate only to be swiftly joined
in exultant death, we have the profounder tragedy
of mutually destroying energies, of grievously
miscalculating men, of failure and frustration
dogging the steps of the strenuous and the wise, of
destiny searching out the fatal weakness of the

strong. To the poet has now been added the reader ; to the master of the pathos of passion the student of the tragedy of universal life.

It is thus by culture and experience—culture limited but concentrated, and experience limited but intense—that the man Shakespeare has been intelligibly made into the dramatist Shakespeare as we find him when he comes to his greatest tasks. For the formation of the supreme artist there was needed alike the purely plastic organism and the lessoning to which it was so uniquely fitted to respond ; lessoning that came without search, and could be undergone as spontaneously as the experience of life itself.[1] In the English version of Plutarch's LIVES, pressed upon him doubtless by the play-making plans of other men, Shakespeare found the most effectively concentrated history of ancient humanity that could possibly have reached him ; and he responded to the stimulus with all his energy of expression

[1] "He was a natural reader : when a book was dull he put it down ; when it looked fascinating he took it up ; and the consequence is, that he remembered and mastered what he read. . . . It is certain that Shakespeare read the novels of his time . . . ; he read Plutarch . . . ; and it is remarkable that Montaigne is the only philosopher that Shakespeare can be proved to have read, because he deals more than any other philosopher with the first impressions of things which exist."—Bagehot, *Literary Studies* ("Shakespeare the Man"), Hutton's ed. i, 81.

because he received it so freely and vitally, in respect alike of his own plasticity and the fact that the vehicle of the impression was his mother tongue. It is plain that to the last he made no secondary study of antiquity. He made blunders which alone might warn the Baconians off their vain quest : he had no notion of chronology : finding Cato retrospectively spoken of by Plutarch as one to whose ideal Coriolanus had risen, he makes a comrade of Coriolanus say it, as if Cato were a dead celebrity in Coriolanus's day ; just as he makes Hector quote Aristotle in Troy.

These clues are not to be put aside with æsthetic platitudes : they are capital items in our knowledge of the man. And if the idolater feels perturbed by their obtrusion, he has but to reflect that where some [1] of the trained scholars around Shakespeare reproduced antiquity with greater accuracy in minor things, tithing the mint and anise and cumin of erudition, they gave us of the central human forces, which it was their special business to realise, mere hollow and tedious parodies. Jonson was a scholar whose variety of classic reading might have constituted him a specialist to-day ; but Jonson's ancients are mostly dead for

[1] Certainly not all. Cp. the author's *Did Shakespeare write "Titus Andronicus"?* pp. 211-213.

us, even as are Jonson's moderns, because they are the expression of a psychic faculty which could neither rightly perceive reality nor finely express what it did perceive. He represents industry in art rather than inspiration. The two contrasted pictures, of Jonson writing out his harangues in prose in order to turn them into verse, and of Shakespeare giving his lines unblotted to the actors—thinking in verse, in the white heat of his cerebration, as spontaneously as he breathed—these historic data, which happen to be among the most perfectly certified that we possess concerning the two men, give us at once half the secret of one and all the secret of the other. Jonson had the passion for book knowledge, the patience for hard study, the faculty for plot-invention ; and withal he produced dramatic work which gives no such permanent pleasure as does Shakespeare's. Our dramatist had none of these studious characteristics ; and yet, being the organism he was, it needed only the culture which fortuitously reached him in his own tongue to make him successively the greatest dramatic master of eloquence, mirth, charm, tenderness, passion, pathos, pessimism, and philosophic serenity that literature can show, recognisably so even though his work be almost constantly hampered by the framework of other men's enterprises, which he was so singularly content to develop or improve. Hence the critical importance of following up the culture which evolved him, and above all, that which finally touched him to his most memorable performance.

VII

THE POTENCY OF MONTAIGNE

IT is to Montaigne, then, that we now come, in terms of our preliminary statement of evidence. When Florio's translation was published, in 1603, Shakespeare was thirty-seven years old, and he had written or refashioned KING JOHN, HENRY IV, RICHARD II, HENRY V, THE MERCHANT OF VENICE, A MIDSUMMER NIGHT'S DREAM, TWELFTH NIGHT, AS YOU LIKE IT, ROMEO AND JULIET, THE MERRY WIVES OF WINDSOR, and JULIUS CÆSAR. It is very likely that he knew Florio, being intimate with Jonson, who was Florio's friend and admirer; and the translation, long on the stocks, must have been discussed in his hearing. Hence, presumably, his immediate perusal of it. Portions of it, as we have seen, he may very well have read or heard of before it was fully printed (necessarily a long task in the then state of the handicraft); but in the book itself, we have seen abundant reason to believe, he read largely in 1603-4.

Having inductively proved the reading, and at the same time the fact of the impression it made, we may next seek to realise deductively what kind of impression it was fitted to make. We can readily see what North's Plutarch could be and was to the sympathetic and slightly-cultured playwright : it was nothing short of a new world of human knowledge ; a living vision of two great civilisations, giving to his universe a vista of illustrious realities beside which the charmed gardens of Renaissance romance and the bustling fields of English chronicle-history were as pleasant dreams or noisy interludes. He had done wonders with the chronicles ; but in presence of the long muster-rolls of Greece and Rome he must have felt their insularity ; and he never returned to them in the old spirit. But if Plutarch could do so much for him, still greater could be the service rendered by Montaigne. The difference, broadly speaking, is very much as the difference in philosophic reach between JULIUS CÆSAR and HAMLET, between CORIOLANUS and LEAR.

For what was in its net significance Montaigne's manifold book, coming thus suddenly, in a complete and vigorous translation, into English life and into Shakespeare's ken ? Simply the most living literature then existing in Europe. This is not the place in which to attempt a systematic estimate of the most enduring of French writers, who has stirred to their best efforts some of the ablest of French critics ; but I must needs try to indicate briefly, as I see it, his significance in general European culture.   And I would put it that Montaigne is really, for the civilised world at this day, what Petrarch has been too enthusiastically declared to be—the first of the moderns.   He is so as against even the great Rabelais, because Rabelais misses directness, misses universality, misses lucidity, in his gigantic mirth ; he is so as against Petrarch, because he is emphatically an impressionist where Petrarch is a framer of studied compositions ; he is so as against Erasmus, because Erasmus also is a framer of artificial compositions in a dead language, where Montaigne writes with absolute spontaneity in a language not only living but growing.   Only Chaucer, and he only in the CANTERBURY TALES, can be thought of as a true modern before Montaigne ; and Chaucer is there too English to be significant for all Europe.   The high figure of Dante is decisively medieval : it is the central point in later medieval literature.   Montaigne was not only a new literary phenomenon in his

own day : he remains so still ; for his impres-
sionism, which he carried to such lengths in
originating it, is the most modern of literary
inspirations ; and all our successive literary and
artistic developments are either phases of the
same inspiration or transient reactions against it.
Where literature in the mass has taken centuries
to come within sight of the secret that the most
intimate form of truth is the most interesting, he
went, in his one collection of essays, so far towards absolute self-expression that our practice is
still in the rear of his, which is quite too unflinch-
ing for contemporary nerves. Our *bonne foi* is
still sophisticated in comparison with that of the
great Gascon. Of all essayists who have yet
written, he is the most transparent, the most
sincere even in his stratagems, the most discursive,
the most free-tongued, and therefore the most
alive. A classic commonplace becomes in his hands
a new intimacy of feeling : where verbal commonplaces have, as it were, glazed over the surface
of our sense, he probes through them to rouse
anew the living nerve. And there is no theme
on which he does not some time or other dart his
sudden and searching glance. It is truly said of
him by Emerson that " there have been men with
deeper insight ; but, one would say, never a man

with such abundance of thoughts : he is never dull, never insincere, and has the genius to make the reader care for all that he cares for. Cut these words and they bleed ; they are vascular and alive." Such a voice, speaking at Shakespeare's ear in an English nearly as racy and nervous as the incomparable old-new French of the original, was in itself a revelation. And it spoke to one for whom, as player and as playwright, it had come to be an imperative need to substitute a living and lifelike speech for the turgid and unreal rhetoric of the would-be academics who had created the English drama as he found it ; one who, after his narrative poems had won success, turned his back once for all on the prolixities of the school of Spenser.

I have said above that we seem to see passing from Montaigne to Shakespeare a vibration of style as well as of thought ; and it would be difficult to overstate the importance of such an influence. A writer affects us often more by the pulse and pressure of his speech than by his matter. Some such action is indeed the secret of all great literary reputations ; and in no author of any age are the cadence of phrases and the beat of words more provocative of attention than in Montaigne. They must have affected Shake-

speare as they have affected so many others ; and
in point of fact his work, from HAMLET forth,
shows a gain in nervous tension and .pith, fairly
attributable in part to the stirring impact of the
style of Montaigne, with its incessancy of stroke,
its opulence of colour, its hardy freshness of figure
and epithet, its swift, unflagging stride. Seek in
any of Shakespeare's earlier plays for such a
strenuous rush of feeling and rhythm as pulses
through the soliloquy :

"How all occasions do inform against me,"

and you will gather that there has been wrought
a technical change, no less than a moral and an
intellectual. The poet's nerves have felt a new
impulsion.

But it was not merely a congenial felicity and
energy of utterance that Montaigne brought to
bear on his English reader, though the more we
consider this quality of spontaneity in the essayist
the more we shall realise its perennial fascination.
The culture-content of Montaigne's book is more
than even the self-revelation of an extremely
vivacious and reflective intelligence : it is the
living quintessence of all Latin criticism of life,
and of a large part of Greek ; a quintessence as
fresh and pungent as the essayist's expression of

his special individuality. For Montaigne stands out among all the humanists of the epochs of the Renaissance and the Reformation in respect of the peculiar directness of his contact with Latin literature. Other men must have come to know Latin as well as he ; and hundreds could write it with an accuracy and facility which, if he were ever capable of it, he must, by his own confession, have lost before middle life,[1] though he read it perfectly to the last. But he is the only modern man whom we know to have learned Latin as a mother tongue ; and this fact was probably just as important in psychology as was the similar fact, in Shakespeare's case, of his whole adult culture being acquired in his own language. It seems to me, at least, that there is something significant in the facts : (1) that the man who most vividly brought the spirit or outcome of classic culture into touch with the general European intelligence, in the age when the modern languages first decisively asserted their birthright, learned his Latin as a living and not as a dead tongue, and knew Greek literature almost solely by trans-lation ; (2) that the dramatist who of all of his craft has put most of breathing vitality into his pictures of ancient history, despite endless

[1] Cp. the *Essais*, ii, 17 ; iii, 2. (Edit. cited, vol. ii. pp. 40, 231.)

inaccuracies of detail, read his authorities only
in his own language ; and (3) that the English
poet who in our own period has most intensely
and delightedly sympathised with the Greek spirit
—I mean Keats—read his Homer only in an
English translation.

As regards Montaigne, the full importance of
the fact does not seem to me to have been
appreciated by the critics.   Villemain, indeed, who
perhaps could best realise it, remarked in his
youthful *éloge* that the fashion in which the elder
Montaigne had his child taught Latin would
bring the boy to the reading of the classics with
an eager interest where others had been already
fatigued by the toil of grammar ; but beyond
this the peculiarity of the case has not been much
considered.   Montaigne, however, gives us details
which seem full of suggestion to scientific educa-
tionists.   " Without art, without book, without
grammar or precept, without whipping, without
tears, I learned a Latin as pure as my master
could give " ; and his first exercises were to turn
bad Latin into good.[1]   So he read his Ovid's
METAMORPHOSES at seven or eight, where other
forward boys had the native fairy tales ; and a
wise teacher led him later through Virgil and

---

[1] *Essais*, i, 25 ; cp. i, 48.   (Edit. cited, vol. i, pp. 304, 429.)

Terence and Plautus and the Italian poets in the same freedom of spirit. Withal, he never acquired any facility in Greek,[1] and, refusing to play the apprentice where he was accustomed to be master,[2] he declined to construe in a difficult tongue ; read his Plutarch in Amyot ; and his Plato, doubtless, in the Latin version. It all goes with the peculiar spontaneity of his mind, his reactions, his style ; and it was in virtue of this undulled spontaneity that he was fitted to be for Shakespeare, as he has since been for so many other great writers, an intellectual stimulus unique in kind and in potency.

This fact of Montaigne's peculiar influence on other spirits, comparatively considered, may make it easier for some to conceive that his influence on Shakespeare could be so potent as has been above asserted. Among those whom we know him to have acted upon in the highest degree—setting aside the disputed case of Bacon—are Pascal, Montesquieu, Rousseau, Flaubert, Emerson, and Thoreau. In the case of Pascal, despite his uneasy assumption that his philosophy was contrary to Montaigne's, the influence went so far that the PENSEÉS again and again set forth Pascal's doctrine in passages taken almost literally from the Essays.

[1] *Essais*, ii, 4. (Edit. cited, i, 380.)   [2] *Ib.* ii, 10. (Edit. cited, i, 429.)

Stung by the lack of all positive Christian credence in Montaigne, Pascal represents him as "putting all things in doubt"; whereas it is just by first putting all things in doubt that Pascal justifies his own credence. The only difference is that where Montaigne, disparaging the powers of reason by the use of that very reason, used his "doubt" to defend himself alike against the atheists and the orthodox Christians, Catholic or Protestant, himself standing simply to the classic theism of antiquity, Pascal seeks to demolish the theists with the atheists, falling back on the Christian faith after denying the capacity of the human reason to judge for itself. The two procedures were of course alike fallacious; but though Pascal, the more austere thinker of the two, readily saw the invalidity of Montaigne's as a defence of theism, he could do no more for himself than repeat the process, disparaging reason in the very language of the essayist, and setting up in his turn his private predilection in Montaigne's manner. In sum, his philosophy is just Montaigne's, turned to the needs of a broken spirit instead of a confident one— to the purposes of a chagrined and exhausted convertite instead of a theist of the stately school of Cicero and Seneca and Plutarch. Without Montaigne, one feels, the PENSÉES might never have been written : they represent to-day, for all vigilant readers, rather the painful struggles of a wounded intelligence to fight down the doubts it has caught from contact with other men's thought than any coherent or durable philosophic construction.

It would be little more difficult to show the debt of the ESPRIT DES LOIS to Montaigne's inspiration, even if we had not Montesquieu's avowal that " In most authors I see the man who writes : in Montaigne, the man who thinks." [1] That is precisely Montaigne's significance, in sociology as in philosophy. His whole activity is a seeking for causes ; and in the very act of undertaking to " humble reason " he proceeds to instruct and re-edify it by endless corrective comparison of facts. To be sure, he departed so far from his normal *bonne foi* as to affect to think there could be no certainties while parading a hundred of his own, and with these some which were but pretences ; and his pet doctrine of daimonic fortune is not ostensibly favourable to social science ; but in the concrete, he is more of a seeker after rational law than any humanist of his day. In discussing

---

[1] *Pensées Diverses.* Less satisfying is the further *pensée* in the same collection : " Les quatre grand poëtes, Platon, *Malebranche*, *Shaftesbury*, Montaigne."

sumptuary laws, he anticipates the economics of the eighteenth and nineteenth çenturies, as in discussing ecclesiastical law he anticipates the age of tolerance ; in discussing criminal law, the work of Beccaria ; in discussing *a priori* science, the protest of Bacon ; and in discussing education, many of the ideas of to-day. And it would be difficult to cite, in humanist literature before our own century, a more comprehensive expression of the idea of natural law than this paragraph of the APOLOGY :

"If nature enclose within the limits of her ordinary progress, as all other things, so the beliefs, the judgments, the opinions of men ; if they have their revolutions, their seasons, their birth, and their death, even as cabbages ; if heaven doth move, agitate, and roll them at his pleasure, what powerful and permanent authority do we ascribe unto them ? If, by uncontrolled experience, we palpably touch [orig. " Si par experience nous touchons à la main," *i.e.* nous maintenons, nous prétendons : an idiom which Florio has not understood] that the form of our being depends of the air, of the climate, and of the soil wherein we are born, and not only the hair, the stature, the complexion, and the countenance, but also the soul's faculties . . . in such manner that as fruits and beasts do spring up diverse and different, so men are born, either more or less warlike, martial, just, temperate, and docile ; here subject to wine, there to theft and whoredom, here inclined to superstition, there addicted to misbelieving. . . . If sometimes we see one art to flourish, or a belief, and sometimes another, by some heavenly influence ; . . . men's spirits one while flourishing, another while barren, even as fields are seen to be, what become of all those goodly prerogatives wherewith we still flatter ourselves ?" [1]

All this, of course, has a further bearing than Montaigne gives it in the context, and affects his own professed theology as it does the opinions he attacks ; but none the less, the passage strikes alike at the dogmatists and at the pragmatists of all the preceding schools, and hardily clears the ground for a new inductive system. And in the last essay of all he makes a campaign against bad laws which unsays many of his previous sayings on the blessedness of custom.

In tracing his influence elsewhere, it would be hard to point to an eminent French prose-writer who has not been affected by him. Sainte-Beuve finds [2] that La Bruyère "at bottom is close to Montaigne, in respect not only of his style and his skilfully inconsequent method, but of his way of judging men and life"; and the literary heredity from Montaigne to Rousseau is recognised by all who have looked into the matter. The temperaments are profoundly different ; yet the style of Montaigne had evidently taken as deep a hold of the artistic consciousness of Rousseau as had the doctrines of the later writers on whom he drew for his polemic. But indeed he found in

[1] Edition cited, i, 622-623. (Morley's Florio, pp. 294-295.)
[2] *Port-Royal*, 4ième édit., ii, 400, *note*.

the essay on the Cannibals the very theme of his first paradox ; in Montaigne's emphatic denunciations[1] of laws more criminal than the crimes they dealt with, he had a deeper inspiration still ; in the essay on the training of children he had his starting-points for the argumentation of ÉMILE ; and in the whole unabashed self-portraiture of the Essays he had his great exemplar for the CONFESSIONS. Even in the very different case of Voltaire, we may go at least as far as Villemain and say that the essayist must have helped to shape the thought of the great freethinker ; whose PHILOSOPHE IGNORANT may indeed be connected with the APOLOGY without any of the hesitation with which Villemain suggests his general parallel. In fine, Montaigne has scattered his pollen over all the literature of France. The most typical thought of La Rochefoucauld is thrown out[2] in the essay[3] DE L'UTILE ET DE L'HONNESTE ; and the most modern-seeming currents of thought, as M. Stapfer remarks, can be detected in the passages of the all-discussing Gascon.

Among English-speaking writers, to say

---

[1] B. III, Ch. 13.

[2] "In the midst of our compassion, we feel within I know not what bitter sweet touch of malign pleasure in seeing others suffer." (Comp. La Rochefoucauld, *Pensée* 104.)

[3] B. III, Ch. 1.

nothing of those who, like Sterne and Lamb, have been led by his example to a similar felicity of freedom in style, we may cite Emerson as one whose whole work is coloured by Montaigne's influence, and Thoreau as one who, specially developing one side of Emerson's gospel, may be said to have found it all where Emerson found it, in the Essay OF SOLITUDE.[1] The whole doctrine of intellectual self-preservation, the ancient thesis "flee from the press and dwell in soothfastness," is there set forth in a series of ringing sentences, most of which, set in Emerson or Thoreau, would seem part of their text and thought. That this is no random attribution may be learned from the lecture on "Montaigne : the Sceptic," which Emerson has included in his REPRESENTATIVE MEN. "I remember," he says, telling how in his youth he stumbled on Cotton's translation, "I remember the delight and wonder in which I lived with it. It seemed to me as if I had myself written the book in some former life, so sincerely it spoke to my thought and experience." That is just what Montaigne has done for a multitude of others, in virtue of his prime quality of spontaneous self-expression. As Sainte-Beuve has it, there is a Montaigne in all of us. Flaubert,

[1] B. I, Ch. 38.

we know, read him constantly for style ; and no less constantly " found himself" in the self-revelation and analysis of the Essays.

After all these testimonies to Montaigne's seminal virtue, and after what we have seen of the special dependence of Shakespeare's genius on culture and circumstance, stimulus and initiative, for its evolution, there can no longer seem to an open mind anything of mere pseudo-paradox in the opinion that the Essays are among the sources of the greatest expansive movement of the poet's mind, the movement which made him—already a master of the whole range of passional emotion, of the comedy of mirth and the comedy and tragedy of sex—the great master of the tragedy of the moral intelligence.[1]   Taking the step from JULIUS

[1] In vol. xvii (new Ser. vol. x), No. 3 (1902), of the Publications of the Modern Language Association of America, I find, in a study by Miss E. R. Hooker of the relation of Montaigne to Shakespeare (p. 317), a summary description of the thesis of this work as a theory "that *all the greatness of Shakespeare, both in thought and in style*, was due to the influence of Montaigne." One would have expected from a student a little more discrimination of propositions. " Theories like these," says Miss Hooker, " need no discussion." They certainly do not ; and the sole discussion called for by Miss Hooker's assertion is a reference to the above passage, to the account of Shakespeare given above, pp. 37, 38, 53, 65, 96, 119, 125, 149, 153-160, and to the remarks below, pp. 179, 183, 184, 196, 200, 222, which all stand substantially as in the original edition.   One modification has been made above, to reduce the passage to consistency with earlier passages which note the necessary concurrence of moving personal experience with literary influence.   Genius is of course assumed all along as the *conditio sine qua non.*

CÆSAR to HAMLET as corresponding to this movement in his mind, we may say that where the first play exhibits the concrete perception of the fatality of things, "the riddle of the painful earth"; in the second, in its final form, the perception has emerged in philosophic consciousness as a pure reflection. The poet has in the interim been revealed to himself; what he had perceived he now conceives. And this is the secret of the whole transformation which the old play of HAMLET has received at his hands. Where he was formerly the magical sympathetic plate, receiving and rectifying and giving forth in inspired speech every impression, however distorted by previous instruments, that is brought within the scope of its action, he is now in addition the inward judge of it all, so much so that the secondary activity tends to overshadow the primary.

The old HAMLET, it is clear, was a tragedy of blood, of physical horror. The least that Shakespeare, at this age, could have done with it, would be to overlay and transform the physical with moral perception; and this has already been in part done in the First Quarto form. The mad Hamlet and the mad Ophelia, who had been at least as much comic as tragic figures in the older play,[1] are

[1] See Mr. Corbin's able study, *The Elizabethan Hamlet*, 1895.

12

already purified of that taint of their barbaric birth, save in so far as Hamlet still gibes at Polonius and jests with Ophelia in the primitive fashion of the pretended madman seeking his revenge. But the sense of the futility of the whole heathen plan, of the vanity of the revenge to which the Christian ghost hounds his son, of the moral void left by the initial crime and its concomitants, not to be filled by any hecatomb of slain wrongdoers—the sense of all this, which is the essence of the tragedy, though so few critics seem to see it, clearly emerges only in the finished play. The dramatist is become the chorus to his plot, and the impression it all makes on his newly active spirit comes out in soliloquy after soliloquy, which hamper as much as they explain the action. In the old prose story, the astute barbarian takes a curiously circuitous course to his revenge, but at last attains it. In the intermediate tragedy of blood, the circuitous action had been preserved, and withal the revenge was attained only in the general catastrophe, by that daimonic "fortune" on which Montaigne so often enlarges.

For Shakespeare, then, with his mind newly at work in reverie and judgment, where before it had been but perceptive and reproductive, the theme was one of human impotence, failure of will, weariness of spirit in presence of over-mastering fate, recoil from the immeasurable evil of the world. Hamlet becomes the mouthpiece of the all-sympathetic spirit which has put itself in his place, as it had done with a hundred suggested types before, but with a new inwardness of comprehension, a self-consciousness added to the myriad-sided consciousness of the past.   Hence an involution rather than an elucidation of the play.   There can be no doubt that Shakespeare, in heightening and deepening the theme, has obscured it, making the scheming barbarian into a musing pessimist, who yet waywardly plays the mock-madman as of old, and kills the " rat " behind the arras ; doubts the Ghost while acting on his message ; philosophises with Montaigne and yet delays his revenge in the spirit of the Christianised savage who fears to send the praying murderer to heaven.   There is no solution of these anomalies : the very state of Shakespeare's consciousness, working in his subjective way on the old material, made inevitable a moral anachronism and contradiction, analogous in its kind to the narrative anachronisms of his historical plays.   But none the less, this tragedy, the first of the great group which above all his other work make him immortal, remains perpetually fascinating, by virtue even of that " pale cast of thought " which has " sicklied it o'er " in the sense of making it too intellectual for dramatic unity and strict dramatic success. Between these undramatic, brooding soliloquies which stand so aloof from the action, but dominate the minds of those who read and meditate the text, and the old sensational elements of murder, ghost, fencing and killing, which hold the interest of the crowd—in virtue of these constituents, HAMLET remains the most familiar Shakespearean play.

This very pre-eminence and permanence, no doubt, will make many students still demur to the notion that a determining factor in the framing of the play was the poet's perusal of Montaigne's Essays. And it would be easy to overstate that thesis in such a way as to make it untrue. Indeed, M. Chasles has, to my thinking, so overstated it. Had I come to his main proposition before realising the infusion of Montaigne's ideas in HAMLET, I think I should have felt it to be as excessive in the opposite direction as the proposition of Mr. Feis. Says M. Chasles : [1]

"This date of 1603 [publication of Florio's translation] is instructive ; the change in Shakespeare's style dates from this very year. Before 1603, imitation of Petrarch, of Ariosto, and of Spenser is evident in his work : after 1603, this coquettish copying of Italy has disappeared ; no more crossing rhymes, no more sonnets and concetti. All is

---

[1] *L'Angleterre au seizième siècle*, p. 133.

reformed at once. Shakespeare, who had hitherto studied the ancients only in the fashion of the fine writers of modern Italy, . . . now seriously studies Plutarch and Sallust, and seeks of them those great teachings on human life with which the chapters of Michael Montaigne are filled. Is it not surprising to see Julius Cæsar and Coriolanus suddenly taken up by the man who has just (*tout à l'heure*) been describing in thirty-six stanzas, like Marini, the doves of the car of Venus ? And does not one see that he comes fresh from the reading of Montaigne, who never ceased to translate, comment, and recommend the ancients . . . ? The dates of Shakespeare's Coriolanus, Cleopatra, and Julius Cæsar are incontestable. These dramas follow on from 1606 to 1608, with a rapidity which proves the fecund heat of an imagination still moved."

All this must be revised in the light of a more correct chronology. Shakespeare's Julius Cæsar dates, not from 1606 but from 1600 or 1601, being referred to in Weever's Mirror of Martyrs, published in 1601, to say nothing of the reference in the third Act of Hamlet itself, where Polonius speaks of such a play. And, even if it had been written after 1604, it would still be a straining of the evidence to ascribe its production, with that of Coriolanus and Antony and Cleopatra, to the influence of Montaigne, when every one of these themes was sufficiently obtruded on the Elizabethan theatre by North's translation of Amyot's Plutarch. As a matter of fact, a play on Julius Cæsar was known as early as 1579 ; and there were many others.[1]   Any one who will compare CORIOLANUS with North's translation will see that Shakespeare has followed the text down to the most minute and supererogatory details, even to the making of blunders by putting the biographer's remarks in the mouths of the characters.   The comparison throws a flood of light on Shakespeare's mode of procedure ; but it tells us nothing of his perusal of Montaigne. Rather it suggests a return from the method of the revised HAMLET, with its play of reverie, to the more strictly dramatic method of the chronicle histories, though with a new energy and concision of presentment.   The real clue to Montaigne's influence on Shakespeare beyond HAMLET, as we have seen, lies not in the Roman plays, but in MEASURE FOR MEASURE.

There is a misconception involved, again, in M. Chasles's picture of an abrupt transition from Shakespeare's fantastic youthful method to that of HAMLET and the Roman plays.   He overlooks the intermediate stages represented by such plays as ROMEO AND JULIET, HENRY IV, HENRY V, KING JOHN, TWELFTH NIGHT, MUCH ADO, the MERCHANT OF VENICE, and AS YOU LIKE IT,

---

[1] Halliwell-Phillipps, *Outlines of the Life of Shakespeare*, 1885, p. 497.

all of which exhibit a great advance on the methods of LOVE'S LABOUR'S LOST, with its rhymes and sonnets and " concetti." The leap suggested by M. Chasles is exorbitant : such a headlong development would be unintelligible. Shakespeare had first to come practically into touch with the realities of life and character before he could receive from Montaigne the full stimulus he actually did undergo. Plastic as he was, he none the less underwent a normal evolution ; and his early concreteness and verbalism and externality had to be gradually transmuted into a more inward knowledge of life and art before there could be superimposed on that the mood of the thinker, reflectively aware of the totality of what he had passed through.

Finally, the most remarkable aspect of Shakespeare's mind is not that presented by CORIOLANUS and ANTONY AND CLEOPATRA, which with all their intense vitality represent rather his marvellous power of reproducing impressions than the play of his own criticism on the general problem of life. For the full revelation of this we must look rather in the great tragedies, notably in LEAR, and thereafter in the subsiding movement of the later serious plays. There it is that we learn to give exactitude to our con-

ception of the influence exerted upon him by
Montaigne, and to see that, even as in the cases
of Pascal and Montesquieu, Rousseau and Emerson,
what happened was not a mere transference or
imposition of opinions, but a living stimulus, a
germination of fresh intellectual life, which
developed under new forms. It would be strange
if the most receptive and responsive of all the
intelligences which Montaigne has touched should
not have gone on differentiating itself from his.

VIII

WHAT then is the general, and what the final relation of Shakespeare's thought to that of Montaigne? How far did the younger man approve and assimilate the ideas of the elder ; how far did he reject them, how far modify them ? In some respects this is the most difficult part of our inquiry, were it only because Shakespeare is firstly and lastly a dramatic writer. But he is not only that : he is at once the most subjective, the most sympathetic, and the most self-withholding of dramatic writers. Conceiving all situations, all epochs, in terms of his own perception and his own psychology, he is yet the furthest removed from all dogmatic design on the opinions of his listeners ; and it is only after a most vigilant process of moral logic that we can ever be justified in attributing to him this or that thesis of any one of his personages, apart from the general ethical sympathies which must be taken for granted.

Much facile propaganda has been made by the device of crediting him in person with every religious utterance found in his plays—even in the portions which analytical criticism proves to have come from other hands.   Obviously we must look to his general handling of the themes with which the current religion deals, in order to surmise his attitude to that religion.   And in the same way we must compare his general handling of tragic and moral issues, in order to gather his general attitude to the doctrine of Montaigne.

At the very outset, we must make a clean sweep of the strange proposition of Mr. Jacob Feis—that Shakespeare deeply disliked the philosophy of Montaigne, and wrote HAMLET to discredit it.   It is hard to realise how such a hopeless misconception can ever have arisen in the mind of any one capable of making the historic research on which Mr. Feis seeks to found his assertion.   If there were no other argument against it, the bare fact that the tragedy of HAMLET existed before Shakespeare, and that he was, as usual, simply working over a play already on the boards, should serve to dismiss such a wild hypothesis.   And from every other point of view, the notion is equally preposterous.   No human being in Shakespeare's day could have gathered from HAMLET such a criticism of Montaigne as Mr. Feis reads into it by means of violences of interpretation which might almost startle Mr. Donnelly. Even if men blamed Hamlet for delaying his revenge, in the manner of the ordinary critical moralist, they could not possibly regard that delay as a kind of vice arising from the absorption of Montaignesque opinions. In the very year of the appearance of Florio's folio, it was a trifle too soon to make the assumption that Montaigne was demoralising mankind, even if we assume Shakespeare to have ever been capable of such a judgment. And that assumption is just as impossible as the other. According to Mr. Feis, Shakespeare detested such a creed and such conduct as Hamlet's, and made him die by poison in order to show his abhorrence of them—this, when we know Hamlet to have died by the poisoned foil in the earlier play. On that view, Cordelia died by hanging in order to show Shakespeare's conviction that she was a bad daughter ; and Desdemona by stifling as a fitting punishment for adultery. The idea is beneath serious discussion. Barely to assume that Shakespeare held Hamlet for a pitiable weakling is a sufficiently shallow interpretation of the play ; but to assume that he made him die by way of condign punishment for his opinions is merely ridiculous. Once for all, there is absolutely nothing in Hamlet's creed or conduct which Shakespeare was in a position to regard as open to didactic denunciation.

The one intelligible idea which Mr. Feis can suggest as connecting Hamlet's conduct with Montaigne's philosophy is that Montaigne was a Quietist, preaching and practising withdrawal from public broils. But Shakespeare's own practice was on all fours with this. He sedulously held aloof from all meddling in public affairs ; and when he had gained a competence he retired, at the age of forty-seven, to Stratford-on-Avon. Mr. Feis's argument brings us to the very crudest form of the good old Christian verdict that if Hamlet had been a good and resolute man he would have killed his uncle out of hand, whether at prayers or anywhere else, and would then have married Ophelia, put his mother in a nunnery, and lived happily ever after.[1] And to that edifying assumption Mr. Feis adds the fantasy that Shakespeare dreaded the influence of Montaigne as a deterrent from the retributive slaughter of guilty uncles by wronged nephews.

In the hands of Herr Stedefeld, who in 1871

[1] This seems to be the ideal implied in the criticisms even of Mr. Lowell and Mr. Dowden.

anticipated Mr. Feis's view of HAMLET as a sermon against Montaigne, the thesis is not a whit more plausible. Herr Stedefeld entitles his book :[1] " Hamlet : a Drama-with-a-purpose (TENDENZ-DRAMA) opposing the sceptical and cosmopolitan view of things taken by Michael de Montaigne " ; and his general position is that Shakespeare wrote the play as " the apotheosis of a practical Christianity," by way of showing how any one like Hamlet, lacking in Christian piety, and devoid of faith, love, and hope, must needs come to a bad end, even in a good cause. We are not entitled to charge Herr Stedefeld's thesis to the account of religious bias, seeing that Mr. Feis in his turn writes from the standpoint of a kind of Protestant freethinker, who sees in Shakespeare a champion of free inquiry against the Catholic conformist policy of Montaigne ; while strictly orthodox Christians have found in Hamlet's various allusions to deity, and in his " As for me, I will go pray," a proof alike of his and of Shakespeare's steadfast piety. Against all such eccentricities and superficialities of exegesis alike our safeguard must be a broad common-sense induction.

We are entitled to say at the outset, then, only

[1] *Hamlet : ein Tendenzdrama Sheakspere's* [*sic* throughout book] *gegen die skeptische und cosmopolitische Weltanschauung des Michael de Montaigne*, von G. F. Stedefeld, Kreisgerichtsrath, Berlin, 1871.

this, that Shakespeare at the time of working over
HAMLET and MEASURE FOR MEASURE in 1603-1604
had in his mind a great deal of the reasoning in
Montaigne's Essays ; and that a number of the
speeches in the two plays reproduce portions of
what he had read.   We are not entitled to assume
that these portions are selected as being in agreement with Shakespeare's own views : we are here
limited to saying that he put certain of Montaigne's
ideas or statements in the mouths of his characters
where they would be appropriate.   It does not
follow that he shared the feelings of Claudio as to
the possible life of the soul after death.   And when
Hamlet says to Horatio, on the strangeness of the
scene with the Ghost :

> " And therefore as a stranger give it welcome !
> There are more things in heaven and earth, Horatio,
> Than are dreamt of in our philosophy "—

though this may be said to be a summary of the
whole drift of Montaigne's essay,[1] THAT IT IS
FOLLY TO REFER TRUTH OR FALSEHOOD TO OUR
SUFFICIENCY ; and though we are entitled to
believe that Shakespeare had that essay or its
thesis in his mind, there is no reason to suppose
that the lines convey Shakespeare's own belief in
ghosts.   Montaigne had indicated his doubts on

[1] B. I, Ch. 26.

that head even in protesting against sundry denials of strange allegations ; and it is dramatically fitting that Hamlet in the circumstances should say what he does. On the other hand, when the Duke in MEASURE FOR MEASURE, playing the part of a friar preparing a criminal for death, gives Claudio a consolation which contains not a word of Christian doctrine, not a syllable of sacrificial salvation or sacramental forgiveness or a future life, we are entitled to infer from such a singular negative phenomenon, if not that Shakespeare rejected the Christian theory of things, at least that it formed no part of his habitual thinking. It was the special business of the Duke, posing in such a character, to speak to Claudio of sin and salvation, of forgiveness and absolution. Such a notable omission must at least imply disregard on the part of the dramatist. It is true that Isabella, pleading to Angelo in the second Act, speaks as a believing Christian on the point of forgiveness for sins ; and again that the Duke speaks[1] of the unrepentant Barnardine as a priest might :

> " A creature unprepared, unmeet for death,
> And to transport him in the mind he is
> Were damnable " ;

and the versification in these passages is quite

[1] Act II, Sc. 3.

Shakespearean. But a solution of the anomaly is to be found here as elsewhere in the fact that Shakespeare was working over an existing play ;[1] and that in ordinary course he would, if need were, put such speeches as the religious pleading of Isabella into his own magistral verse just as he would touch up the soliloquy of Hamlet on the question of killing his uncle at prayers—a soliloquy which we know to have existed in the earlier forms of the play. The writer who first made Isabella plead religiously with Angelo would have made the Duke counsel Claudio religiously. The Duke's speech to Claudio, then, is to be regarded as Shakespeare's special insertion ; and it is to be taken as negatively exhibiting his opinions.

In the same way, the express withdrawal of the religious note at the close of HAMLET— where in the Second Quarto we have Shakespeare making the dying prince say " the rest is silence " instead of " heaven receive my soul," as in the First Quarto—may reasonably be taken to express the same agnosticism on the subject of a future life as is implied in the Duke's speech to Claudio. It cannot reasonably be taken to suggest a purpose of holding Hamlet up to blame as an unbeliever,

---

[1] It is not disputed that the plot existed beforehand in Whetstone's *Promos and Cassandra* ; and there was probably an intermediate drama.

because Hamlet is made repeatedly to express himself, in talk and in soliloquy, as a believer in deity, in prayer, in hell, and in heaven. These speeches are mostly reproductions of the old play, the new matter being in the nature of the pagan allusion to the "divinity that shapes our ends." What is definitely Shakespearean is just the agnostic conclusion. And the Sonnets point in the same direction. Sonnet cxlvi cannot be made to bear the orthodox interpretation so often forced upon it ; and the general note of the Sonnets on death is a negation of the idea of a future state. [1]

Did Shakespeare, then, derive this agnosticism from Montaigne ? What were really Montaigne's religious and philosophic opinions? We must consider this point also with more circumspection than has been shown by most of Montaigne's critics. The habit of calling him "sceptic," a habit initiated by the Catholic priests who denounced his heathenish use of the term "Fortune," and strengthened by various writers from Pascal to Emerson, is a hindrance to an exact notion of the facts, inasmuch as the word "sceptic" has passed through two phases of significance, and may still have either. In the original sense of the term, Montaigne is a good

[1] Cp. Tyler, *Shakespeare's Sonnets*, 1890, Ch. x.

13

deal of a "sceptic," because the main purport of
the APOLOGY OF RAIMOND SEBONDE—certainly
an inconsistent performance—appears to be the
discrediting of human reason all round, and the
consequent shaking of all certainty, religious or
other. And this method strikes not only indirectly but directly at the current religious
beliefs ; for Montaigne indicates a lack of belief
in immortality,[1] besides repeatedly ignoring the
common faith where he would naturally be
expected to endorse it, as in the nineteenth and
fortieth essays hereinbefore cited, and in his
discussion of the Apology of Socrates. As is
complained by Dean Church : [2] " His views, both
of life and death, are absolutely and entirely
unaffected by the fact of his profession to believe
the Gospel." That profession, indeed, partakes
rather obviously of the nature of his other formal
salutes [3] to the Church, which are such as
Descartes felt constrained to make in a later generation. His profession of fidelity to Catholicism,

---

[1] Edit. Firmin-Didot, i, 590.

[2] *Oxford Essays*, p. 279. Sterling, from his Christian-Carlylese
point of view, declared of Montaigne that " All that we find in him
of Christianity would be suitable to apes and dogs rather than to
rational and moral beings " (*London and Westminster Review*, July
1838, p. 346).

[3] Sainte-Beuve has noted how in the essay *Of Prayers* he added
many safeguarding clauses in the later editions.

again, is rather his way of showing that he saw no superiority of reasonableness in Protestantism, than the expression of any real conformity to Catholic ideals ; for he indicates alike his aversion to heretic-hunting and his sense of the folly of insisting on the whole body of dogma. When fanatical Protestants, uncritical of their own creed, affected to doubt the sincerity of any man who held by Catholicism, he was naturally piqued. But he was more deeply piqued, as Naigeon has suggested, when the few but keen freethinkers of the time treated the THEOLOGIA NATURALIS of Sebonde, which Montaigne had translated at his father's wish, as a feeble and inconclusive piece of argumentation ; and it was primarily to retaliate on such critics—who on their part no doubt exhibited some ill-founded convictions while attacking others—that he penned the APOLOGY, which assails atheism in a familiar fashion, but with a most unfamiliar energy and splendour of style, as a manifestation of the foolish pride of a frail and perpetually erring reason. For himself, he was, as we have said, a classic theist, of the school of Cicero and Seneca ; and as regards that side of his own thought he is not sceptical, save in so far as he nominally protested against all attempts to bring deity down to human conceptions, while himself doing that very thing, as every theist needs must.

Shakespeare, then, could find in Montaigne the traditional deism of the pagan and Christian world, without any colour of specifically Christian faith, and with a direct lead to unbelief in a future state. But, whether we suppose Shakespeare to have been already led, as he might be by the initiative of his colleague Marlowe, an avowed atheist, to agnostic views on immortality, or whether we suppose him to have had his first serious lead to such thought from Montaigne, we find him to all appearance carrying further the initial impetus, and proceeding from the serene semi-Stoicism of the essayist to a deeper and sterner conception of things. It lay, indeed, in the nature of Shakespeare's psychosis, so abnormally alive to all impressions, that when he fully faced the darker sides of universal drama, with his reflective powers at work, he must utter a pessimism commensurate with the theme. This is part, if not the whole, of the answer to the question " Why did Shakespeare write tragedies ? "[1] The whole answer can hardly be either Mr. Spedding's, that the poet wrote his darkest tragedies

[1] See Mr. Spedding's essay, so entitled, in the *Cornhill Magazine*, August 1880.

in a state of philosophic serenity,[1] or Dr. Furnivall's, that he "described hell because he had felt hell."[2] But when we find Shakespeare writing a series of tragedies, including an extremely sombre comedy (MEASURE FOR MEASURE), after having produced mainly comedies and history-plays, we must conclude that the change was made of his own choice, and that whereas formerly his theatre took its comedies mostly from him, and its tragedies mostly from others, it now took its comedies mostly from others and its tragedies from him.

Further, we must assume that the gloomy cast of thought so pervadingly given to the new tragedies is partly a reflex of his own experience, which would seem to have included deep psychic perturbation on the side of sex, but also in large part an expression of the philosophy to which he had been led by his reading, as well as by his life. For we must finally avow that the pervading thought in the tragedies outgoes the simple artistic needs of the case. In OTHELLO we have indeed a very strictly dramatic array of the forces of wrong —weakness, blind passion, and pitiless egoism; but there is already a full suggestion of the over-

[1] Art. cited, *end*.
[2] Note cited by Mr. Spedding. Cp. Introd. to *Leopold* Shakespeare, p. lxxxvii.

whelming energy of the element of evil ; and in LEAR the conception is worked out with a desperate insistence which carries us far indeed from the sunny cynicism and prudent scepticism of Montaigne.   In no other version of the Lear story is tragedy so accumulated : the suicide of Cordelia which in the old legend followed by Spenser was long subsequent to her succour of her father, is here altered to a violent death which hastens his. And the thought throughout is as dark as the action.   Twice in the Essays, it is true, we meet with the note of gloom struck in the lines :

> " As flies to wanton boys are we to the Gods :
> They kill us for their sport " :

and I think the essayist's words were in Shakespeare's mind when he wrote ; but the gloom of Montaigne's page is as a passing cloud compared with that of the play.   And since there is no pretence of balancing that mordant saying with any decorous platitude of Christian Deism, we are led finally to the inference that Shakespeare sounded a further depth of philosophy than Montaigne's unembittered "cosmopolitan view of things."   Instead of reacting against Montaigne's " scepticism," as Herr Stedefeld supposes, he produced yet other tragedies in which the wrongdoers and the wronged alike exhibit less and not more of Christian faith than

Hamlet,[1] and in which there is no hint of any such faith on the part of the dramatist, but, on the contrary, a sombre persistence in the presentment of unrelieved evil. The utterly wicked Iago has as much of religion in his talk as any one else in OTHELLO, using the phrases " Christian and heathen," " God bless the mark," " Heaven is my judge," " You are one of those that will not serve God, if the devil bid you," " The little godliness I have," " God's will," and so forth ; the utterly wicked Edmund in LEAR, as we have seen, is made to echo Montaigne's " sceptical " passage on the subject of stellar influences, spoken with a moral purpose, rather than the quite contrary utterance in the APOLOGY, in which the essayist, theistically bent on abasing human pretensions, gives to his scepticism the colour of a belief in those very influences.[2] There is here, clearly, no pro-religious thesis. The whole drift of the play shows that Shakespeare shares the disbelief in stellar control, though he puts the expression of the disbelief in the mouth of a villain ; though he makes the honest Kent, on the other hand, declare that " it is the stars . . . that govern our conditions ";[3] and

[1] Lear once (iii, 4) says he will pray ; but his religion goes no further.

[2] See the passage cited above in section III in connection with *Measure for Measure.*   [3] Act IV, Sc. 2.

though he had previously made Romeo speak of
"the yoke of inauspicious stars," and the Duke
describe mankind as "servile to all the skiey
influences," and was later to make Prospero, in the
TEMPEST,[1] express his belief in "a most auspicious
star." In the case of Montaigne, who goes on yet
again to contradict himself in the APOLOGY itself,
satirising afresh the habit of associating deity with
all human concerns, we are driven to surmise an
actual variation of opinion—the vivacious intelligence springing this way or that according as
it is reacting against the atheists or against the
dogmatists. Montaigne, of course, is not a
coherent philosopher : the way to systematic
philosophic truth is a path too steep to be climbed
by such an undisciplined spirit as his, "sworn
enemy to obligation, to assiduity, to constancy" ;[2]
and the net result of his APOLOGY for Raimond
Sebonde is to upset the system of that sober theo-
logian as well as all others. Whether Shakespeare,
on the other hand, could or did detect all the
inconsistencies of Montaigne's reasoning, is a point
on which we are not entitled to more than a surmise ; but we do find that on certain issues on which
Montaigne dogmatises very much as did his predecessors, Shakespeare applies a more penetrating

[1] Act I, Sc. 2.   [2] B. I, Ch. 20.

logic, and explicitly reverses the essayist's verdicts. Montaigne, for instance, carried away by his master doctrine that we should live " according to nature," is given to talking of " art " and " nature " in the ordinary Aristotelian manner, carrying the primitive commonplace indeed to the length of a pseudo-paradox. Thus in the essay on the Cannibals,[1] speaking of " savages," he protests that

" They are even savage, as we call those fruits wild which nature of herself and of her ordinary progress hath produced, whereas indeed they are those which ourselves have altered by our artificial devices, and diverted from their common order, we should rather call savage. In those are the true and more profitable virtues and natural properties most lively and vigorous " ;[2]

deciding with Plato that

"all things are produced either by nature, by fortune, or by art ; the greatest and fairest by one or other of the two first ; the least and imperfect by this last."

And in the APOLOGY,[3] after citing some as arguing that

" Nature by a maternal gentleness accompanies and guides " the lower animals, "as if by the hand, to all the actions and commodities of their life," while, "as for us, she abandons us to hazard and fortune, and to seek by art the things necessary to our conservation,"

though he proceeds to insist on the contrary that " nature has universally embraced all her creatures,"

[1] B. I, Ch. 30. [2] Edit. Firmin-Didot, i, 202.
[3] *Ibid.* pp. 477-478.

man as well as the rest, and to argue that man is
as much a creature of nature as the rest—since
even speech, "if not natural, is necessary"—he
never seems to come within sight of the solution
that art, on his own showing, is just nature in a
new phase.   But to that point Shakespeare proceeds at a stride in the WINTER'S TALE, one of
the latest plays (? 1611), written about the time
when we know him to have been reading or
re-reading the essay on the Cannibals.   When
Perdita refuses to plant gillyflowers in her garden,

> "For I have heard it said
> There is an art which in their piedness shares
> With great creating nature,"

the old king answers :

> "Say there be :
> Yet nature is made better by no mean,
> But nature makes that mean ; so o'er [? e'en] that art
> Which you say adds to nature, is an art
> That nature makes.   You see, sweet maid, we marry
> A gentle scion to the wildest stock
> And make conceive a bark of baser kind
> By bud of nobler race : This is an art
> Which does mend nature—change it rather ; but
> The art itself is nature."

It is an analysis, a criticism, a philosophic demonstration ; and the subtle poet smilingly lets us see
immediately that he had tried the argument on
the fanatics of "nature," fair or other, and knew

them impervious to it. " I'll not put," says
Puritan Perdita, after demurely granting that " so
it is "—

> " I'll not put
> The dibble in earth to set one slip of them."

It is a fine question whether in this case the
suggestion came to Shakespeare from Bacon, who
developed nearly the same idea as to nature and
art in a whole series of the writings which cul-
minated in the NOVUM ORGANUM and DE
AUGMENTIS SCIENTIARUM. In Bacon's English
ADVANCEMENT OF LEARNING (1605) it is put
thus : [1]

" From the wonders of nature is the nearest intelligence
and passage towards the wonders of art ; for it is no more
but by following and as it were hounding nature in her
wanderings, to be able to lead her afterwards to the same
place again."

In his English FILUM LABYRINTHI, which is
a version of his Latin COGITATA ET VISA, dated
by Spedding about 1607, the idea stands thus :

" The original inventions and conclusions of nature,
which are the life of all that variety, are not many, nor
deeply fetched ; and . . . the rest is but the subtile and
ruled motion of the instrument and hand." [2]

Thus far the thesis is barely perceptible in germ.

---

[1] B. II (Routledge's ed. of *Works*, p. 80).
[2] *Filum Labyrinthi, sive, Formula Inquisitionis. Ad Filios*, Ch. 3.

But in the Latin tractate DESCRIPTIO GLOBI IN-
TELLECTUALIS, which is proved by an astronomical
allusion [1] to have been at least partly written in
1612, we have it set forth, not, indeed, quite
lucidly, but with emphasis :

" I am the rather induced to set down the history of arts
as a species of natural history, because it is the fashion to
talk as if art were something different from nature, so that
things artificial should be separated from things natural, as
differing totally in kind ; whence it comes that most writers
of natural history think it enough to make a history of
animals or plants or minerals, without mentioning the
experiments of mechanical arts (which are far the most
important for philosophy) ; and not only that, but another
and more subtle error finds its way into men's minds ; that
of looking upon art merely as a kind of supplement to nature ;
which has power enough to finish what nature has begun or
correct her when going aside, but no power to make radical
changes, and shake her in the foundations ; an opinion which
has brought a great deal of despair into human concerns.
Whereas men ought on the contrary to have a settled conviction that things artificial differ from things natural, not in
form or essence, but only in the efficient ; that man has in
truth no power over nature except that of motion—the
power, I say, of putting natural bodies together or separating
them—and that *the rest is done by nature working within.*
Whenever therefore there is a possibility of moving natural
bodies towards one another or away from one another, man
and art can do everything ; when there is no such possibility,
they can do nothing.   On the other hand, provided this
motion to or from, which is required to produce any effect,

---

[1] The allusion to the "nova stella in pectore Cygni qui jam
per duodecim annos integros duravit" (cap. 7).   This star was
discovered by Jansen in 1600.

be duly given, *it matters not whether it be done by art and human means, or by nature unaided by man;* nor is the one more powerful than the other." [1]

This is almost identical with the well-known passage in the later DE AUGMENTIS [2] (published in 1623). The first book of that is substantially the same as the English of the ADVANCEMENT; but the second book is in the Latin greatly modified, and the above is one of the entirely new passages.

It appears then that between 1605 and 1612 Bacon's thought had played freshly on the subject, whether of his own motion or on a stimulus from without. And that he had heard of some discussion on the point is suggested by a passage which occurs a few sentences before that above cited :

"I will make the division of natural history according to the force and condition of nature itself; which is found in three states, and subject as it were to three kinds of regimen. For nature is either free, and allowed to go her own way and develop herself in her ordinary course ; that is when she works by herself, without being any way obstructed or wrought upon ; as in the heavens, in animals, in plants, and in the whole array of nature ;—or again she is forced and driven quite out of her course by the perversities and

---

[1] Trans. rev. by Spedding. (Routledge's one-vol. ed. of Bacon, 1905, pp. 678-9.)
[2] B. II, c. 2. (Edit. cited, p. 427.)

insubordination of wayward and rebellious matter, and by
the violence of impediments ; as in monsters and heteroclites
of nature ;—or lastly, she is constrained, moulded, translated,
and made as it were new by art and the hand of man ;
as in things artificial. For in things artificial nature seems
as it were made, whereby a new array of bodies presents
itself, and a kind of second world. Natural history therefore
treats either of the *liberty* of nature or her *errors* or her *bonds*.
*And if any one dislike that arts should be called the bonds of
nature, thinking they should rather be counted as her deliverers
and champions, because in some cases they enable her to fulfil her
own intention by reducing obstacles to order ; for my part I do
not care about these refinements and elegancies of speech ;* all I
mean is, that nature, like Proteus, is forced by art to do that
which without art would not be done ; call it which you
will,—force and bonds, or help and perfection. I will
therefore divide natural history into history of generations,
history of preter-generations, and history of arts, which I
also call mechanical and experimental history."

The effect of these sentences is distinctly to
suggest that an objection to his own way of putting
things had come to Bacon from without ; and
that at the time of writing the sentences last
quoted he had not fully assimilated the thought,
since he is still insisting on nature's *errors* and
bonds, according to his original formula in the
ADVANCEMENT : "Nature in course ; nature
erring or varying ; and nature altered or wrought."
The passage which follows (the first cited) seems
to develop the new view on a new perception ;
and though the old definitions are still adhered to

in a somewhat altered form, the chapter concludes on the new note :

"Therefore *as nature is one and the same, and her power extends through all things, nor does she ever forsake herself,* these three things should by all means be set down as alike subordinate only to nature ; namely, the course of nature ; the wandering of nature ; and art, or nature with man to help. And therefore in natural history all these things should be included in one continuous series of narratives. . . ."

Following up the clue, we find some reason to query whether the whole chapter was written at the same time. The next work, in order of publication, in which Bacon handles the theme is the Novum Organum (1620), where on the first page we have the passage [1] which Spedding translates :

"Nature to be commanded must be obeyed ; and that which in contemplation is as the cause is in operation as the rule.

"Towards the effecting of works all that man can do is to put together or put asunder natural bodies. The rest is done by nature working within."

—the theorem of the ostensibly later idea in the Descriptio, with the stress laid on the emphatic closing sentence. Again, however, there arises a problem of imperfect assimilation, for, later in the same book,[2] Bacon appears to repent of his admission, referring in a hostile fashion to "the

[1] B. I, Aph. iii, iv. [2] Aph. lxxv.

notion that composition only is the work of man, and mixture of none but nature." It will be found, too, that in the final DE AUGMENTIS there is the same conflict of ideas, the notion that man is merely an assistant to nature being blamed (in the fashion of the DESCRIPTIO) as a doctrine of despair, whereas that is precisely the purport of the proposition with which the passage closes. The discord is never resolved, and we seem bound to conclude that Bacon continued to move among two or three opinions—one conventional, and held by him in 1605 (that nature can " err " and be put in " bonds ") ; another, entertained and affirmed, though without rejecting the other, about 1612 (that nature is one throughout, man merely trafficking in her operations) ; and a third, entertained perhaps at the same time (though never really reconciled) with the second, and re-affirmed, in apparent reaction against it, in the later works : namely, that man's power over nature is unlimited. To the last there is in-coherence. All might be cleared up by putting it that in " assisting " nature man *is* using, employ-ing, and controlling her—obeying in order to be obeyed, as it is put in the Aphorism at the outset of the NOVUM ORGANUM ; but the two lines of thought never properly blend. The residual impression is that set up by the Descriptio, that about 1612 the idea of the continuity or universality of nature came to Bacon from without, and that while it strongly impressed him, and never left him, it always remained a separate item in his consciousness. In the final recast of the doctrine in the De Augmentis he even omits the phrase about "nature working within."

The whole matter is thus somewhat obscure; but the date of 1612 is suggestively prominent. Seeing, then, that the Winter's Tale was performed, in all likelihood, in 1610, and certainly in 1611, and published in 1612,[1] would it not appear that Bacon's larger idea had been suggested to him by the dramatist?

There are so many possibilities that we have no right to a decided opinion. On the one hand, the main thesis may have been framed by some anti-Aristotelian before Bacon. John Mill supposed[2] that the definition of man's power over nature—which he does not credit to Bacon—was "first illustrated and made prominent as a fundamental principle of political economy" by his father; whereas it had been so used by Verri and noted by Destutt de Tracy, both of whom

---

[1] Fleay, p. 65 ; Lee, 2nd ed., p. 251.
[2] *Principles of Polit. Econ.* B. I, Ch. 1, § 2, *note.*

14

were quoted by M'Culloch in his earlier
"Principles." Even a later parentage has been
assigned to it in the same connection. If, then,
the fact of such a series of utterances could be
overlooked by such a student as Mill in our own
day, a pre-Baconian utterance of the same truth
may easily have been forgotten. Indeed, as Ellis
points out in a note on the passage in the NOVUM
ORGANUM, the phrase as to nature "working
within" seems to follow Galen, who, in his treatise
DE NATURALIBUS FACULTATIBUS, contrasts the
inward workings of nature with the outward
operations of art. In Bacon's day, the Galenic
lore was still familiar to physicians ; and from
one of these he may have had his idea, though it
must be admitted that he paid much less heed to
current scientific thought than he has the air of
doing ; since he never once makes mention of
Harvey's new doctrine of the circulation of the
blood, which had been put in currency as early as
1615, and this by the court physician. To new
physiology the new Instaurator paid as little heed
as to the new astronomic demonstrations of Kepler.

On the other hand, we have Dr. Rawley's
testimony : "I myself have seen at least twelve
copies of the INSTAURATION revised year by year,
one after another ; and every year altered and

amended in the frame thereof; till at last it came to that model in which it was committed to the press."[1]   In the face of this, who shall confidently say that Bacon's precise and trenchant wording of the idea was independent of Shakespeare's ?

What seems certain is that Shakespeare lived in a circle in which Bacon's themes were in some degree canvassed.   The lines in Hamlet's epistle :

> "Doubt thou the stars are fire ;
> Doubt that the sun doth move,"

tell of two of the special problems of the DESCRIPTIO GLOBI INTELLECTUALIS and of others of Bacon's treatises ; and when we remember how ardent and intimate was Ben Jonson's admiration for the great Chancellor, we can fairly infer that his doctrines would come in the way of Shakespeare. The poets who met at the Mermaid could hardly have missed conversing on such topics.   And there is another distinct and concrete ground for surmising that in some indirect way specific propositions, out of the line of commonplace, passed between Bacon's circle and Shakespeare's.   In TROILUS AND CRESSIDA occurs the famous anachronism of Hector's allusion to Aristotle :

> "Young men, whom Aristotle thought
> Unfit to hear moral philosophy."[2]

---

[1] *Life of Bacon*, prefixed to the *Instauratio Magna* in 1656.
[2] Act II, Sc. 2.

Bacon could not have committed the anachronism, but he had either preceded or followed Shakespeare in the error—or rather the current convention—of putting "moral" where Aristotle had put "political"[1]—an error repeated in the Latin DE AUGMENTIS eighteen years later.[2] Spedding, taking it for granted that Shakespeare copied the mistake of Bacon, yet remarked that the Italian writer Malvezzi, in his DISCORSI SOPRA CORNELIO TACITO (published in 1622), made precisely the same mistake.[3]   Mr. Lee further points out that "moral" was actually held in Bacon's day to be a proper equivalent for "political" as used by Aristotle, the phrase having been so rendered in a manuscript note of the period on a French translation of the ETHICA.[4]   This is fairly enough put as a rebuttal of the inference drawn by the Bacon-Shakespeare sectaries, that the two passages under notice came from the same pen. A more decisive rebuttal, however, lies in the bare notation of the extravagant anachronism in the play.   Bacon could make more serious slips than the rendering of Aristotle's "political" by "moral," but he could hardly have made Hector quote Aristotle at the siege of Troy.

[1] *Advancement of Learning*, B. II.   Edit. cited, p. 146.
[2] B. VII, Ch. 3.   Edit. cited, p. 575.   [3] *Id.* p. 146.
[4] *Life*, pp. 370-71, *note*.

There remains Spedding's reasonable suggestion that Shakespeare in TROILUS AND CRESSIDA, published in 1609, was quoting from the ADVANCEMENT OF LEARNING. In respect of dates of issues, the position is unchallengeable ; but we now know that TROILUS AND CRESSIDA was written a number of years before it was printed ; and in all likelihood is to be dated 1602 or 1603.[1] It is now arguable, therefore, that Bacon's allusion to Aristotle was made on the strength of witnessing TROILUS AND CRESSIDA in 1602 or 1603, as he very well might, seeing that the play was performed about that time by the Lord Chamberlain's men, who frequently played before the Court in the midwinter season.[2]

The notion that Bacon was the imitator, unlikely enough in itself, receives countenance from the fact that in every other instance which has been noted of resemblance or correspondence between the thought of the two writers, the order is the same. The question whether the stars are true fires is discussed by Bacon only in 1612 ; and we have seen how on the question of nature and art he comes to the true view only after

[1] Cp. Fleay, *Life*, pp. 24, 44-5, 61-2, 136, 146, 160, 220-22 ; Lee, p. 225.
[2] Fleay, pp. 136, 142, 146, etc.

Shakespeare,[1] and even then retreats from it. And
in yet another case we find Bacon following
Shakespeare in point of time on a line of thought
on which their utterances suggest a point of
contact. As has been pointed out by an adherent
of the Baconian view[2] of the plays, there is a
marked resemblance between a paragraph in
Bacon's essay OF GREAT PLACE and a passage in
CYMBELINE. Shakespeare has :

> "The art o' the Court
> As hard to leave as keep : whose top to climb
> Is certain falling, or so slippery that
> The fear's as bad as falling."[3]

Bacon has :

"The standing is slippery : and the regress is either a down-
fall or at least an eclipse, which is a melancholy thing."

And the thought further chimes in the contexts.
Now, the essay OF GREAT PLACE appears for the
first time in the edition of 1612 ; while the play
was certainly on the boards as early as 1611.
Here again, then, the presumption of priority is in
Shakespeare's favour, if we can assume imitation
in the case of so exoteric a thought. And yet

[1] I have suggested elsewhere that the "probability" is that the
idea reached Shakespeare from Bacon through Ben Jonson ; but
this was written without due regard to the chronological data.

[2] *Baconiana*, Oct. 1908, p. 244.

[3] Act III, Sc. 3.

again, in the case of the somewhat slight parallels between Perdita's speech on flowers and Bacon's essay OF GARDENS, pointed out by Spedding in his notes on that essay, the play is the prior document, the essay being one of the later additions, not found in the edition of 1597.

When all is said, of course, we have no right to pass beyond hypothesis ; and even if we do not stress the unlikeliness of Bacon's echoing a lax phrase about Aristotle which he had heard in a play [1]—coupled too with a staring anachronism— there is more plausibility in another very natural hypothesis. Such ideas might very well pass unwritten from circle to circle, even on very different social planes. Ben Jonson, whom we know to have been on terms of some respectful intimacy with Bacon, was likely enough, àpropos of current events, to say at times the same thing in talk with Bacon and in talk with his friends at the tavern. And some such intellectual mediation seems to have taken place ; for even if we decide that the twisted tag from Aristotle was really a current commonplace in that form, we can hardly come to the same conclusion in regard to the

---

[1] It may be argued, of course, that Shakespeare, reading the *Advancement* after he had written *Troilus*, inserted the passage in the MS. But there is no trace of any other echo, and this hypothesis would be even less plausible than the other.

parallel utterances on the theme of nature and art. In that case, Jonson is eminently likely to have been the middleman, especially if, as has been not unwarrantably suggested, his was one of the " good pens " employed by Bacon to put some of his later works into Latin. The suggestion that such a thought should have reached Bacon in such a fashion may seem a *lèse-majesté* to the high Baconians ; and indeed, as we have said, it may well have reached him from some other source. But it does not appear to have been his before it was Shakespeare's ; and as to the problem, in turn, of the poet's originality in this connection, we can but say finally that Shakespeare has grasped the particular truth here in question more firmly than Bacon ever did, and phrased it once for all with perfect lucidity and consistency.

Be the thought primarily his or not, Shakespeare has put the philosopheme into consummately dramatic and rhythmic speech, with a perfect appreciation of the issue, and has visibly made it part of his own philosophy. The mind which could thus easily pierce below the inveterate fallacy of three thousand years of conventional speech may well be presumed capable of rounding Montaigne's philosophy wherever it collapses, and of setting it aside wherever it is arbitrary. Certain it is that we can never convict Shakespeare of bad reasoning in person; and in his later plays we never seem to touch bottom in his thought. The poet of VENUS AND ADONIS seems to have deepened beyond the plummet-reach even of the deep-striking intelligence that first stirred him to philosophise.

And yet, supposing this to be so, there is none the less a lasting community of thought between the two spirits, a lasting debt from the younger to the elder. Indeed, we cannot say that at all points Shakespeare outwent his guide. It is a haunting reflection that they had possibly one foible in common; for we know Montaigne's little weakness of desiring his family to be thought ancient, of suppressing the fact of its recent establishment by commerce; and we have evidence which seems to show that Shakespeare sought zealously,[1] despite rebuffs, the formal constitution of a coat-of-arms for his family. It may have been, of course, that he was seeking to please some one else. On the other hand, there is nothing in Shakespeare's work—the nature of the case indeed forbade it—to compare in democratic outspokenness with Montaigne's essay[2] OF THE INEQUALITY AMONG US. The Frenchman's hardy

---

[1] Fleay's *Life*, pp. 138, etc.   [2] B. I, Ch. 42.

saying [1] that "the souls of emperors and cobblers are all cast in one same mould" could not well be echoed in Elizabethan drama ; and indeed we cannot well be sure that Shakespeare would have endorsed it, with his habit of taking kings and princes and generals and rich ones for his leading personages.   But then, on the other hand, we cannot be sure that this was anything more than a part of his deliberate life's work of producing for the English multitude what that multitude cared to see, and catching London with that bait of royalty which commonly attracted it.   It remains doubtful whether his extravagant idealisation and justification of Henry V—which, though it gives so little pause to some of our English critics, moved M. Guizot to call him a mere John Bull in his ideas of international politics —was really an expression of his own thought. As regards the prologues to the play, I affirm with confidence that they are not Shakespeare's work, having no community of diction and rhythm with his undisputed verse of that date.   The presumption is that they were written for the revival of the play in the autumn of 1599,[2] when the faction of Essex were working on the bellicose instincts of the people.   That Shakespeare left the trumpet-

---

[1] B. II, Ch. 12.   (Edit. cited, i, 501.)   [2] Fleay's *Life*, p. 35.

ing to be done by another hand seems doubly significant. It is notable that he never again in his plays strikes the note of blatant patriotism. And the poets of that time, further, seem to have been privately very far from serious reverence with regard to their Virgin Queen ; so that we cannot be sure that Shakespeare, paying her his fanciful compliment,[1] was any more sincere about it than Ben Jonson, who would do as much while privately accepting the grossest scandal concerning her.[2] It is certainly a remarkable fact, finally, that Shakespeare abstained from joining in the poetic outcry over her death, incurring reproof by his silence.[3]

However all that may have been, we find Shakespeare, after his period of pessimism, viewing life in a spirit which could be expressed in terms of Montaigne's philosophy. He certainly shaped his latter years in accordance with the essayist's ideal. We can conceive of no other man in Shakespeare's theatrical group deliberately turning his back, as he did, on the many-coloured London life when he had means to enjoy it at leisure, and seeking to possess his own soul in Stratford-on-

---

[1] *Midsummer Night's Dream*, Act II, Sc. 2.

[2] See his Conversations with Drummond of Hawthornden.

[3] Halliwell-Phillipps, *Outlines of the Life of Shakespeare*, 5th ed. p. 175.

Avon, in the circle of a family which had already
lived so long without him. It is highly probable,
indeed, that his health was already shattered by
the nervous malady which marks the signatures to
his will,[1] and which doubtless hastened his death ;
but it was still open to him to dwell in London.
Thus his retirement, rounding with peace the
career of manifold and intense experience, is a
main fact in Shakespeare's life, and one of our
clues to his innermost character. Emerson, never
quite delivered from Puritan prepossessions,
though so often superior to them, avowed his
perplexity over the fact "that this man of
men, he who gave to the science of mind a
new and larger subject than had ever existed,
and planted the standard of humanity some
furlongs forward into Chaos—that he should not
be wise for himself : it must even go into the
world's history that the best poet led an obscure (!)
and profane life, using his genius for the public
amusement." [2] If this were fundamentally so
strange a thing, one might have supposed that the
transcendentalist would therefore "as a stranger
give it welcome." Approaching it on another
plane, one finds nothing specially perplexing in

[1] Cp. J. F. Nisbet, *The Insanity of Genius,* 1891, pp. 151-59.
[2] *Representative Men : Shakespeare, the Poet.*

the matter. Shakespeare's personality was an uncommon combination ; but was not that what should have been looked for? And where, after all, is the evidence that he was " not wise for himself " ?[1] Did he not make his fortune where most of his rivals failed ? If he was "obscure," how otherwise could he have been less so ? How could the bankrupt tradesman's son otherwise have risen to fame? Should he have sought, at all costs, to become a lawyer, and rise perchance to the seat of Bacon, and incur the temptation of eking out his stipend by gifts? If it be conceded that he must needs try literature, and such literature as a man could live by ; and if it be further conceded that his plays, being so marvellous in their content, were well worth the writing, where enters the " profanity " of having written them, or of having

[1] Mr. Appleton Morgan and others have created a needless difficulty on this head. In his *Shakespeare in Fact and Criticism*, Mr. Morgan writes (p. 316) : " I find him . . . living and dying so utterly unsuspicious that he had done anything of which his children might care to hear, that he never even troubled himself to preserve the manuscript of or the literary property in a single one of the plays which had raised him to affluence." As I have already pointed out, and as was pointed out a century and a half ago by Farmer, there is no reason to suppose that Shakespeare could retain the ownership of his plays any more than did the other writers who supplied his theatre. They belonged to the partnership. Besides, he could not possibly have published as *his* the existing mass, so largely made up of other men's work. His fellow-players did so without scruple after his death, being primarily bent on making money.

acted in them, "for the public amusement"?
Even wise men seem to run special risks when
they discourse on Shakespeare : Emerson's essay
has its own anomaly.

It is indeed fair to say that Shakespeare must
have drunk a bitter cup in his life as an actor.
It is true that that calling is apt to be more
humiliating than another to a man's self-respect,
if his judgment remain both sane and sensitive.
We have the expression of it all in the Sonnets :[1]

> " Alas ! 'tis true, I have gone here and there,
>   And made myself a motley to the view,
>   *Gored mine own thoughts, sold cheap what is most dear,*
>   *Made old offences of affections new.*"

It is impossible to put into fewer and fuller
words the story, many a year long, of sordid
compulsion laid on an artistic nature to turn its
own inner life into matter for the stage.   But he
who can read Shakespeare might be expected to
divine that it needed, among other things, even
some such discipline as that to give his spirit its
strange universality of outlook.   And he who
could esteem both Shakespeare and Montaigne
might have been expected to note how they drew
together at that very point of the final retirement,
the dramatic caterer finally winning, out of his

---

[1] Sonnet cx.   Compare the next.

earnings, the peace and self-possession that the essayist had inherited without toil. He must, one thinks, have repeated to himself Montaigne's very words :[1] " My design is to pass quietly, and not laboriously, what remains to me of life ; there is nothing for which I am minded to make a strain : not knowledge, of whatever great price it be." And when he at length took himself away to the quiet village of his birth, it could hardly be that he had not in mind those words of the essay[2] OF SOLITARINESS :

" We should reserve a storehouse for ourselves . . . altogether ours, and wholly free, wherein we may hoard up and establish our true liberty, the principal retreat and solitariness, wherein we must go alone to ourselves. . . . We have lived long enough for others, live we the remainder of all life unto ourselves. . . . Shake we off these violent hold-fasts which elsewhere engage us, and estrange us from ourselves. The greatest thing of the world is for a man to know how to be his own. It is high time to shake off society, since we can bring nothing to it. . . ."

A kindred note is actually struck in the 146th Sonnet,[3] which tells of revolt at the expenditure of

[1] B. II, Ch. 10. [2] B. I, Ch. 38.

[3] This may be presumed to have been written between 1603 and 1609, the date of the publication of the Sonnets ; but, as we have seen, the point is much disputed. Mr. Minto argues that, " the only sonnet of really indisputable date is the 107th, containing the reference to the death of Elizabeth " (*Characteristics*, as cited, p. 220). If this could be settled, other sonnets could be dated in turn. As the first 126 sonnets makes a series, it is reasonable to take those remaining as of later date.

inner life on the outward garniture, and exhorts the soul to live aright :

> " Then, soul, live thou upon thy servant's loss,
>   And let that pine to aggravate thy store ;
>   Buy terms divine in selling hours of dross ;
>   Within be fed, without be rich no more :
>   So shalt thou feed on death that feeds on men,
>   And death once dead, there's no more dying then "

—an echo of much of Montaigne's discourse, hereinbefore cited.[1]

In perfect keeping with all this movement towards peace and contemplation, and in final keeping, too, with the deeper doctrine of Montaigne, is the musing philosophy which lights, as with a wondrous sunset, the play which one would fain believe the last of all. At the end, as at the beginning, we find the poet working on a pre-existing basis, re-making an old play ; and at the end, as at the beginning, we find him picturing, with an incomparable delicacy, new ideal types of womanhood, who stand out with a fugitive radiance from the surroundings of mere humanity ; but over all alike, in the TEMPEST,

---

[1] It more particularly echoes, however, two passages in the nineteenth essay : " There is no evil in life for him that hath well conceived how the privation of life is no evil. To know how to die, doth free us from all subjection and constraint." " No man did ever prepare himself to quit the world more simply and fully . . . than I am fully assured I shall do. The deadest deaths are the best."

there is the fusing spell of philosophic reverie. Years before, in HAMLET, he had dramatically caught the force of Montaigne's frequent thought that daylight life might be taken as a nightmare, and the dream life as the real. It was the kind of thought to recur to the dramatist above all men, even were it not pressed upon him by the essayist's reiterations:

"Those which have compared our life unto a dream, have happily had more reason so to do than they were aware. When we dream, our soul liveth, worketh, and exerciseth all her faculties, even and as much as when it waketh. . . . We wake sleeping, and sleep waking. In my sleep I see not so clear, yet can I never find my waking clear enough, or without dimness. . . . Why make we not a doubt whether our thinking and our working be another dreaming, and our waking some kind of sleeping?" [1]

"Let me think of building castles in Spain, my imagination will forge me commodities and afford me means and delights wherewith my mind is really tickled and essentially gladded. How often do we pester our spirits with anger or sadness by such shadows, and entangle ourselves into fantastical passions which alter both our mind and body? . . . Enquire of yourself, where is the object of this alteration? Is there anything but us in nature, except subsisting nullity? over whom it hath any power? . . . Aristodemus, king of the Messenians, killed himself upon a conceit he took of some ill presage by I know not what howling of dogs. . . . It is the right way to prize one's life at the right worth of it, to forego it for a dream." [2]

---

[1] B. II, Ch. 12.   [2] B. III, Ch. 4 (end).

". . . Our reasons do often anticipate the effect and have the extension of their jurisdiction so infinite, that they judge and exercise themselves in inanity, and to a not being. Besides the flexibility of our invention, to frame reasons unto all manner of dreams ; our imagination is likewise found easy to receive impressions from falsehood, by very frivolous appearances." [1]

Again and again does the essayist return to this note of mysticism, so distant from the daylight practicality of his normal utterance. And it was surely with these musings in his mind that the poet made Prospero pronounce upon the phantasmagoria that the spirits have performed at his behest. It has been suggested that the speech proceeds upon a reminiscence of four lines in the Earl of Stirling's DARIUS (1604), lines in themselves very tolerable, alike in cadence and sonority, but destined to be remembered by reason of the way in which the master, casting them into his all-transmuting alembic, has remade them in the fine gold of his subtler measure. The Earl's lines run :

" Let greatness of her glassy scepters vaunt ;
    Not scepters, no, but reeds, soon bruised, soon broken ;
And let this wordly pomp our wits enchant ;
    All fades, and scarcely leaves behind a token.
Those *golden palaces*, those *gorgeous* halls,
    With furniture superfluously fair ;
Those stately courts, those *sky-encountering* walls,
    Evanish all like vapours in the air."

---

[1] B. III, Ch. 11, near end.

The passage may very well have given Shakespeare his cue; but as it happens there is another possible source in a passage of Kyd's translation of Garnier's CORNELIA,[1] published in 1594 :

> " O *lofty towers*, O stately battlements
> O *glorious temples*, O proud *palaces*,
> And you brave walls, bright heaven's masonry
> Grac'd with a thousand kingly diadems."

Here the verbal coincidences are a little more noticeable, though the idea of the vanishing of all is not developed as in Stirling's lines. In any case, the sonorities of one or the other set of verses [2]

---

[1] Act IV, Sc. 2, 5-8.

[2] Echoes of this kind may derive proximately from Spenser :

> " My pallaces possessèd of my foe,
> My cities sacked, and their sky-threating walls
> Racèd and made smooth fields."
>
> (*Faerie Queene*, B. V, c. x, st. 33.)

> " High towers, faire temples, goodlie theaters
> Strong walls, rich porches, princelie pallaces . . .
> All these (O pitie !) now are turned to dust. . . ."
>
> (*The Ruines of Time*, st. 14.)

> " Triumphant Arcks, spires, neighbours to the sky. . . ."

> " These haughtie heapes, these palaces of olde,
> These walls, these arcks, these baths, these temples hie. . . ."
>
> (Version of Bellay's *Ruines of Rome*, st. 7 and 27.)

> " All his glory gone
> And all his greatness vapourèd to nought."
>
> (*Ruines of Time*, st. 32.)

> " All that in this world is great or gay
> Doth as a vapour vanish and decay."
>
> (*Id.* st. 8.)

If any should resent the suggestion that Shakespeare's muse was

seem to have vibrated in the poet's brain amid
the memories of the prose which had suggested
to him so much ; and the verse and prose alike
are raised to an immortal movement in the great
lines of Prospero :

> " These our actors,
> As I foretold you, are all spirits, and
> Are melted into air, into thin air.
> And like the baseless fabric of this vision,
> The cloud-capped towers, the gorgeous palaces,
> The solemn temples, the great globe itself,
> Yea, all which it inherit, shall dissolve
> And, like this unsubstantial pageant faded,
> Leave not a wrack behind. *We are such stuff*
> *As dreams are made on*, and our little life
> Is rounded with a sleep."

In the face of that large philosophy, it seems an
irrelevance to reason, as some do, that in the earlier
scene in which Gonzalo expounds his Utopia of
incivilisation, Shakespeare so arranges the dialogue
as to express his own ridicule of the conception.
The interlocutors, it will be remembered, are
Sebastian and Antonio, the two villains of the
piece, and Alonso, the king who had abetted the
usurping brother. The kind Gonzalo talks of
the ideal community to distract Alonso's troubled

ever spurred in this fashion, what do they make of the echo of Lyly's
song on the lark (*Alexander and Campaspe*, Act V, Sc. 1) :

> " How at heaven's gate she claps her wings " ;

in " Hark, hark, the lark at heaven's gate sings," and in Sonnet xxix.

thoughts ; Sebastian and Antonio jeer at him ; and Alonso finally cries, "Pr'ythee, no more, thou dost talk nothing to me." Herr Gervinus is quite sure that this was meant to state Shakespeare's prophetic derision for all communisms and socialisms and peace congresses, Shakespeare being the fore-ordained oracle of the political gospel of his German commentators, on the principle of "*Gott mit uns.*" And it may well have been that Shakespeare, looking on the society of his age, had no faith in any Utopia, and that he humorously put what he felt to be a valid criticism of Montaigne's in the mouth of a surly villain : he has done as much elsewhere. But he was surely the last man to have missed seeing that Montaigne's Utopia was no more Montaigne's personal political counsel to his age than As You Like It was his own ; and, as regards the main purpose of Montaigne's essay, which was to show that civilisation was no unmixed gain as contrasted with some forms of barbarism, the author of CYMBELINE was hardly the man to repugn it, even if he amused himself by putting forward Caliban [1] as the real "cannibal," in contrast to Montaigne's. He had given his impression of certain aspects of civilisation in HAMLET,

---

[1] In all probability this character existed in the previous play, the name being originally, as was suggested last century by Dr Farmer, a mere variant of "Canibal."

MEASURE FOR MEASURE, and KING LEAR. As his closing plays show, however, he had reached the knowledge that for the general as for the private wrong the sane man must cease to cherish indignation. That teaching, which he could not didactically impose, for such a world as his, on the old tragedy of revenge which he recoloured with Montaigne's thought, he found didactically enough set down in the essay OF DIVERSION : [1]

> " Revenge is a sweet pleasing passion, of a great and natural impression : I perceive it well, albeit I have made no trial of it. To divert of late a young prince from it, I told him not he was to offer the one side of his cheek to him who had struck him on the other in regard of charity ; nor displayed I unto him the tragical events poesy bestoweth upon that passion. There I left him and strove to make him taste the beauty of a contrary image ; the honour, the favour, and the good-will he should acquire by gentleness and goodness ; I diverted him to ambition."

And now it is didactically uttered by the wronged magician in the drama :

> " Though with their high wrongs I am struck to the quick,
>   Yet with my nobler reason, 'gainst my fury,
>   Do I take part ; the rarer action is
>   In virtue than in vengeance. . . ."

The principle now pervades the whole of Prospero's polity ; even the cursed and cursing Caliban had

[1] B. III, Ch. 4.

before been recognised [1] as a necessary member of it :

> " We cannot miss him ; he does make our fire,
> Fetch in our wood ; and serves in offices
> That profit us " ;

and the plotting Caliban, like the plotting villains, is finally forgiven. It is surely not unwarrantable to pronounce, then, in sum, that the poet who thus watchfully lit his action from the two sides of passion and sympathy was in the end at one with his "guide, philosopher, and friend," who in that time of universal strife and separateness could of his own accord renew the spirit of Socrates, and say : [2] "I esteem all men my compatriots, and embrace a Pole even as a Frenchman, subordinating this national tie to the common and universal." Here, too, was not Montaigne the first of the moderns ?

[1] Act II, Sc. 2.   [2] B. III, Ch. 9.

THE ORIGINALITY OF SHAKESPEARE

(1898)

I

THE foregoing attempt to trace part of the intellectual development of Shakespeare elicited from the newspaper press, among a number of unexpectedly favourable comments, several protests; and one of these is so superior to the rest, at once in deliberateness and in seriousness of tone, that it seems warrantable to take it as a competent if not a typical statement of the conservative case. It is needless to specify the newspaper sources of this and any other criticisms I may deal with : suffice it 'to call the principal antagonist " Critic A," and to label the others in series. And first as to the general notion of originality, concerning which critic A thus concludes :

" On the whole, too much is said in these days, by Mr. Robertson and others, of Shakespeare's lack of invention. He invented admirably whenever he pleased—is not ' A MID-SUMMER NIGHT'S DREAM, for example, to all intents an invention, and a perennially beautiful one? But beyond this (we intend no paradox) his choice of themes was so inspired that it amounted to invention. The themes of his five great tragedies, ROMEO, HAMLET, MACBETH, OTHELLO, LEAR, were equally open to his contemporaries; but it was he, not they, who saw in them the type-tragedies of the world. It is quite a mistake to assume that it is merely his workmanship that makes these plays great. The greatness lies very largely in the subjects. We look in vain among his fellows, not only for such workmanship, but for such themes. He chose them; others passed them by; and such choice is in a very true sense invention. Ben Jonson was infinitely more at home than he in Roman history; but while Ben laboured away at the episodes of CATILINE and SEJANUS, Shakespeare went straight to the world-historic themes of JULIUS CÆSAR and ANTONY AND CLEOPATRA. If it be lack of invention that enables a man to create ROMEO AND JULIET, OTHELLO, and KING LEAR, then lack of invention is the essential gift of the world-dramatist."

In examining this deliverance, we need not stay long over the last sentence, which hardly justifies a serious discussion. No one, so far as I am aware, has ever argued that lack of invention "enabled" Shakespeare to write his tragedies; but if it *were* argued that the highest faculty for imaginative and poetic dramatisation of character and feeling was haply correlative with defect of faculty for plot-framing—that the gift of Shakespeare and the gift of Scribe are not likely to go together—then the critic's fling would still be a mere verbalism or petulance, leaving the matter as it was, though he apparently supposes it to be a *reductio ad absurdum*. Let us then take his other points one by one.

1. For the proposition that Shakespeare "invented admirably *whenever he pleased*" the critic offers only the evidence of one play—one out of thirty-seven—and that juvenile, fantastic, unvital, turning on fairy tricks and cross-purposes, yet withal in the way and manner of the customary comedy of mistaken identity.

2. While naming ROMEO, HAMLET, MACBETH, OTHELLO, LEAR, as tragedy-motives taken up by Shakespeare and disregarded by his contemporaries, the critic incidentally shows himself to be perfectly well aware of the notorious fact that at least two of the five *had* been handled by other men before Shakespeare. Beyond question, HAMLET had been a popular success before Shakespeare took it up. The CHRONICLE HISTORY OF KING LEIR was certainly on the stage before Shakespeare's tragedy, and was clearly the suggestion for that. As regards ROMEO AND JULIET, again, there is good reason to surmise a pre-Shakespearean play. Such a conservative critic as Mr. Grant White sees "quite unmistakeable" signs of a pre-Shakespearean hand in the early quarto, and frames the theory "that in 1591 Shakespeare and one or

more other 'practitioners for the stage' composed a ROMEO AND JULIET in partnership, and that in 1596 Shakespeare 'corrected, augmented, and amended' it." Mr. Fleay, going further, holds that the first form of the play was written by Peele about 1593. Whether or not that view is adopted, no student, I apprehend, will take the line of arguing, with critic A, that Shakespeare alone was capable of seeing the strength of the story as a tragic theme for the stage. Next, as to MACBETH, we have the opinion of the Cambridge editors that certain portions of the first Act, in particular those of which Mr. Arnold pronounced the style detestable, are by another hand than Shakespeare's. On that view, Shakespeare may have either worked over a previous play, or proceeded on another man's beginning. Neither alternative can logically be excluded by the *a priori* principle of critic A.

Concerning OTHELLO, lastly, the extravagance of the general assumption of critic A can easily be realised by any one who will take the trouble to read Marston's MALCONTENT, published, and enlarged by Webster, in 1604. In that play the motive of jealousy—albeit jealousy well-founded— is handled with so many resemblances to some of the Iago scenes in OTHELLO that it is hardly possible to doubt that one dramatist has had the other's work in mind. Apart from that, the coincidence that in both plays there are characters named Bianca and Emilia, and in each case of similar type, can hardly be accidental. And as Marston seems all along to have in some degree imitated Shakespeare — as his early poem PYGMALION was clearly suggested by the VENUS AND ADONIS, and his plays contain various Shakespearean echoes, while he noticeably follows Shakespeare's lead in blank verse — the natural presumption is that before writing the MALCONTENT he had seen OTHELLO. On that view there can no longer be any question that OTHELLO must be dated as early as 1604. But now there arises a difficulty. Imitative as the Elizabethans were, is it likely that on the very heels of the first production of OTHELLO, Marston would sit down to write a play in which whole scenes of that were parallelled, and in which two of its character-names for light women were duplicated ? His plot is widely different : would he not have taken the trouble to avoid such coincidences ? We are not entitled to a decided opinion, there being no proofs either way ; but we are left at least free to surmise that there may have been an older play on which both dramatists worked in 1604. And when I read in OTHELLO such passages as Iago's speech over his swooning victim :

> " Thus credulous fools are caught ;
> And many worthy and chaste dames even thus,
> All guiltless, meet reproach,"

I can more easily believe that they belong to either an earlier or a later hand than conceive them Shakespeare's. An accomplished Shakespearean scholar and editor, too, strongly conservative in his general attitude, assured me recently that he had decided against Shakespeare's authorship of the rhyming lines spoken by the Duke and Brabantio in Act I, Scene 3. Now, there are sententious couplets very like these in the MALCONTENT, as in the soliloquy of Malevole after he has aroused the jealousy of Pietro :

> " Lean thoughtfulness, a sallow meditation,
> Suck thy veins dry, distemperance rob thy sleep !
> The heart's disquiet is revenge most deep :
> He that gets blood, the life of flesh but spills,
> But he that breaks heart's peace, the dear soul kills."

> " Duke, I'll torment thee now ; my just revenge
> From thee than crown a richer gem shall part :
> Beneath God, naught's so dear as a calm heart."

What is the solution ? Be it what it may, it will never be reached on the line of an *a priori* decision that none but Shakespeare could appreciate the dramatic value of certain themes, execution apart.

The theatrical effect of Othello's deluded jealousy is doubtless greater than that of Pietro's, which proceeds on true information ; but the dramatist who used the latter motive could perfectly well have employed the former.

3. It follows from the foregoing that there is no force whatever in the crowning claim of critic A that " it is quite a mistake to assume that it is merely Shakespeare's workmanship " that makes his plays great. The dictum, indeed, that " the greatness lies very largely in the subjects," is surely quite the queerest compliment ever paid to any man. Idolatry, it would seem, can "give points" to iconoclasm. On behalf of Shakespeare I affirm on the contrary that it is just his " workmanship," at its best, that sets him so far above all his rivals. It is when I contrast those lines of Malevole's above cited with Iago's

> " Not poppy nor mandragora,
> Nor all the drowsy syrups of the world,
> Shall ever med'cine thee to that sweet sleep
> Which thou ow'dst yesterday,"

that I feel the indescribable spell of his presence : a comparison of mere subjects leaves me unmoved. Shakespeare, working in the way of business (as I conceive) over a variety of old or ill-made plays, took at times bad subjects as well as good—witness

16

his part in PERICLES ; and could at times fail to
rise completely to the height of a good subject—
witness his insufficient share in TIMON.   It is one
of the capital perplexities of the student that he
apparently could write at times, especially in his
first period, as badly as other men ; nay, that some
of his best plays include passages which we could
cordially credit to underlings, while other men's
plays have passages which we should have
thought very tolerable in his.   Take, for instance,
Pietro's speech in the scene of the MALCONTENT
(ii, 2) in which he and his attendant courtiers
wait to surprise his unfaithful wife :

" My lords, the heavy action we intend
    Is death and shame, two of the ugliest shapes
    That can confound a soul ; think, think of it :
    I strike, but yet, like him that 'gainst stone walls
    Directs, his shafts rebound in his own face ;
    My lady's shame is mine, O God, 'tis mine !
    Therefore I do conjure all secrecy :
    Let it be as very little as may be,
    Pray ye, as may be.
    Make frightless entrance, salute her with soft eyes,
    Stain naught with blood : only Ferneze dies,
    But not before her brows.   O gentlemen,
    God knows I love her !   Nothing else, but this :—
    I am not well : if grief, that sucks veins dry,
    Rivels the skin, casts ashes in men's faces,
    Be-dulls the eye, unstrengthens all the blood,
    Chance to remove me to another world,
    As sure I once must die, let *him* succeed :

I have no child : all that my youth begot
Hath been your loves, which shall inherit me :
Which as it ever shall, I do conjure it
Mendoza may succeed : he's nobly born ;
With me of much desert. . . .
    . . . Your silence answers, ' Ay ' :
I thank you—come on now. O, that I might die
Before her shame's display'd ! would I were forc'd
To burn my father's tomb, unheal [1] his bones
And dash them in the dirt, rather than this !
This both the living and the dead offends :
Sharp surgery where naught but death amends."

Not only is the execution here somewhat Shake-spearean, as regards alike the versification and the phrasing, but the theme—a *grounded* jealousy —is just as worthy of Shakespeare's hand as the passion of Othello. Is not the tragedy of a weak man's agony under a real betrayal as " typical " as that of the stronger man who slays his wife under a delusion ? Would not the former indeed make the better " type-tragedy " of the two ?

In fine, no considerate student will, after due reflection, dispute that Shakespeare could have wrought as great effects with some of the themes of his contemporaries which he did not chance to touch as he did with those which came to his hand ; and that they, on the converse, would in all likelihood have done no better with his best

[1] *Unheal* = uncover, dig up. Cp. *Faerie Queene*, B. II, c. xii, st. 64.

themes than they did with their own.   Even
where they caught some of the knack of his
nervous rhythms, they could not ape his instinc-
tive judgment, his strange catholicity of sympathy,
the electric intensity of his utterance at his
supreme moments.   If we put choice of subject
on one side, and all aspects of execution on the
other as " workmanship," then these things are
matters of workmanship ;   and they decide the
issue.

4. It may be well, however, to note in conclusion that as regards the Elizabethan treatment
of Roman history, pronounced upon by critic A,
he is again entirely astray.   Ben Jonson's resort
to Sejanus and Catiline as subjects was in all
probability dictated by the very fact that that of
Cæsar was already so fully taken up ;   and the
assertion that Shakespeare " went straight " to the
two latter is mere unjustified asseveration.   In
the case of JULIUS CÆSAR as of so many other
plays, he was following other men's lead.   It is
on record that a Latin play on the death of Cæsar
was performed at Oxford as early as 1582.   And
so far was this subject from being disregarded by
Shakespeare's contemporaries that, as the critic
might have learned from almost any modern
editor's introduction, it was handled by a group

of playwrights in 1602, and by the Earl of Stirling in 1604, to say nothing of the CÆSAR AND POMPEY produced in 1607.

Nor is this all. There is good ground for surmising, with Mr. Fleay, that the existing Shakespearean play is a condensation of a previous play in two parts—a view which receives strong independent support from Craik's prior remark that, looking to the treatment, "it might almost be suspected that the complete and full-length Cæsar had been carefully reserved for another drama." If, as Craik says, "the first figures, standing conspicuously out from all the rest, are Brutus and Cassius," there is double reason for supposing something to have disappeared. And that something is much more likely to have been some earlier playwright's work than to have been Shakespeare's. But when we closely scan the very first scene of the existing play, in particular the longer speeches of Marullus and Flavius, we find, I think, small reason to be confident that the earlier matter has wholly disappeared. The versification and the phraseology there are perfectly within the reach of several of Shakespeare's immediate predecessors in tragedy, as will appear from a few of the samples of their style hereinafter given. In short, even the workmanship of considerable portions of the existing play might quite reasonably be credited to smaller men, while the extant treatment of the nominal theme is positively inadequate, so much so that Mr. Fleay's hypothesis on its bare *prima facie* merits outweighs the thin reasonings by which Ulrici seeks to establish a " unity of idea " in the drama. The " type-tragedy " argument is thus in this case doubly invalid.

Nor is our critic more accurate in his implication that the theme of Antony and Cleopatra was special to Shakespeare in his day. Taking up the first annotated edition that comes to hand, I read that " Daniel wrote a tragedy, CLEOPATRA, which was published in 1594 ; and the Countess of Pembroke's TRAGEDIE OF ANTONIE, which was translated from the French,[1] appeared in 1595." *Solvuntur tabulae.*

II

FROM the incautious critic, however, comes a grave charge of incaution. It is after animadverting on the bulk of the passages adduced by

---

[1] *I.e.* from the *Marc Antoine* of Garnier, who also wrote a *Porcie*, dealing with the civil wars of Rome, and a *Cléopâtre*. And a still earlier French dramatist, Jodelle, had written a *Cléopâtre captive* !

me to show Montaigne's influence on Shakespeare that critic A writes :

" In the violence of his reaction against the old uncritical habit of accepting everything as pure Shakespeare that was bound between the boards of SHAKESPEARE'S WORKS, Mr. Robertson goes to the other extreme of assuming that in practically all his dramas we must be on the look-out for non-Shakespearean passages, survivals of the old plays he worked over. Mr. Robertson even finds in this theory a simple explanation of Shakespeare's carelessness as to the publication of his plays :

" ' He could not possibly have published as his the existing mass, so largely made up of other men's work. His fellow-players did so without scruple after his death, being simply [1] bent on making money.'

" Now this is an extravagantly exaggerated statement. Had Shakespeare been his own editor, he might not have included TITUS ANDRONICUS and HENRY VIII in the first folio, and he might have had his doubts about the three parts of HENRY VI, and perhaps even RICHARD III and TIMON OF ATHENS ; but we are not aware of any reason for thinking that enough non-Shakespearean work survived in any other of the thirty-six plays to make the most scrupulous precisian hesitate to claim their authorship. In the majority of cases there is no ground for suspecting that Shakespeare had any earlier play to work upon ; and in the cases in which an earlier play has come down to us — for instance, the TAMING OF THE SHREW, MEASURE FOR MEASURE, KING LEAR, and KING JOHN — we find that Shakespeare entirely re-created the work and made it his own. We are at a loss to imagine Mr. Robertson's reasons for thinking that ' there

---

[1] This expression I admit to have been unduly strong ; and I have substituted " primarily." The preface shows the players to have had a kindly concern for their great colleague's fame.

was probably an intermediate drama' between Whetstone's
PROMOS AND CASSANDRA and MEASURE FOR MEASURE. He
will not even leave to Shakespeare Macbeth's

> 'I have lived long enough : my way of life
> Is fallen into the sear, the yellow leaf,' etc.

but 'decides' (to use an expression of which he is very
fond) that Shakespeare 'in all probability was again only
perfecting some previous declamation.'"

I am glad to take this opportunity of giving
assent, *pro tanto*, to Mr. J. F. Nisbet's suggestion [1]
that Shakespeare's closing years at Stratford may
have been years of bad health ; and that his malady,
whatever it was, could suffice to prevent his carrying out any such purpose as he might be supposed
to harbour of editing and publishing his plays,
supposing him to have been at liberty to do so.
It is an old surmise of my own that the tremulous-
ness of his later signatures, of which the Baconians
make so much, may have been due to some nervous
trouble. Taine's closing thought, that he died
early because the stress of his imaginative life had
prematurely outworn him, thus coincides with
some of the objective clues. It remains, however,
difficult to take it for certain that Shakespeare
retired on account of sheer ill-health when we have
absolutely no contemporary hint to that effect ;
and it remains, I think, impossible to dispute that

[1] *The Insanity of Genius,* 1891, p. 151 sq.

in all likelihood the plays were the property of the theatre partnership. We are thus shut up once more to the question of what Shakespeare could regard as his own share in the plays afterwards published under his name.

It will be observed that critic A, to begin with, admits, though with surprising hesitation, the heterogeneous character of seven plays out of the thirty-six in the Folio—nearly a fifth part of the whole. He thus in effect fully concedes that Shakespeare " could not possibly have published as his the existing mass," and that it was somewhat " largely " made up of other men's work. As regards the remaining twenty-nine plays, however, he is " not aware of any reason for thinking " that anything but a trifle of non-Shakespearean work is to be found in them. It thus becomes necessary to supplement his information.

" It is scarcely credible, but it is a fact," to use one of critic A's phrases, that he not only attributes to Shakespeare the whole of TROILUS, but sees nothing of the collaborator's hand in the TAMING OF THE SHREW. Because in the latter case the extant early play shows little connection with the quasi-Shakespearean, he takes it for granted that the latter is wholly Shakespeare's. Now, the process by which the presence of alien work in the plays may be proved is necessarily lengthy, and it is out of the question to expound it here ; but as against our critic's oracular " we are not aware of any reason " it may suffice to point to the consensus of the experts.   Mr. Grant White, conservative as he is, pronounces that in the SHREW " three hands at least are traceable : that of the author of the old play, that of Shakespeare himself, and that of a co-laborer."   Mr. Fleay, on his different lines, arrives likewise at the conclusion that the play reveals three writers ; [1] and so does Dr. Furnivall. How any student can find the play homogeneous I cannot understand.   I do not applaud the flings by which Mr. White assumed at times to close a dispute over the authorship of a given passage : his way of proclaiming that those who differ from him are clearly unqualified to judge, must tend to provoke not only opposition but disrespect for the belletrist temperament and methods.   But when a critic professes to see absolutely nothing non-Shakespearean in the TAMING OF THE SHREW, I confess I am somewhat at a loss how to deal with him.

Of TIMON OF ATHENS, as to which critic· A writes that " perhaps even " there Shakespeare has

---

[1] One of these he supposes to be Lodge (*Life of Shakespeare*, p. 23) ; and I think the play has still traces either of Lodge's or Greene's diction.   Cp. *Did Shakespeare write " Titus Andronicus"?* pp. 182-84.

retained foreign matter, it is enough to say that practically all the modern editors declare it to come from different hands. And though it is not so generally recognised that there is alien work in TROILUS AND CRESSIDA, I believe that few good readers, since Steevens published his suspicions, have denied the difficulty of tracing Shakespeare throughout the fifth Act. If then we add TROILUS and the SHREW to critic A's seven exceptions, and further add the clearly heterogeneous PERICLES, which is not in the First Folio, and which is now hardly disputed over save as to the precise fractions of it written by Shakespeare, we have ten plays recognised by scholars as only in part Shakespearean —that is, more than a quarter of the "existing mass." Needless to say, the disputed phrase is now justified twice over : the "existing mass" means just all the plays as published.

But expert criticism has gone further still, though critic A seems to be unaware of it. No English editors rank higher than Messrs. Clark and Wright, who have avowed their belief that (1) the existing HAMLET contains a good deal of the pre-Shakespearean play, not much modified, and (2) that MACBETH as it stands has non-Shakespearean matter—added, they think, after the play was planned. Mr. Fleay takes a similar view. In the latter play, as it happens, the portion which Arnold pronounced "detestable" comes under suspicion, and one would expect the idolaters to be glad so to explain it away. To me it seems inconceivable that Shakespeare should have written the crude rants of the second scene at a time when he was capable of the immortal utterance of the supreme moments of the play ; and it is a natural sequence to assume that he would not have published the whole with his name as it stands. In the character not of "scrupulous precisian" but of man of simple common-sense, I take it, he would have preferred to excise or rewrite the inferior parts before putting his name to the whole.

In the same way, as regards HAMLET, however ready be the idolaters to endorse the play as it stands, a careful student will concede that a good deal of the comic dialogue is within the measure of Shakespeare's colleagues, and that even some of the speeches in verse smack strongly of his predecessors. Dr. Furnivall, we know, appealed to "every man and woman with a head" to repudiate the notion that Shakespeare could possibly have drawn from another play even the groundwork of such scenes as those between the king and queen and the courtiers, and Hamlet and the players, the praying scene, Hamlet's scene with his mother, and so on.   Possibly critic A would take that side ; but I incline to think that the simple tactic of Dr. Furnivall's argument is already out of date, and that the mass of students will turn their backs on it.   Not only will they find it quite conceivable that in scene after scene Shakespeare was painting over a predecessor's work : they will admit, I think, that such blank verse as the Ghost's speech to Hamlet is nearer to the style of previous writers than to that of Hamlet's speech to Horatio just before the Ghost's appearance, and his address to the Ghost itself.

If any reader should demur to this finding, let me invite his attention to the matter and manner of some lines from the opening speech of the Ghost in the Second Part of the SPANISH TRAGEDY (1592), the work of Thomas Kyd, who was in all probability the author of the old HAMLET. This view, first thrown out by Malone, and accepted by many later writers, has been pretty well established by Mr. Fleay and by Dr. Gregor Sarrazin, in his essay on Kyd.[1]   To say nothing of the many resemblances of structure and plot [2]

[1] *Thomas Kyd und sein Kreis ; eine litterar-historische Untersuchung,* von Gregor Sarrazin.   Berlin (Felber), 1892.

[2] In *Soliman and Perseda* the conclusion is one of duel and poison, and there is an earlier passage referring to the use of a poisoned rapier in combat.   In the *Spanish Tragedy* we find a ghost, a play within a play, embassies for tribute, and so forth, and

between HAMLET, on the one hand, and SOLIMAN
AND PERSEDA and the SPANISH TRAGEDY on the
other, Herr Sarrazin has pointed out several
coincidences of phrase which, collectively considered, cannot well be accidental.   Thus in
SOLIMAN AND PERSEDA we have the line :

> " Importing health and wealth to Soliman " ;

and in HAMLET (v, 2) :

> " Importing Denmark's health and England's too."

Again, in the First Quarto HAMLET (Sc. xi, l.
106) we have :

> " I will *conceal, consent,* and do my best
> What stratagem soe'er thou shalt *devise* " :

which curiously corresponds with this passage in
the SPANISH TRAGEDY :

> " *Bellimperia.*
> Hieronimo, I will *consent, conceale,*
> And aught, that may effect for thine availe,
> Join with thee to revenge Horatio's death.
>
> *Hieronimo.*
> O then, *whatsoever I devise*
> Let me entreat you, grace my practices."

Such an echoing of oneself is no less common a
feature of the Elizabethan dramatists than their
echoing of each other ; and as the old HAMLET

the central theme is revenge. As to the probable presence of
Greene's as well as Kyd's hand in *Soliman* see the author's *Did
Shakespeare write " Titus Andronicus"* ? pp. 151, 153, 155-7, 166-7.

is not known to have been printed, we can only conclude that Shakespeare had his predecessor's manuscript to work upon, unless we prefer to suppose that he was echoing Kyd's other plays—a very difficult hypothesis. Given then these actual survivals of Kyd's text, we are entitled to ask whether Shakespeare has not retouched some passages of Kyd that are *not* verbally paralleled in Kyd's surviving plays. It has been often observed that the style and rhythm of much of HAMLET are not those of Shakespeare's manner about 1603, and are markedly different from those of other parts of the drama. Compare then the Ghost's address to his son with the style of the speech of Kyd's Ghost in the earlier play :

> " When this eternal substance of my soul
>   Did live imprisoned in my wanton flesh
>   Each in their function serving other's need,
>   I was a courtier in the Spanish court.
>   My name was Don Andrea ; my descent
>   Though not ignoble, yet inferior far
>   To gracious fortunes of my tender youth :
>   For there in prime and pride of all my years,
>   By duteous service and deserving love,
>   In secret I possess'd a worthy dame
>   Which hight sweet Bellimperia by name.
>   But, in the harvest of my summer's joys,
>   Death's winter nipp'd the blossoms of my bliss,
>   Forcing divorce betwixt my love and me. . . .

> In keeping on my way to Pluto's court
> Through dreadful shades of ever-glooming night,
> I saw more sights than thousand tongues can tell. . . .
>
> The left-hand path, declining fearfully
> Was ready downfall to the deepest hell,
> Where bloody furies shake their whips of steel
> And poor Ixion turns an endless wheel. . . .
>
> 'Twixt these two ways I trod the middle path
> Which brought me to the fair Elysian green ;
> In midst whereof there stands a stately tower,
> The walls of brass, the gates of adamant. . . ."

Let it be granted that the diction and rhythm here are inferior to those of the Ghost's address in HAMLET ; but is there not in the two speeches a resembling diffuseness of manner ; and would it have taken much touching from Shakespeare to work the one up to the level of the other ?   I am not here staking anything on the resemblance alleged : I am merely citing it to illustrate the unreasonableness of the assumption that in such a play as HAMLET, certainly written over an earlier one, we can at all points be equally sure of possessing the unmitigated art of Shakespeare. And there are other considerations which tell in the same way.   The opening speech of Marston's FIRST PART OF ANTONIO AND MELLIDA runs :

> " Heart, wilt not break ! and thou abhorrèd life
> Wilt thou still breathe in my enragèd blood ;

Veins, sinews, arteries, why crack ye not,
Burst and divulst with anguish of my grief !
Can man by no means creep out of himself
And leave the slough of viperous grief behind ? "

When we compare this with Hamlet's

" Hold, hold, my heart,
And you, my sinews,"

and the soliloquy

" O that this too, too solid flesh would melt,"

it is hardly possible to doubt that the imitative Marston had his eye on some such speeches. But Marston's play was published in 1602, and is known to have existed in 1601, and that date carries us back beyond the First Quarto, in which (1603) we find Shakespeare beginning to transform the old HAMLET. Are we then unreasonable, whether or not we suppose the MALCONTENT to point to a previous form of OTHELLO, if we suggest that ANTONIO AND MELLIDA was written with an eye to the HAMLET which served as foundation for Shakespeare's ? In the speech above cited, though the movement of " Burst and divulst " is somewhat like that of " Thaw and resolve itself," the versification is of the early sort ; but in 1602 Marston was capable of a rhythm much more nearly comparable with that of Shakespeare's middle period : witness the

17

speech of Antonio at the tomb of his father in
Part II, Act III, Scene i :

" Set tapers to the tomb, and lamp the church.
    Give me the fire.—Now depart and sleep.

[Exeunt Pages.

I purify the air with odorous fume.
Grave, vaults and tombs, groan not to bear my weight ;
Cold flesh, bleak trunks, wrapt in your half-rot shrouds,
I press you softly with a tender foot.
Most honour'd sepulchre, vouchsafe a wretch
Leave to weep o'er thee.   Tomb, I'll not be long
Ere I creep in thee, and with bloodless lips
Kiss my cold father's cheek.   I prithee, grave,
Provide soft mould to wrap my carcase in."

This passage, which so readily recalls the similar
scene in ROMEO AND JULIET, is not far below
Shakespeare's medium style : the more reason then
to suppose that in the speech cited from the First
Part Marston was imitating a pre-Shakespearean
workman.[1]

A similar problem forces itself on us in the
play of MEASURE FOR MEASURE, concerning which
critic A cannot imagine my reasons for surmising
that there may have been an intermediate drama
between the Shakespearean play and that of
Whetstone, on which it is founded.   I have put
this view no higher than a suggestion of prob-

---

[1] Since this was written, Professor A. C. Bradley has usefully
employed Marston's imitations as a partial test of the date of
Macbeth (*Shakespearean Tragedy*, Note B.B.).

ability ; but there are several grounds for it. First, the rhymed speech of the Duke,

> " He who the sword of heaven will bear "
> (Act III, Sc. 2),

is not at all in Shakespeare's manner at that or any other period, and is entirely incongruous with his blank-verse work in the same play. Neither is it found in PROMOS AND CASSANDRA. Was it then added after the play left Shakespeare's hand ? This may have happened ; but it seems *prima facie* likelier that it was restored or retained from an intermediate play than that it was invented by Shakespeare's colleagues. This surmise is at least countenanced by a study of some of the blank verse, such as Isabella's speech,

> " He hath a garden circummured with brick "
> (Act IV, Sc. 1),

which is so widely diverse from the rhythms of the main scenes ; and by the fact that while Isabella's pleading to Angelo, though in Shakespeare's verse, is in terms of Christian theology, the Duke's speech to Claudio and Claudio's in reply (both connected by me with matter in Montaigne) are in terms of pure paganism, though the Duke is playing a friar's part. Yet again, some at least of the prose farce of the play, such as the talk of Elbow in Act II, Scene 1, is singularly poor trash to come from

Shakespeare at the very height of his powers, and smacks as much of another hand as do the rhymed platitudes above mentioned.   Granting that the question remains open, I incline to think that the vigilant reader will lean more towards my surmise than to the confidence of critic A, who sees nothing in the whole play but unmitigated Shakespeare.

It is perhaps unnecessary, after all this, to ask whether Shakespeare would have consented to publish as his the vision scene in CYMBELINE, now given up by most editors, though some critics are still capable, with Mr. Lowell, of ascribing it to him on the strength of such a line as " the all-dreaded thunder-stone."   But when we realise, as we soon can, that such sonorities of phrase were within the power of a dozen Elizabethans, and that we have now noted at least thirteen plays—more than a third of the thirty-seven—in which some alien matter has been retained or added, we shall see cause to admit not only that a writer very far from being a precisian would in Shakespeare's place have scrupled to publish the existing mass of plays as his own, but that in regard to yet other plays, such as the early COMEDY OF ERRORS [1]

---

[1] Pronounced by Mr. Fleay to be "founded on a previous version, in which another pen was concerned" (*Life*, p. 26).   Note that in the first scene the double-endings are only 2 per cent ; in the second over 24 per cent.

and King John, we have at least no right to set down the whole as unquestionably Shakespeare's. Critic A, we have seen, finds nothing extraneous in King John. I will not labour that point in this connection, but will merely transcribe a few speeches from King John (Act II, Scene 2) as it stands, and ask the reader to compare them with a few sample harangues from Greene and Peele. It is one of the bewilderments of criticism that an instructed reader should profess to find the true Shakespearean ring. in such forcible-feeble declamations as these :

> " *French Herald*
> You men of Angiers, open wide your gates,
> And let young Arthur, Duke of Bretagne, in,
> Who by the hand of France this day hath made
> Much work for tears in many an English mother,
> Whose sons lie scattered on the bleeding ground ;
> Many a widow's husband grovelling lies,
> Coldly embracing the discolour'd earth ;
> And victory, with little loss, doth play
> Upon the dancing banners of the French,
> Who are at hand, triumphantly display'd,
> To enter conquerors and to proclaim
> Arthur of Bretagne—England's king and yours.
>
> *English Herald*
> Rejoice, you men of Angiers, ring your bells ;
> King John, your king and England's, doth approach
> Commander of this hot malicious day ;
> Their armours, that march'd hence so silver bright,
> Hither return all gilt with Frenchmen's blood ;

There stuck no plume in any English crest
That is removed by a staff of France ;
Our colours do return in those same hands
That did display them when we first march'd forth ;
And, like a jolly troop of huntsmen, come
Our lusty English, all with purpled hands,
Dyed in the dying slaughter of their foes :
Open your gates and give the victors way. . . .

King John

France, hast thou yet more blood to cast away ?
Say, shall the current of our right run on ?
Whose passage, vexed with thy impediment,
Shall leave his native channel and o'erswell
With course disturb'd even thy confining shores,
Unless thou let his silver water keep
A peaceful progress to the óceán."

Whatever be thought of their genuineness, as compared with many of the surrendered passages in the HENRY VI plays, I have no hesitation in saying that they are easily within the scope of the men who wrote the following :

" The fairest flower that glories Africa,
    Whose beauty Phœbus dares not dash with showers,
    Over whose climate never hung a cloud,
    But smiling Titan lights the horizon,—
    Egypt is mine, and there I hold my state
    Seated in Cairo and in Babylon.
    From thence the beauty of Angelica
    Whose hue's as bright as are those silver doves
    That wanton Venus mann'th upon her fist,
    Forc'd me to cross and cut th' Atlantic seas
    To oversearch the fearful óceán."

Greene's ORLANDO FURIOSO, *beginning.*

" Meanwhile we'll richly rig up all our fleet
　　More brave than was that gallant Grecian keel
　　That brought away the Colchian fleece of gold ;
　　Our sails of sendal spread into the wind ;
　　Our ropes and tacklings all of finest silk,
　　Fetch'd from the native looms of labouring worms,
　　The pride of Barbary, and the glorious wealth
　　That is transported by the western bounds ;
　　Our stems cut out of gleaming ivory ;
　　Our planks and sides fram'd out of cypress-wood
　　That bears the name of Cyparissus' change,
　　To burst the billows of the ocean-sea,
　　Where Phœbus dips his amber-tresses oft,
　　And kisses Thetis in the day's decline ;
　　That Neptune proud shall call his Tritons forth
　　To cover all the ocean with a calm :
　　So rich shall be the rubbish of·our barks
　　Ta'en here for ballast to the ports of France,
　　That Charles himself shall wonder at the sight.
　　Thus, lordings, when our banquetings be done
　　And Orlando espousèd to Angelica
　　We'll furrow through the moving ócean
　　And cheerly frolic with great Charlemagne."

Greene's ORLANDO FURIOSO, *end.*

I do not argue that there is any close likeness,
save here and there, between the KING JOHN
speeches and these last : what I urge is that if
Shakespeare wrote the whole of KING JOHN about
1596 he was half the time doing no better work
than had been done by Greene and by Peele in
1594. Had we found in KING JOHN such lines
as the following, none of us, I think, would have

pronounced them inferior to those above copied
from the Shakespearean play :

> " Now hath the sun display'd his golden beams
>   And, dusky clouds dispers'd, the welkin clears,
>   Wherein the twenty-colour'd rainbow shows."

> " O deadly wound that passeth by mine eye,
>   The fatal poison of my swelling heart !
>   O fortune constant in unconstancy !
>   Fight, earthquakes, in the entrails of the earth,
>   And eastern whirlwinds in the hellish shades !
>   Some foul contagion of th' infected heaven
>   Blast all the trees, and in their cursèd tops
>   The dismal night-raven and tragic owl
>   Breed, and become foretellers of my fall,
>   The fatal ruin of my name and me ! "

>   Peele's BATTLE OF ALCAZAR, Act I, Sc. 1 and 2.

Even the versification here is better than much of
what the idolaters are willing to call Shakespeare's.
Let the open-minded reader, then, judge for
himself whether Shakespeare's greatness is the
better affirmed by the course of clinging as long
as possible to every shred of the matter that has
been preserved under his name, or by the methods
of comparative analysis and inference from the
accepted evidence, which lead us to pronounce
much of the plays as ungenuine as it is unworthy
of him, leaving untouched by doubt precisely those
portions which set him so far above all rivalry.

III

HAD then Shakespeare, it will be asked, no "original" faculty whatever? Does not the very idea of greatness in a sense involve that of originality? I answer that it certainly does, and that the originality of Shakespeare lay precisely in his power (*a*) of transforming and upraising other men's crude creations, (*b*) of putting admirably imagined characters and admirably turned speech where others put unplausible puppets and unreal rhetoric, and (*c*) of rising from the monotonous blank-verse of his predecessors to a species of rhythm as inherently great as that of Milton at his skilfullest, and more nervously powerful, because more dramatic. To the strenuous Marlowe is due the credit of forcing the fortunate norm of blank-verse on the English stage, in opposition to rival playwrights, like Greene, who only reluctantly came round; but Marlowe's verse as such (be it said with all respect to the high authority of Mr. Symonds) is much less remarkable in relation to earlier and contemporary samples than is Shakespeare's later verse in relation to Marlowe's. Peele used blank

verse in parts of his ARRAIGNMENT OF PARIS in
1584, and in 1585 for his short " Device of the
Pageant borne before Woolstone Dixi, Lord Maior
of the Citie of London," two or three years before
TAMBURLAINE was written, though he had mainly
used rhyme in the ARRAIGNMENT ; and Marlowe's
blank measure is only a more orotund and poetic
form of Peele's and Greene's, hardly more distinguishable in structure from theirs than is theirs
from that of GORBODUC.   Here is its normal
cadence :

> " Weep, Heavens, and vanish into liquid tears !
> Fall, stars that govern his nativity,
> And summon all the shining lamps of heaven
> To cast their bootless fires to the earth
> And shed their feeble influence in the air ;
> Muffle your beauties with eternal clouds,
> For hell and darkness pitch their pitchy tents,
> And death with armies of Cimmerean spirits
> Gives battle 'gainst the heart of Tamburlaine ! "
>
> TAMBURLAINE, Part II, Act V, Sc. 3.

This kind of verse, as Mr. Symonds has well
remarked, is framed on the basis of the couplet ;
it is " end-stopped," and is blank only in the
sense of lacking rhyme.   No doubt a development
from this to the Miltonic species, with " the sense
variously drawn from verse to verse," was bound
to come ; and Marston and Beaumont quickly

assimilated Shakespeare's principle of variation, which he did not hit upon till after years of practice in the early style ; but it *was* Shakespeare, so far as I can see, who stamped that principle on the art ; and he remains to the end the supreme dramatic master of it. To have done this alone would be to show artistic originality of the rarest kind. The metrical gift of Shakespeare, indeed, though slow to be perfected, sets him apart from his coevals and successors as markedly as his sense of dramatic fitness and reality, so much so that perhaps our dominant sensation as to the difference between him and them is in terms of rhythms. The best of them is chronically outright unmetrical, so that in no one of them all, from Jonson to Massinger, can we ever read far—in some of them we cannot read a speech—without feeling that they keep measure by effort or by acquired habit, and can lapse more easily than they can sustain it. Not one of them but fatigues or jars the rhythmic ear ; of Shakespeare alone can we say : "The characteristic of his verse is that it is naturally, unobtrusively, and enduringly musical." [1] And when to that endowment we add the marvellous felicity of perception and conception with which he gives speech to his personages, we

[1] Symonds, *Blank Verse*, p. 29.

have surely credited originality enough to endow
the greatest of all men of letters. Such and no
other was the originality of Homer (man or
clan), of Virgil, of Dante, and of Goethe as
revealed in FAUST. The uniqueness of Shakespeare, I repeat, lay not, as critic A so strangely
contends, in his choice of themes, but in his
treatment of them. The expression of feminine
character, for instance, in Marston or in Middleton
at their best is so raw, so unsubtle, so indelicate, so
unconvincing, that we nearly always wince at their
touch ; and to turn from them to Shakespeare's
women is like passing from the music of Morocco
to that of Mozart, from a cracked flute to a fine
oboe, from a lacquered tray to a perfect mirror.
Mr. Watson has admirably phrased the sensation
with which one goes from Marlowe's best to
Shakespeare's :

> " How grateful, after gong and cymbal's din
> The continuity, the long slow slope
> And vast curve of the gradual violin ! "

That holds good nearly all round. Beaumont
and Fletcher indeed catch at times not a little of
the pathos and the tenderness with which the
master endowed his women's voices ; but they
never rose to the tense strain of Imogen and

Hermione. Nor is Shakespeare's mastery to be measured only on the side of pathetic passion and tender truth. There are in the Elizabethan drama a hundred flights of sounding declamation from impassioned men ; but the strongest of them rings thin and slight beside Macbeth's " Thou canst not say I did it," or Coriolanus's " You common cry of curs," where the very air seems to pulsate with horror or with rage, and the reader's sense stirs as if under the touch of a spirit. Shakespeare, as has been so often said, seems to work in the very stuff of human nature, fusing it in poetry, where other men do but contrive more or less tolerable imitations in another medium. That, one would think, is originality enough and to spare !

IV

If so much be agreed upon, there ought to be little difficulty in coming to an understanding over the issue as to Shakespeare's literary indebtedness to other men's thought where he is not merely adapting or reshaping a previous play. Critic A demurs strongly to certain phrases of mine which seem to suggest that such reminiscence on the dramatist's part is frequent.   I again quote him at length :

"We urge Mr. Robertson to narrow his argument from verbal similarities, and to check the habit into which he has insensibly glided of writing as though every passage in Shakespeare must have some external 'source,' if only we could unearth it.   For instance, speaking of the Duke's exhortation to Claudio in MEASURE FOR MEASURE, Mr. Robertson says : 'The thought itself is not new or out-of-the-way ; it is nearly all to be found suggested in the Latin classics ; but . . . it is difficult to doubt that Montaigne is for Shakespeare *the source*.'   Such an expression clearly implies that there must necessarily be *a* source ; whereas the man who was capable of finding the words of this superb indictment of life was surely no less capable of finding the ideas.   It is very probable that by the time he wrote MEASURE FOR MEASURE, Shakespeare had digested and assimilated Montaigne's thoughts upon life and death, just as he had doubtless taken in, at first, second or third hand, the ideas of fifty other thinkers ; but the process of assimilation had (to all appearance) been perfect, and there is no reason to suppose that he was here reproducing, consciously *or unconsciously*, either Montaigne or any one else.   Observe that Mr. Robertson is not at this point merely discussing Montaigne's general influence on Shakespeare, but is trying to prove by means of parallel passages the poet's intimate knowledge of the essayist's text.   The passages he adduces in this instance prove less than nothing.   When we find Montaigne describing life as 'but a twinkling in the infinite course of an eternal night,' and when we find that Shakespeare in no way reproduces such a strong and characteristic image, which would so exactly have suited his purpose, the legitimate inference is, not that Shakespeare had Montaigne in mind, but that he had, for the moment, forgotten him.   Mr. Robertson next gives a page of parallels from Montaigne to Claudio's famous speech, 'Ay, but to die, to go we know not where,' etc. It is scarcely credible, but it is a fact, that all the passages cited treat of one form or another of metempsychosis—the one possibility to which Claudio makes no allusion ! "

The words " or unconsciously " are italicised by me as virtually stultifying the rest of the passage ; but I shall let pass that confusion, and meet the rest of the argument on its merits. First of all, the phrase " writing as though *every* passage of Shakespeare must have some external source " is the merest extravagance in itself, and has the effect of suppressing essential parts of the case. There was no pretence on my part that for every part of Shakespeare there must be an outside source : the position was that a certain passage showed many affinities to Montaigne, and also to some of the Latin classics, but that it was probably from Montaigne and not from the classics that Shakespeare had drawn his line of thought. On this point it may be well to remind the reader that Shakespeare has actually been shown beyond question to have echoed other writers even where he is not adapting a play. What may or may not be such an imitation is set forth for students in Mr. Ward's table of the passages in which Shakespeare's Shylock follows Marlowe's Barabas.

JEW OF MALTA
First appearance of Barabas.
He enumerates his argosies.
Act I, Sc. 1.

" These are the blessings pro-
mised to the Jews,
And herein was old Abraham's
happiness," etc.
Ib.

" You have my goods, my money,
and my wealth," etc.
". . . You can request no
more "
(Unless you wish to take my life).
Act I, Sc. 2.
" What, bring you Scriptures to
confirm your wrongs ? "
Ib.

" Oh, my girl,
My gold, my fortune, my
felicity !

. . . . . .

Oh, girl, oh, gold, oh, beauty,
oh, my bliss ! "
Act II, Sc. 1.
Barabas and Slave (against hearty
feeders in general).
Act II, Sc. 1.
" I learned in Florence how to
kiss my hand,
Heave up my shoulders when
they call me dog
And duck as low as any barefoot
friar."
Act II, Sc. 3.

MERCHANT OF VENICE
First appearance of Shylock.
He enumerates the argosies
of Antonio.
Act I, Sc. 3.
Passage about Jacob, with a
reference to Abraham,
ending :
" This was a way to thrive, and
he was bless'd ;
And *thrift* is blessing, if men
steal it not."
Ib.
Greatly improved in Shylock's
speech :
" Nay, take my life and all,"
etc.
Act IV, Sc. 1.

" The devil can cite Scripture
for his purpose."
Act I, Sc. 3.
" My daughter ! O my ducats !
—O my daughter !

. . . . . .

Justice ! the law ! my ducats,
and my daughter ! "
Act II, Sc. 8.
Shylock and Launcelot Gobbo.
Act II, Sc. 5.

" Still have I borne it with a
patient shrug ;
For sufferance is the badge of all
our tribe.
You call me misbeliever, cut-
throat dog . . ."
Act I, Sc. 3.

It seems to me an open question whether Shakespeare was here again working up another man's sketch, or simply copying what had been found to be effective touches in another play. As Mr. Ward notes, the situation of the eloping daughter of the Jew and the father's outcry is found also in Jonson's THE CASE IS ALTERED (1599), and was thus handled as common property. If we take the first view, the MERCHANT OF VENICE is one more composite play. If the other, we must admit that Shakespeare could copy his guide Marlowe at times as closely as he himself was copied by Marston. Such a possibility must be insisted on as against critics who ignore both alternatives. Critic A, on the other hand, admits not only the indisputable transcription from Montaigne in the TEMPEST, but some of the verbal reminiscences of the Essays in HAMLET. His claim that Shakespeare was " no less capable of finding the ideas " is thus a mere forensic flourish. He might as well argue that Shakespeare was capable of finding the ideas in Prospero's speech, " Ye elves of hills," which we know to be a paraphrase from Golding's translation of Ovid's METAMORPHOSES. Shakespeare was certainly capable of inventing dialogue quite as effective as the above-cited items from the MERCHANT OF VENICE ; but it is pretty

18

clear that he did not invent these. Now, the very ground for surmising that he had Montaigne's writing in mind when he penned the Duke's exhortation to Claudio is that he has there framed a catena of stoical comments on life and death, and that such a catena is found repeatedly in Montaigne, whom, as critic A admits, he was studying about the time he adapted MEASURE FOR MEASURE. Doubtless he might have met with such a catena in some English book or play that drew upon Seneca ; and if such a source can be shown, with closer correspondences, my Montaigne parallels fall to the ground. But either way the surmise as to a "source" would be established, and critic A would be rebutted. And as the Montaigne parallels are at times strikingly close, they are for the present certainly not disposed of by saying that Shakespeare *could* have dispensed with such seeds of reflection. Another critic signing himself "B," who considers the book "rather sulky" in style, and obscurely likens its critical method to the process of reading a book by travelling down the index—a critic who is further much incensed by the expression "Christian platitudes" — yet pronounces as regards these parallels that "The coincidences are many and close, not in words only ; but as regards the

Duke's singularly cool and unchristian mode of handling the matter, they are absolute Montaigne."

The confusion of our first critic's reasoning comes out flagrantly and fatally in his remark that I was "not at this point merely discussing Montaigne's general influence on Shakespeare, but trying to prove by means of parallel passages the poet's intimate knowledge of the essayist's text." In point of fact, there is not a single word in my book about such "intimate knowledge"; and the passages under notice are adduced precisely to prove Montaigne's "general influence" on the dramatist. Critic A takes the singular course of adjuring me to prove only Shakespeare's bare contact with Montaigne by a few verbal parallels, and then to claim a general influence without giving any textual proofs whatever. His judicial principle seems to be, "Heads, I win; tails, you lose." He implicitly admits a probable general influence, while denying that the very signs of the influence are such, because they are not precise verbal parallels. "Where," he goes on,

"Where are we to find the ghost of a resemblance between Hamlet's

'O God! I could be bounded in a nutshell, and count myself a king of infinite space, were it not that I have bad dreams'—

and Montaigne's

' Man possesseth goods in imagination and evils essentially. We have had reason to make the powers of our
imagination to be of force, for all our felicities are but in
conceit, and as it were in a dream.'

Mr. Robertson injures a good case by giving it such crazy
and superfluous buttresses. His point is to prove that Shakespeare devoured Florio's translation immediately on its appearance in 1603, and to suggest that he had not previously read
Montaigne either in the original or in Florio's manuscript.
Now to establish Shakespeare's acquaintance with Florio's
text he need only produce one or two verbal identities which
it is impossible to regard as fortuitous. Such identities are
ready to hand. The most convincing to our mind occur in
the well-worn phrases 'A consummation devoutly to be
wished,' and 'There a divinity that shapes our ends, Rough
hew them how we will.' The fact of Shakespeare's acquaintance with Montaigne in the years 1603-4 being thus established, Mr. Robertson ought to leave dubious and far-fetched
verbal parallels alone, and study Montaigne's general influence,
by way of action and reaction, on Shakespeare's thought.
His unconvincing parallels are doubly dangerous to his
argument, for it would certainly be easy to find similar
vague resemblances between passages in Montaigne and
earlier plays of Shakespeare, and thus to upset (in appearance)
the theory that Montaigne came in at this particular juncture
as a new and determining influence in the poet's development."

How then, in the name of common sense, is a
" general influence " ever to be proved? The
passages in which the critic cannot see the ghost
of a resemblance are verbally different but essentially similar statements of a peculiar thought :
" Happiness lies in the dream-life : I should be
happy if my dreams were good "; and this

thought, I pointed out, occurs repeatedly in Montaigne, the sentence cited being given as a "type" of others, some of which are cited later in the book. All this the critic sweeps aside because there is no exact verbal parallel : all general parallels are for him "dubious," though it is exactly for general parallels that his argument asks.

Thus suicidal in his main position, critic A commits mere critical felony in his subordinate reasonings. Because Shakespeare does not use verbatim a certain striking phrase, he decides that Shakespeare cannot have seen or remembered it. This from the champion of the dramatist's originality ! Now, a moment's reflection will show that the phrase in question would *not* have suited Shakespeare's purpose at all, since not only is it rhetorically incongruous with the figures of the Duke's speech, but it is contrary in effect. The Duke is trying to reconcile Claudio to death, and the particular phrase in question, calling life a twinkling in the midst of eternal night, suggests that the life is at least better than the night ! I transcribed it in its place rather than mutilate the sentence ; but I did not suppose it could be argued upon as has been done by critic A. In his remarks on the parallels drawn by me between Montaigne and Claudio's

speech on death he is still further astray ; and his
" scarcely credible " exclamation gives a pleasing
emphasis to his fiasco. In the first place, it is
simply not true that all the passages cited from
Montaigne treat of metempsychosis. They specify
(1) a mere ascending of souls to heaven and a re-
descending ; (2) Origen's theory of a perpetual
transition " from a good to a bad estate " ; (3) a
" reconjoining " of the good soul " unto that star
or planet unto which he is assigned " ; (4) a " stay-
ing in the deceased bodies wherewith to animate . . .
worms . . . which are said to engender from
the *corruption* of our members " ; (5) a becoming
" immortal without any science or knowledge " ; (6)
a passage or change of condemned men's souls
into devils ; (7) a locating of souls for punishment and purification in extreme cold. If the sixth
item be held to come under the head of metempsychosis, then Claudio speaks of metempsychosis,
for he reproduces that item in his speech. One is
at a loss for comment on such a tissue of error.
Against the seven allusions cited, there are in my
extracts only two or three sentences specifying
metempsychosis ; and here again the critic's contention is all astray, for that is precisely the item
that would *not* suit Shakespeare's purpose. He is
making Claudio recoil in affright from the chances

of life after death ; and the old fancy of metempsychosis, so far from being frightful, is to an
unsophisticated intelligence apt to be almost
fascinating. In any case, it would certainly set up
no shock of sympathetic horror in an Elizabethan
audience [1] if Claudio had been made to cite it ; and
some would assuredly have laughed where it was
desired that they should be thrilled.

I am at a loss, finally, to comment on the
declaration that "it would certainly be easy" to
find between Montaigne's Essays and the earlier
plays of Shakespeare resemblances such as those I
have cited. This "we could an' if we would"
method of demonstration has obvious advantages
over mine ; and I can but avow my difficulty in
confuting a critic who, thus affirming that it would
be easy to produce a decisive rebuttal, does not
even attempt to produce it. Why does he not
actually give himself that easy triumph? I on my
part sifted my memory to find parallels between
the Essays and the plays before HAMLET, and I
could recall only a few semblances of borrowing,
which, as I have shown, disappear on comparative
analysis.[2] It seems warrantable, in the circum-

---

[1] Marston in *Antonio and Mellida* (Pt. II, Act III, Sc. 1) intro-
duces the idea as a familiar one, and not as a shocking conception.

[2] An accomplished student of Montaigne has since called my
attention to the resemblance between Henry's speech " Upon the

stances, to wait till my critic makes good his assertion.[1]

As regards his remaining objections to details in my series of parallels, I need only say that he has obscured the issue over Macbeth's speech beginning " I have lived long enough." He is good enough at the outset to pronounce my book " eminently rational and suggestive " in method ; but, giving way to the itch for negation, and conforming to the average method of English journalistic criticism, which consists in showing as little as possible of the other man's case in order to leave the way easier for your own, he has not only avoided noticing a number of parallels which show verbal and other coincidences of a very close kind, but has contrived to suggest that I ascribe imitation in some Shakespearean passages at random, thus leaving the rationality of my method far from clear.

King " in *Henry V*, and much of Montaigne's essay *Of Inequality* (i, 42). But this speech as it happens was added to the play after 1600. See above p. 112.

[1] I do not, of course, profess such a recollection of Montaigne's text, even after repeated perusals, as entitles me to deny that such parallels may be produced. In the first edition of *Montaigne and Shakespeare* (p. 62) I said I did not remember in the Essays any parallels to certain passages cited from *Troilus and Cressida* and *Measure for Measure*. I have since found [and noted in the present edition] three parallels in the essays *Of Coaches* (iii, 6) and *Of Vanity* (iii, 9), the latter containing a quotation from Cicero which may have been in Shakespeare's view instead of the passage I cited from Seneca. Doubtless many other parallels remain to be noted by students.

As a matter of fact, Macbeth's speech had been traced by other students before me to one of Hercules in Seneca, cited in my pages ; and the resemblance is too striking to be put aside.   What I have suggested on that head is that Shakespeare had "in all probability"—I did *not* "decide" in this connection—found the speech in some previous play, and was not copying Seneca at first hand.   I may here add that Marston, whom I cited as copying another speech of the Senecan Hercules in his INSATIATE COUNTESS, clearly had his eye on the original, for he copies it minutely in the lines :

> "What Tanais, Nilus, or what Tigris swift
> What Rhenus ferier than the cataract" ;

hence my surmise that, though his play was not published till 1613, his lines about the sea and the sanguinolent stain may have been written without knowledge[1] of Shakespeare's "the multitudinous seas incarnadine."   I will readily grant, however, that in view of his indubitable imitations of Shakespeare, above noticed, it may well be argued that, though he is clearly reproducing Seneca at first hand, he was set to it by the knowledge that

[1] Marston, says Mr. Bullen, "seems to have entered the Church, and to have abandoned the writing of plays, about the year 1607." His play on that view was at least six years old when published, and may have been more.

Shakespeare's great lines were a paraphrase at second hand, and by the hope of doing as well with the help of the original. In any case, the presumption that Shakespeare had seen or heard some other paraphrase of both speeches remains unaffected. It is as consequent as critic A makes it out gratuitous.

A similar rebuttal is easily made as regards the objection of a third critic, who follows A's method of evading the cumulative argument, and of crying out against one or two particular parallels. After thus objecting on mere general grounds to one, critic C goes on to say that

"Another palpable instance of forcing is the effort to trace the phrase 'discourse of reason' to Florio's Montaigne. It is admitted that the phrase occurs in English books before 1600, yet we are told that it is 'difficult to doubt' that it comes to Shakespeare from Florio, although to most readers the doubt will not only be easy but inevitable and persistent."

Now, the grounds for my surmise were concrete and coercive, whereas the critic's doubt rests on the mere disposition to cavil. My "difficulty" lay in the fact that the phrase, though not exactly rare, is exotic in English to start with ; that it has been traced only in a few books, most of which Shakespeare was not at all likely to have read, and none of which is he known to have read ; and that it *never occurs in his works before the Second Quarto of*

HAMLET,[1] which he recast at a time when we know him to have been making acquaintance with Florio's newly published " Montaigne," wherein the phrase occurs *at least four times*, several of them in passages that he gives other signs of having read. How any one, with these facts before him, can " persist " in assuming that Shakespeare got the phrase from another source, I cannot understand.

When all the concrete issues are disposed of, however, there may remain some force in one general objection made by critic A to my argument—the objection, namely, that I do not make it clear whether in my opinion Shakespeare's study of Montaigne caused or merely coincided with the great expansive movement of his mind represented by the stride from JULIUS CÆSAR to HAMLET and LEAR. " The truth," says the critic, " probably lies midway between these extreme statements. We may safely say that Montaigne *contributed to* the perfect ripening of Shakespeare's intellect ; and this we take to be

[1] The *New Dictionary*, citing the phrase in *Hamlet*, gives the date 1602, presumably because the play was then entered in the Stationers' Register, though not published till 1603. But the Quarto of 1603, which is our only clue to the text as it stood in 1602, has " *devoid of* reason " where we now read " that wants discourse of reason." This was pointed out by Charles Knight, who supposed the latter phrase to be of Shakespeare's invention. It is clear that we cannot date it earlier than the Second Quarto, 1604.

Mr. Robertson's real position, though in the ardour of discussion he sometimes writes as though he thought ' caused ' the juster term." Doubtless I have insufficiently treated of the problem thus raised : it is one on which it is hard to pronounce crisply and with confidence. On reconsideration, however, I am not disposed to recede from any of my expressions which leant more to the notion of " cause " than to that of simple " contribution," seeing that they are qualified by sufficient mention of those forces of experience and primary genius which were equally essential. Putting aside mere " coincidence " as a nugatory conception, I should say that Shakespeare's study of Montaigne seems to have been one of the determinants in his greatest development, and one without which he might have missed something of his highest utterance. If this still sounds excessive ; if the reader would fain hold with a fourth critic that " Shakespeare was probably more profoundly influenced by the events of his own life than by any reading," and would fain dispute " the special dependence of Shakespeare's genius on culture and circumstance, stimulus and initiative," I can but recur persistently to the manifold proofs that Shakespeare's mind developed late ; that it moved on paths already made ; that it was profoundly affected by its culture, though it did not seek culture very sedulously ; and that, in particular, his most successful effort alike in the comic and the tragic vein was by way of bettering other men's. Critic D agrees with me that " his avocation of actor developed his sympathies and the capacity of interpreting and interpenetrating the thoughts of others " ; adding that " he had living intercourse with men who were greater than their books." Then, if these things count, why should not proportional weight be allowed to what critic D agrees with me in pronouncing "simply the most living book then existing in Europe " ? The impact and impulse of a great and comprehensive book are surely more potent, more searching, more persuasive, than those of any personality save one that is inordinately magnetic ; and neither " Kind Kit Marlowe " nor " Rare Ben Jonson " seems to have been exactly a king of men, magnetic and masterful as both were.

The more carefully we collate the facts, the more ground do we see for conceiving Shakespeare as differentiated from other men not by his inventive and strictly " creative " faculty, but by his unparalleled plasticity and receptivity and responsiveness, happily balanced by a fine sanity of judgment, which last was yet not the ruling element in his life. On no theory of the Sonnets does their author figure as a self-poised and self-determining type; and I continue to find it patently unlikely that a man of marked originality of character and deep intellectual bias would have taken to acting for a calling as Shakespeare did, or that a mind innately or independently capable of LEAR and the TEMPEST should at twenty-nine have struck no deeper than VENUS AND ADONIS and THE RAPE OF LUCRECE, and should for years have been content to manipulate and supplement the declamations of the Greenes and Peeles, with whatever facility. We are really constrained to think that had not they and Marlowe led the way, and had not the old HAMLET and LEAR lain to his hand, stirring his mobile genius to transcend them, his performance would have been very different in matter and manner, and different for the worse. Mr. Ward, no iconoclast and no radical in these matters, deliberately affirms [1] that "while Shakespeare's genius nowhere exerted itself with more transcendent force and marvellous versatility" than in LEAR, "it nowhere found more promising materials ready to its command" than those

[1] *History of English Dramatic Literature*, i. 126.

supplied by the previous play. And the same critic, citing Charles Lamb's remark that "the reluctant pangs of abdicating royalty in EDWARD II. furnished hints which Shakespeare scarcely improved in his RICHARD II.," adds, "I really do not know what is to be added to this observation."[1] These judgments, it seems to me, are in harmony with the foregoing argument, and with the main view set forth in "Montaigne and Shakespeare." As for the claim that Shakespeare "mastered and made his own" that which he received, it in no way gainsays these judgments. It was in fact part of my own thesis.

A similar reply may be made to critic B, who, after objecting that I have deductively built up "a life of the dramatist which, if we possessed many more documents, would be still in the highest degree problematical," goes on to say that my theory of Montaigne's seminal influence "is an explanation not deep enough, not so intimate and personal as we demand." That is to say, "we" demand an exposition ten times more problematical than mine, which has just been vetoed for being problematical! I shall be as glad as other people to receive an "intimate and personal" account of Shakespeare's mental history;

[1] *History of English Dramatic Literature*, p. 198.

and to that end I leave critic B to answer his own questions :

> "What does he make of possible undercurrents, flowing from the first beneath a surface they were afterwards to chequer and trouble ? What of reticences waiting for the moment to speak ? What of slight events, never set down anywhere, which might have furnished motive or material to work upon in a mind so preternaturally alive at all points ? "

What indeed ? Is it to be supposed that any one will deny the conceivable potency of " slight events," of " reticences waiting," of " possible under-currents " in Shakespeare's evolution ? Critic B incidentally imputes to me " a certain disdain of the transcendental," whatever that may be ; and I am free to confess that if the above specifications of possibilities constitute a " transcendental " elucidation of the problem in hand, I do not see my way to set a high value on his method, as a substitute for that which I have followed, and which he so oddly likens to the appreciation of a book from its index. Many things, of a surety, must have counted in the growth of Shakespeare's thought and genius : I did but seek to trace out one factor which seemed at once tangible and decisive, leaving it to whoso will or can to attain a fuller interpretation. " We fall back," says critic B, " upon Shakespeare's genius as a psychological reality, and upon his life experience, of which we know so little, as the sufficient reason why he wrote tragedies at least. And we hold that he saw further into the meaning of the world than even Michel de Montaigne." Well, I had actually said as much as this, only arguing further that the reading of Montaigne had determined much of the intellectual colouring of some of the greatest of the tragedies, and had thus given a special atmosphere to Shakespeare's inner life.

And when all is said, what is there in this line of thought that need mortify the humanist, or discord with any large philosophy of things ? Our thesis comes to this, that the rarest genius is but a complex of faculty, fed and stirred by previous accomplishment ; that all mastery roots in lower precedent ; and that every masterpiece implicates in itself the past attainment of a thousand minor men. Is it not already a commonplace of history that an age of bards must have gone to evolve Homer ; and centuries of painting, culminating in an immense florescence of kindred power, to make possible Titian and Leonardo ? But for Italian trials of blank verse, Surrey might not have essayed it in English : but for his and Sackville's and Peele's, Marlowe's might not have been ; but for Marlowe, what should we have

19

had from Shakespeare? The law is universal. Goethe has memorably described himself as a formative plexus of countless various streams of literary force : " every one of my writings," he declared, " has been furnished to me by a thousand different persons, a thousand things : " why should we grudge to think of Shakespeare as his congener, with whatever higher status? France is not loth to make a similar avowal as to Molière, who lays such liberal hands on the plays of his predecessors.[1] Pondering it all, we are irresistibly reminded of the great and liberal code of the all-influencing Montaigne himself : " That which a man rightly knows and understands, he is the free disposer of at his own full liberty, without any regard to the author from whom he had it, or fumbling over the leaves of his book." That is to say, the very uniqueness, the very universality of Montaigne, came of his having availed himself of all the ideas that he met with on his way, and made his wine of all men's fruitage. In our crowded day, to be sure, the ethic is different : it had need be, lest we should wrong each other. But it is none the less a stimulating and reconciling thought that the supremacy of the work of our greatest man of letters is largely the outcome of his

[1] Cp. Stapfer, *Molière et Shakespeare*, ed. 1887, p. 207.

untroubled willingness to adopt other men's plans and performance, wherever he could turn them to good account, he having the while no thought of becoming immortal by such means. That such a thing should once have been done is haply more than a magnificent rebuke to our little vanities and narrow ambitions : it may be a premonition of what a greater and happier age shall achieve with full consciousness, and with scientific purpose.

THE LEARNING OF SHAKESPEARE

I [1]

I⊤ was in the eighteenth century, so often arraigned for its low appreciation of Shakespeare, that there arose the conception of him as a master not only of his own tongue but of Latin and Greek ; and that opinion, albeit much shaken by the powerful criticism of Dr. Richard Farmer in 1767, continues to be zealously maintained from generation to generation. Latterly it has been affirmed with equal confidence by two internecine groups, the maintainers of Bacon's authorship of the plays, and the traditionally orthodox Shakespeareans who most vehemently oppose them. One recent writer on the orthodox side, it is true, sees a danger in the conflict. "Shakespeareans," writes Mr. Gervais, "will do well not to ridicule the Baconian claims, . . . for we certainly owe the Baconians a debt of gratitude for insisting on the learning with which the plays abound." [2] That thesis is,

[1] On this theme see the Introduction to the present volume, and pp. 75-76, 82-83, 85-86, 97-104, 119-131 above.

[2] F. P. Gervais, *Bacon not Shakespeare*, 1901, p. 4.

indeed, the foundation of the Baconian case, which, as Mr. Gervais notes, runs thus: "The plays show wide learning. William Shakespeare the actor, with his education and opportunities, could never have acquired that learning. We find it in Bacon's works. Therefore Bacon was the author." [1] And the Baconians further have this point in common with some of their "dearest foes," for instance, the late Professor Churton Collins, that they assign to Shakespeare all the plays ascribed to him in the first folio, attempting no critical discrimination. It is significant, then, that a rational critical method is found to involve conflict with the two positions alike.

One of the orthodox school to whom the advice of Mr. Gervais might fitly have been administered was the late Professor John Fiske, who in a vigorous article [2] affirmed with equal confidence the learning of the author of the plays and the folly of the Baconians who turn to Bacon in the effort to account for that learning. Holding the views he did, Professor Fiske necessarily failed to appreciate the measure of real excuse for the first resort to the Baconian hypothesis, as apart from persistence in the claim that it is proved.

[1] F. P. Gervais, *Bacon not Shakespeare*, 1901, p. 1.
[2] *The Atlantic Monthly*, November 1897.

With Professor Ten Brink, he acknowledged explicitly enough that the idolatrous methods of many of the commentators prepared the way for the denial that the man Shakespeare could have produced the works which bear his name. Yet he held confidently by a belief which belongs to the idolatrous conception of Shakespeare ; and he avowed it without any critical reference to the countervailing evidence and arguments. At the same time, he omitted to note the radically important change set up in the critical conception by the knowledge that Shakespeare not only had little or no share in the historical plays long ago seen to reveal other hands, but had wrought upon and partly embodied other men's work in some of the greater tragedies, and had in yet other cases merely interpolated, adapted, and partly revised other men's plays. True, these points of the higher or lower criticism are still more or less in reasonable dispute, and their thorough handling would carry us far from the simple issue as to the alleged Baconian authorship ; so that, though a critic who lays such stress as did Professor Fiske on the argument from style in Homer might be expected to face them, he did not exactly impair his answer to the Baconians by ignoring them. But when, thus ignoring such considerations, he endorsed a proposition which ordinarily rests on the indiscriminate acceptance of all the plays as authentic, he set up a seriously imperfect case.

The proposition in question is that Shakespeare was a good classical scholar. Lowell, a generation ago, had ventured the much more moderate thesis : that Shakespeare " may have laid hold of an edition of the Greek tragedians, *Graece et Latine*, and then . . . contrived to worry some considerable meaning out of them." [1] This suggestion, modest in comparison with the speculation which went on before Farmer, the critic sought to substantiate with a series of phraseological parallels which, like those since collected by Professor Churton Collins, make Shakespeare's mind retain unimportant verbal tricks, tags, and saws from the Greek drama without assimilating anything else. [2]

[1] Essay on "Shakespeare Once More " in *Among my Books*, rep. in *The English Poets*, etc. (Camelot Series), 1888, p. 115 sq.

[2] Thus Lowell, while " laying no stress " upon such " trifles," suggests that such a Shakespearean line as

" Unhouseled, disappointed, unaneled "

may be an imitation of such a line as

ἄπειρος, ἀθαλάττωτος, ἀσαλαμίνιος

in the *Frogs* of Aristophanes, and that Milton followed either Shakespeare or the Greek in the line

" Unrespited, unpitied, unreprieved."

Professor Churton Collins (*Studies in Shakespeare*, p. 61) finds a similar parallel in the line

ἄμοιρον, ἀκτέριστον, ἀνόσιον νέκυν

in the *Antigone* (1071). Both Professors had forgotten that Spenser has such lines as

Lowell's parallels have never set up any conviction, being one and all explicable in terms of the general literary and theatrical tradition through Seneca. But Lowell's critical miscarriage did not deter Professor Fiske from advancing a far more extravagant proposition, backed by far less semblance of proof. Here are the Professor's words :

"There was in the town [Stratford-on-Avon] a remarkably good free grammar school, where he [Shakespeare] might have learned the 'small Latin and less Greek' which his friend Ben Jonson assures us he possessed. This expression, by the way, is usually misunderstood, because people do not pause to consider it. Coming from Ben Jonson, I should say that 'small Latin and less Greek' might fairly describe the amount of those languages ordinarily possessed by a member of the graduating class at Harvard in good standing. *It can hardly imply less than the ability to read Terence at sight, and perhaps Euripides less fluently.* The author of the plays, with his unerring accuracy of observation, knows Latin enough at least to use the Latin part of English most skilfully ; at the same time, when he has occasion to use Greek authors, such as Homer or Plutarch, he *usually* prefers an English translation." . . . "It seems clear that he had a good reading acquaintance with French and Italian, though he often uses translations, as, for instance, Florio's version of Montaigne."[1]

"Unpeopled, unmanured, unproved, unpraysed"
        (*Faerie Queene*, B. IV, c. x, st. 5) ;
"Uncombed, uncurled, and carelessly unshed"
        (*Id.* IV, vii, 40) ;
"Unbodièd, unsouled, unheard, unseen"
        (*Id.* VII, vii, 46).

[1] *Atlantic Monthly*, November 1897, pp. 640, 642.

One rejoices to learn that an ordinary graduate of Harvard in good standing can read Terence at sight, and " perhaps Euripides less fluently." The ordinary graduate of good standing in the Old World is believed to fall short of that measure of facility. But however that may be, the assumption that Shakespeare could do these things is so fantastic as to entitle us to retort on Professor Fiske the charge of not having paused to consider the meaning of Jonson's phrase. Such mastery of Latin and Greek as he defines was really not so common in Elizabethan England that it could seem a small thing even in the eyes of Ben Jonson, who in all likelihood read Euripides, not to speak of Aeschylus, much less fluently than he did Terence ; and who can hardly have been so consummately at home in Persius or Plautus as to think little of the power to read Terence at sight. Professor Fiske's judgment is an echo of that of Maginn, who decided that Jonson " only meant to say that Shakespeare's acquirements in the learned languages were small in comparison with those of professed scholars of scholastic fame." [1] Such affirmations are really on a level with the most gratuitous assumptions of the Baconians. Jonson cannot rationally be supposed to

[1] Maginn's *Shakespeare Papers*, ed. New York, 1856, p. 241.

have put such a meaning in such words. He himself, though a widely-read scholar, had no " scholastic fame " ; and to suppose that he would think it worth while, in a commendatory poem, to make light of Shakespeare's Greek and Latin because it was not far above the level of acquirement of most well-educated Englishmen of his day, is nothing short of fantastic.

Yet this extravagant doctrine was not only heightened by Professor Fiske, but further extended by Professor Churton Collins, who, without citing Maginn or Fiske, undertakes " to prove that, so far from Shakespeare having no pretension to classical scholarship, he could almost certainly read Latin *with as much facility as a cultivated Englishman of our own time reads French* ; that with some at least of the principal Latin classics he was intimately acquainted ; that through the Latin language he had access to the Greek classics ; and that of the Greek classics in the Latin versions he had in all probability a remarkably extensive knowledge." [1]

As Professor Fiske outgoes Maginn, Professor Collins outgoes Fiske. He ascribes to Shakespeare, in effect, a greater facility in Latin than is possessed by many professional scholars, because much of

[1] *Studies in Shakespeare*, 1904, pp. 3-4.

Latin is for any man far harder, more elliptic, more obscure than is any modern French for a cultivated modern Englishman.   For the rest, Professor Collins echoes his predecessors :

> "Jonson, we must remember, was a scholar, and posed ostentatiously as a scholar in the technical sense of the term. . . . To him 'small Latin' and 'less Greek' would connote what it would to Scaliger or to Casaubon. . . . We may be quite sure that Jonson would have spoken of the classical attainments of Shelley, of Tennyson, and of Browning in the same way.   And yet it is notorious that these three poets, though they had no pretension to 'scholarship,' were as familiar with the Greek and Roman classics in the original as they were with the classics of their own language."

Thus can the most explicit testimony be reduced to nullity by an advocate with a pet thesis to maintain.   If a Baconian had asked Professor Collins those four questions—

1. At what age, and under what conditions, did Shelley, Tennyson, and Browning acquire their familiarity with the classics ?

2. What was Shakespeare doing at the age at which those poets were doing their leisured reading ?

3. If Ben Jonson would have credited Tennyson with "small Latin and less Greek," what could he have said of Sidney, or Spenser, or Bacon ?

4. Did Jonson ever say anything of the sort concerning university men with no more pro-

fessional scholarship than Tennyson and Browning
—men with whom he was at strife, as Marston,
Dekker, and Daniel?

—it is to be feared the Professor would have given
comfort to the Philistines by his difficulties. Not
only does he impute leisure for wide classical reading to a penniless youth who had to turn play-actor
at twenty-three to provide for his young family :
he makes light of the evidence of THE RETURN
FROM PARNASSUS[1] that Shakespeare was regarded
by university men as much on a level, for scholarship, with his fellow-actors who talked of "that
writer Ovid, and that writer Metamorphosis." Of
this datum he disposes by the conclusion that
"we know from Harrison and others that in the
Elizabethan age . . . a man who was not associated
with the Universities was at once set down as no
scholar." It might have occurred to Professor
Collins that if Shakespeare, without having been
to the University, actually read Latin habitually
and with perfect facility, his fellow-players and
friends would have had a special motive for
proclaiming the fact. From the first step, the
thesis is blocked by difficulties "gross as a
mountain." There is positively no reason for

[1] Pt. II, Act IV, Sc. 3.

supposing that Ben Jonson would have treated as of no account a degree of skill in Latin which was certainly not excelled by Marlowe—witness his faulty translations—or by any of the university playwrights. And when Professor Collins goes on to say that " after his great rival's death, Ben Jonson transformed into an occasion for compliment what he had *no doubt* during Shakespeare's lifetime employed as a means of contemptuous disparagement," we are left asking why the old and ill-warranted imputation against Jonson is thus gratuitously reiterated ; and further, how many of Jonson's associates are likely to have had more scholarship than Professor Collins ascribes to Shakespeare ? In maintaining the fantastic interpretation of Jonson's words which we have been discussing, and justifying it by references to the plays and poems, the two professors, both vehement opponents of the Baconian thesis, have supplied the Baconians in advance with the very kind of testimony they want. How, they ask, could the Stratford lad, beginning at twenty - three a life of play-acting and play-writing, have acquired what all moderns would admit to be a remarkable degree of Latin scholarship ? With one hand the professors have buttressed the edifice which with the other they seek to demolish. And yet other scholars—the late Professor Baynes for one—have pursued the same course.

II

SINCE, however, such critics as Professors Fiske and Collins have seen fit to outgo Maginn; and since there are good reasons for disallowing even the more moderate interpretation of Jonson's line that is contended for by such a critic as the late Professor Baynes, it is necessary to put the question to the test of evidence. Professor Fiske in his article has not done this at all. Professor Baynes at least undertook to do it. In his scholarly and valuable essay on WHAT SHAKESPEARE LEARNT AT SCHOOL he claimed to prove " that Shakespeare was a fair Latin scholar, and in his earlier life a diligent student of Ovid." [1] Unfortunately, he made a fallacious and indeed a careless induction from the evidence he offered ; and still more unfortunately he gave no proper attention to the outstanding evidence on the other side. Such evidence lay to his hand in Farmer's old essay, ON THE LEARNING OF SHAKESPEARE ; but he chose to dismiss it with the verdict that Dr. Maginn in his criticism of that

---

[1] Baynes, *Shakspere Studies and other Essays,* 1894, p. 245.

paper " pierced the pedantic and inflated essay of Farmer into hopeless collapse," and " abundantly exposed the illogical character and false conclusions of Farmer's reasoning."[1]   It is so much the fashion, of late, to disparage Farmer, that it becomes necessary to speak strongly in reply to such a characterisation.   One cannot easily believe that Professor Baynes had Farmer's essay before him as a whole when he thus extolled Maginn's blustering critique.   In any case, I maintain with as much emphasis that the critique is substantially worthless ; that its bullying and vituperative tone stamps it from the outset as a work of passion and prejudice ; and that not in a single case does it really upset an argument of Farmer's.   It only seems to do so by falsifying the propositions assailed.

Farmer was replying to a number of un-critical comments which ascribed all manner of learning to Shakespeare without justification. Professor Baynes admits so much.   In exposing the errors he dealt with, Farmer made a number of supererogatory comments, mostly humorous, and as such perfectly fitting in their place.   These comments Maginn again and again represents as substantive arguments, pretending that Farmer

[1] Baynes, *Shakspere Studies and other Essays*, 1894, pp. 151, 153.

staked his case on his incidental thrusts at the critics he assailed. It is as if, when Professor Fiske remarks on the special absurdity of the crowning Baconian theses that Bacon wrote the plays of Jonson and the essays of Montaigne, one should represent him as arguing that, since Bacon did not write those, he cannot have written the plays attributed to Shakespeare. It is greatly to be regretted that a professor of logic should praise so illaudable a performance. Farmer's particular reasoning is strictly sound so far as it goes : he completely disposes of every item of positive claim for Shakespeare's scholarship with which he deals ; and he sets up a very strong presumption against similar claims that have not been preceded by an application of his tests.

Only in a somewhat loose but inessential sentence of summary does he ever outgo his proofs. He does write that Shakespeare "remembered perhaps enough of his schoolboy learning to put the *hig, hag, hog* into the mouth of Sir Hugh Evans, and might pick up, in the writers of the time, or the course of his conversation, a familiar phrase or two of French and Italian, but his studies were most demonstratively confined to nature and his own language." [1] The "perhaps"

[1] Cited by Baynes, p. 153.

here, and the limited admission which follows it, are certainly much overstrained if meant to be taken otherwise than humorously ; but the closing proposition, turning as it does on the term " studies," is justified by the whole content of the essay.

Professor Collins, in turn, cited the " *hig, hag, hog* " phrase as significant, while admitting that " Farmer certainly, and with much humour too, made havoc of many of the supposed proofs of Shakespeare's learning paraded by Upton and Whalley." Farmer, he further admits, showed that Shakespeare depended entirely on North's translation for his Plutarch matter ; " that for some of his Latin quotations he had gone no further than Lilly's grammar " ; and that in the " elves of hills" passage in the TEMPEST (v, 1), where the commentators had credited the poet with translating Ovid, he was following Golding's English version. It begins :

"Ye elves of hills, of standing lakes, and groves."

The original was found in Ovid's META-MORPHOSES (vii, 197 sq.) :

" Auraeque, et venti, montesque, amnisque, lacusque
Diique omnes nemorum, diique omnes noctis adeste," etc.

But, as Farmer pointed out, Shakespeare clearly must have had before him Golding's popular translation of 1567, which at this point is sufficiently loose :

"Ye airs and winds, ye *elves of hills*, of brooks, of woods alone, Of *standing lakes*," etc.

This is one of the many cases in which Farmer logically and convincingly rebutted the mistaken claims of the commentators ; and Maginn's rejoinder is naught. He can but argue (and in this plea Professor Collins has followed him) that Shakespeare at several points reproduces some ideas which are in Ovid's lines but not in Golding's version. Now, waiving the possibility that Shakespeare had heard at the Mermaid a discussion on Golding's translation, and assuming that he had actually compared it with the original, we should simply have before us a fact in keeping with Jonson's "small Latin," not at all a proof that he was familiar with the classics. The classical case has so far broken down. But Professor Baynes, after acknowledging it to be "certain" that Shakespeare "well knew this vigorous and picturesque version"[1] of Golding, proceeds to elaborate his claim that Shakespeare followed Ovid at first hand in VENUS AND ADONIS and the RAPE OF LUCRECE, without once checking his opinion by a reference to Golding. Now,

[1] *Shakspere Studies and other Essays,* 1894, p. 206.

such a reference will at once serve to overthrow his claim. Of the parallel passages he cites from Shakespeare and Ovid, he does not pretend that more than a few lines exhibit any close reproduction. These he italicises, and by the test of these his case must stand or fall. In Ovid (METAM. B. viii) he italicises part of the description of the wild boar :

> " Sanguine *et igne micant oculi*, riget ardua cervix :
> *Et setae densis similes hastilibus horrent*,
> [Stantque velut vallum, velut alta hastilia setae] "

and the warning (B. x) of Venus to Adonis :

> " *Non movet aetas*
> *Nec facies, nec quae Venerem movere, leones,*
> *Setigerosque sues, oculosque, animosque ferarum.*"

The corresponding passages italicised in the VENUS AND ADONIS are :

> " *On his bow-back he hath a battle set*
> *Of bristly pikes, that ever threat his foes ;*
> *His eyes like glow-worms shine when he doth fret. . . .*"

> " *Alas, he nought esteems that face of thine,*
> *To whom Love's eyes pay tributary gazes ;*
> *Nor thy soft hands, sweet lips, and crystal eyne. . . .*"

The last line seems to have been italicised by mistake, as it corresponds verbally to nothing in the Latin. But when we turn to Golding we find that his rendering of the first passage corresponds decisively with Shakespeare's lines in a number of terms and images which are special to the translation. First let us note three more lines from Shakespeare's description :

> " His *brawny* sides, with *hairy bristles* arm'd,
> Are *better proof than thy spear's point can enter* ;
> His short thick *neck* cannot be easily harm'd. . . ."

Then compare with the whole, five lines of Golding's version : [1]

> " His eyes did *glister* blood and fire : right dreadful was to see
> His *brawned neck*, right dreadful was his *hair*, which grew *as thick*
> *With pricking points as one of them could well by other stick ;*
> And like a front of armed *pikes* set close in battle 'ray,
> The sturdy *bristles* on his *back* stood staring up alway."

Can it be reasonably doubted that Shakespeare had these lines rather than Ovid's Latin before him when he framed his stanzas? It is true that he applies to the boar's sides Golding's picture of his neck ; but he goes on to give an equivalent account of that ; even seeming to become prosaic in sympathy with his source ; while he clearly follows it in his figures of " pikes " and " battle " ; and in specifying back, neck, bristles and hair ; and in his use of " brawny," to say nothing of the easy step from " glister " to " glow-worms."

In the second passage, again, it is hardly less

---

[1] Spelling modernised.

clear that Shakespeare was following, not the concise Latin but the diffuse translation, if here he can be said to have followed either. For the *aetas* and *facies* of Ovid, Golding gives :

"Thy tender youth, thy beauty bright, thy countnance fair
　　　and brave,"

—a paraphrase in keeping with that of Shakespeare. And even if we set aside this passage altogether, as yielding no clear proof either way, the detailed parallelism of the other serves to settle the point.[1]

There is virtually no basis, again, for Professor Baynes's further assumption that in the RAPE OF LUCRECE Shakespeare is following Ovid at first hand. Here he italicises only one parallel—that

[1] Dr. Anders (*Shakespeare's Books*, 1904, pp. 23-24) makes an oddly erroneous and misleading suggestion as to the passage in the *Midsummer Night's Dream* (iv, 1) in which Hippolyta tells of the baying of the hounds :

"I was with Hercules and Cadmus once
When in a wood of *Crete* they bay'd the bear
With hounds of Sparta."

"In the Latin original" (Ovid, *Metam.* iii, 208, 223-24) "of the Actaeon narrative," says Dr. Anders, "the name Crete (or Creticus, etc.) nowhere occurs"; whereas Golding in his version has "a hound of Crete" and "a sire of Crete." But *Gnosius* (l. 208) and *Dictaeus* (l. 223) both amount to the same thing, though Dr. Anders does not seem to be aware of it. "Dictaean" and "Gnosian" were normal words for "Cretan" among the Latin poets ; and Shakespeare, were he using the original, might no less than Golding prefer "of Crete" to "of Gnosos" or "Dictaean," as one might say "French" instead of "Parisian." Still, as we have seen, it is likely enough that Shakespeare had been using Golding.

between the phrase *quod corrumpere non est . . . hoc magis ille cupit* (FASTI, ii, 765-6) and Shakespeare's lines :

> " Haply that name of ' chaste ' unhappily set
> This bateless edge on his keen appetite."

But the parallel here is not at all close, and the thought involved is one certain to have been emphasised in any version of the story, and likely to have been suggested in almost any allusion to it. It is indeed possible that Shakespeare may have sought to construe the story in Ovid for himself : " small Latin " would fairly suffice for that. It is possible too that at school he had read in the original a good deal of the AENEID, from which (B. ii) is derived the matter concerning the picture of the Fall of Troy, discoursed upon by Lucrece. But, on the other hand, he could avail himself, as Farmer pointed out, of a translation of the AENEID, and it is quite possible that he may have had some translation or adaptation of the part of the FASTI containing the story of Lucrece and Tarquin.

Professor Collins, before following up Professor Baynes's one parallel with a series of five, argues that Farmer " evades or defaces the really crucial tests in the question. Thus he makes no reference to the fact that the RAPE OF LUCRECE is directly

derived from the FASTI of Ovid, of which at that
time there appears to have been no English
version." It is Professor Collins who has evaded
the crucial tests. His "appears" is an indirect
admission, to begin with, that among the many
manuscript translations then in currency there
may very well have been one of the FASTI. It is
not impossible, indeed, that Shakespeare, having
decided to write a "Lucrece" as contrast to the
"Venus," should have had a translation made
for him. But that hypothesis is unnecessary.
After writing "appears," Professor Collins in set
terms (p. 18) avers that there *was* no English
translation of the FASTI, and Shakespeare therefore
must have read it in the original. Yet to this
sentence, finally, he appends a note admitting that
Warton (iv, 241) "says that among Coxeter's
notes there is mention of an English translation
of the FASTI before the year 1570"; and he can
but comment that "the looseness and inaccuracy
of Coxeter's assertions are well known"; that
there is no other record of the translation in
question; and that it is not named in the
Stationers' Register. He does not mention that
in the same passage Warton specifies three
"ballads" (by which may have been meant any
kind of poem) on the legend of Lucrece, published

in 1568, 1569, and 1576 respectively ; or that in the play of EDWARD III [1] the story of Lucrece is spoken of as having tasked

"The vain endeavour of *so many pens*."

Now, the passages cited by Professor Collins are one and all paraphrases of Ovid such as might well occur in a ballad version ; and when he credits Shakespeare with skilfully "interpreting" an obscure line of Ovid about Brutus in four lines based not on Ovid but on another account, he does but indicate fresh ground for surmising that Shakespeare was following a ballad which expanded Ovid's tale. Thus the whole case for his familiarity with the FASTI collapses in uncertainties, faced by contrary probabilities. It is probably unnecessary to dwell upon the further thesis of Dr. Ewig [2] that Shakespeare's poem is based upon Livy [3] no less than upon Ovid, and perhaps uses Chaucer also. The Brutus story is undoubtedly to be referred ultimately to Livy ; but here again the number of possible intermediate sources is such as to exclude the need for supposing Shakespeare to have read Livy. In this connection Dr. Anders may claim to have unconsciously reduced the

---

[1] Act II, Sc. 2, 196-7.
[2] In the German periodical *Anglia*, vol. xxii.
[3] L. i, cc. 57, 58.

classicist thesis to absurdity. " Whether Livy's and Ovid's influence is of a mediate or immediate kind," he writes, " it is impossible to decide with certainty. But," he goes on in the same breath, " I think there ought to be no doubt that Shakespeare had recourse to the Latin writers direct.[1] " There ought, that is, to be no doubt as to a problem which it is impossible to decide with certainty. For the affirmative part of his contradiction Dr. Anders offers no argument whatever. And as it is practically certain that the poet repeatedly used Golding's version of the METAMORPHOSES, which of all Ovid's works is the one he is most likely to have conned in the original at school, we are driven to presume that if he ever tackled the Latin at all, it was only at random or where he could not help it, and that he was thus no " diligent student " in that direction.

We are thus led to reject alike the judgments of Professor Baynes, Professor Fiske, and Professor Collins as to Shakespeare's Latin. Even a man who had learned to read Terence at school could not do it in middle life if he had not kept up the habit of reading Latin ; and there is positively no reason to believe that Shakespeare did so. Professor Collins points to the Latin letters by

[1] *Shakespeare's Books*, 1904, p. 29.

Stratford schoolboys of Shakespeare's day,[1] but even if the schoolmaster had no hand in them, they tell of no likelihood of continued study either by their writers or by Shakespeare. Professor Baynes lays a singular stress on the fact that the Ovidian motto to the VENUS AND ADONIS,

> "Vilia miretur vulgus : mihi flavus Apollo
> Pocula Castalia plena ministret aqua,"

is from the ELEGIES, of which there was then no published English translation. But the quotation is one that might have reached Shakespeare in a hundred ways ; it is likely to have been used by a score of English poets before him ; it might have been furnished to him by Southampton or Florio or Jonson, or any scholarly friend, who could have given him the translation, which, however, "small Latin" could enable him to make for himself. The fact that there was no published translation of the ELEGIES in existence is absolutely irrelevant to the issue: the professor of logic has here reasoned with a laxity of which Farmer is nowhere guilty.

So with Shakespeare's use of the name Titania —applied by Ovid to Diana, Latona, and Circe, as being all descended from the Titans. In this case Professor Baynes does turn to Golding ; and,

[1] Malone's Var. ed. of Shakespeare, vol. i.

finding that he always translates *Titania* (if at all) by "Titan's daughter," decides that Shakespeare must have "studied" the original.[1] Such a slender datum can bear no such breadth of inference. From his schoolmaster, from some poem, from another play, from a collegian friend—from any one of twenty possible sources Shakespeare might have learned that Ovid gave the name *Titania* to the night-goddesses as being of Titan descent. It is pointed out by Farmer that Taylor, the water-poet, who expressly avowed his ignorance of Latin, parades a Latin motto, and makes many classical allusions. This significant circumstance is made light of by Maginn with his customary bluster, and is ignored by Professors Collins and Baynes; but it singly outweighs all Maginn's and Professor Baynes's argumentation, proceeding as that does on the lines of the old "academic apologists," who, on Professor Baynes's admission, "completely outran all critical discretion." The upshot of Professor Baynes's learned and interesting essay is simply this, that Shakespeare at school probably studied certain Latin books as schoolboys do; a circumstance only too notoriously compatible with his forgetting most of his Latin in later life, poet though he

[1] *Shakespeare Studies and other Essays*, 1894, p. 212.

were. After all his disparagement of Farmer, Professor Baynes accepts as "not very far from the truth" the summing up of the humorist who wrote that :

"Although the alleged imitation of the Greek tragedians is mere nonsense, yet there is clear evidence that Shakespeare received the ordinary grammar-school education of his time, and that he had derived from the pain and suffering of several years, not exactly an acquaintance with Greek or Latin, but, like Eton boys, a firm conviction that there are such languages." [1]

And this is "not very far" from the view of Farmer, vituperated by Maginn, concerning whom in turn Professor Baynes concedes that "his position is indeed as extreme on one side as that of the critics he attacked is on the other."

III

No less extreme, then, is the position of Professor Fiske, whose modest concession that Shakespeare "*usually* prefers an English translation of a Greek author" is a sad darkening of counsel.

[1] The passage is from Bagehot's essay on "Shakespeare the Man" (*Prospective Review*, July 1853 ; reprinted in *Literary Studies*, ed. 1895-8, i, 82), one of the sanest judgments that had then been given on Shakespeare. Its defect as a whole consists in its entire failure to recognise in him the element of moral perturbation, of unhappy experience, of pessimism and spiritual pain. But the passage on Shakespeare's culture is eminently just, so far as it goes.

We have seen that, so far as we can ascertain, Shakespeare *always* " preferred " a translation even of a Latin author ; and as to Greek there is not a single plausible case of his using an original. Even Maginn was fain to stake the claim on such a trivial detail as the phrase " oblivious antidote " in MACBETH, where, he argued, the adjective is presumably a rendering at first hand of the Homeric ἐπίληθον (ODYSSEY, δ 221). Like the rest of his dialectic, the proposition is not worth discussing.

Professor Collins, indeed, makes a much more scholarlike attempt to show that Shakespeare actually did make much use of Latin translations of the Greek tragedies; though, as he has first of all suggested that the poet may even have been well grounded in Greek at school, it is not clear why he thus limits his main thesis. Taking it as it stands, we find, as has been partly shown in the introduction to the present volume, and in the opening essay, a series of perfectly inconclusive parallels, in which Shakespeare is credited with going either to Greek originals or to Latin translations of them for sentiments which he could find in any number in Florio's translation of Montaigne ; in English translations from the Latin ; in current collections of proverbs, Latin or English, or in current homiletic literature. And, further, he is even credited with deriving from his habitual reading a tendency to lapse into Greek idiom, as well as to use a number of small Greek turns of phrase—this though the ostensible thesis is that he read Greek authors in Latin versions. A difficulty is set up by the fact that, in regard to a number of proverbial parallels which he quotes, Professor Collins very candidly admits their non-significance for his purpose, while he proceeds to lay serious stress on a number of other parallels of substantially the same character.

It may facilitate a judgment upon the whole problem to reduce to types and groups those of Professor Collins's parallels before discussed, and the others likewise.

1. The passages in TROILUS traced to Plato's FIRST ALCIBIADES are not really derived thence, but from ideas in Cicero and Seneca (some of them copied by the Romans from the Greeks, no doubt), which could have reached Shakespeare in English translations or new works, and some of which lay to his hand in Florio's Montaigne.

2. The passage in LEAR, Act IV, Sc. 6 (Globe ed. ll. 182-4), about the wailing new-born infant, traced to Lucretius (v, 223 sq.), belongs to the

order of universal reflection ; but if it is to be ascribed here to Lucretius we must again see the intermediary in Montaigne, who quotes the original at length [1] besides citing a similar thought from Mexican folk-lore.[2]   And if a source be required for so obvious a remark, we have yet another in Philemon Holland's translation of Pliny's NATURAL HISTORY, published in 1601, where the "wawl and cry" of LEAR is paralleled by "wrawle and cry" in a passage to exactly the same effect.[3]

3. Passages on the brevity and uncertainty of life, and on the tenacity and prestige of custom, cited by Professor Collins as showing Greek influence on the *thought* of Shakespeare, despite his former caveats against coincidences of commonplace and proverb, are to be found by the score in Montaigne, taken mostly from the Greek sources in question through Latin media (see above, pp. 86-91).   Indeed Professor Collins, after dwelling on Greek parallels to the Duke's speech on death in MEASURE FOR MEASURE, tacitly concedes, by a footnote reference, the greater force of the manifold parallelism in Montaigne.

[1] B. II, Ch. 12 : Florio, in Morley's ed. p. 229.

[2] Essay *Of Experience*, B. III, Ch. 13 (Morley's Florio, p. 559).

[3] Prologue to B. VII, cited by Dr. Anders, *Shakespeare's Books*, p. 37.

4. Such philosophemes as the parallel between social government and harmony in music, or the darkening and clogging of the human spirit by the flesh, are of the nature of "commonplaces" in the sense of being everywhere on the tongues of educated men in the Renaissance period. To send Shakespeare direct to Plato's REPUBLIC in the original for the latter, or to Augustine's extract from Cicero's DE REPUBLICA for the former, is to put obvious improbabilities on the footing of certainties. In demurring even to a derivation of Shakespeare's thoughts in MEASURE FOR MEASURE from Montaigne, Professor Collins points out that much of Montaigne's distillation from the Latin classics "had been filtered from them into innumerable works popular among thoughtful people in the fifteenth and sixteenth centuries." [1] This plea, if it is to have any validity against the proved influence from Montaigne, is clearly fatal to the Professor's own general thesis as to Shakespeare's actual familiarity with the classics.

5. The majority of the classical tags in the plays ascribed to Shakespeare are notoriously to be found in plays of which a greater or smaller share is by most critics ascribed to other hands. Thus the classicist argument must stand or fall

[1] *Studies*, p. 294.

with the argument for the wholly Shakespearean authorship of those plays. Professor Collins ascribes to Mr. Cunliffe the opinion that the question as to whether Shakespeare followed the original or the translation of SENECA is so nicely balanced that if the authorship of TITUS ANDRONICUS could be established it would turn the scale. This is an overstatement of Mr. Cunliffe's case, but that may be let pass. Without assenting to the inference that the Senecan phrasing in Shakespeare is ever more than a transmutation of previous Senecan declamation on the English stage, I am content here to let the thesis of Shakespeare's classicism stand or fall with that of his authorship of TITUS ANDRONICUS.

6. One of the most noteworthy of Professor Collins's parallels is that of the expression in HENRY V (i, 1) about the summer grass, " *unseen yet crescive* in his faculty," and Horace's

> " Crescit, occulto velut arbor aevo,
>   Fama Marcelli.
>
> ODES, I, xii, 45-6.

Now, such a reminiscence is one which might be readily granted as possible and even likely in the case of any poet who had read Horace at school ; and the same may be said of the verbal

resemblance between those lines in HENRY V
(iii, 5):

> "The melted snow
> Upon the valley : whose low vassal seat
> The Alps doth spit and void his rheum upon "

and Horace's

> "Furius hibernas cana nive conspuet Alpes."
>
> SAT. II, v, 41.

"Small Latin" could include such items of
reminiscence or quotation. But from the loose
parallel between Osric's talk and two lines in
Juvenal (SAT. iii, 102-3), or between Lear's
"Tremble, thou wretch" (iii, 2) and Juvenal's

> "Hi sunt qui trepidant et ad omnia fulgura pallent
> Quum tonat," etc.
>
> (SAT. xiii, 223 sq),

we are not entitled even to surmise a classical
reminiscence. And where, as in the lines (I
HENRY IV, i, 2):

> "If all the year were playing holidays,
> To sport would be as tedious as to work ;
> But when they seldom come, they wished-for come "

—a sentiment of absolutely universal currency,
and everywhere native—we have really no ground
for tracing them to Juvenal's

> "Facere hoc non possis quinque diebus
> Continuis, quia sunt talis quoque taedia vitae
> Magna : voluptatis commendat rarior usus."
>
> SAT. xi, 206-8.

7. And as little are we entitled to assume that Shakespeare went for so obvious a trope as his

> " Can I believe
> That unsubstantial death is amorous ? "

to the Latin translation of an epigram in the ANTHOLOGY :

> " Pluto, suavissimam amicam
> Cur rapis ?   An Veneris te quoque tela premunt ? "

The idea must have been familiar to every elegist in Elizabethan England.   In Sidney's ARCADIA [1] we have :

> " Nay, even cold death inflamed with hot desire
> Her to enjoy where joy itself is thrall. . . .
> Thus death becomes a rival to us all
> And hopes with foul embracements her to get."

That Shakespeare had read those lines is indeed suggested by the fact that shortly after them occurs the phrase " Let death first die," which recalls the " death once dead " of his 146th sonnet.   But the same image, as Malone showed long ago, is found in this form :

> " Ah, now methinks I see death dallying seeks
> To entertain itself in love's sweet place "

in Daniel's COMPLAINT OF ROSAMOND, 1582. Probably it is to be found in other Elizabethan poems.

[1] Lib. II, verse dialogue between Plangus and Basilius, ed. 1627, p. 146.

8. The suggested parallel, again, between Macbeth's "To-morrow and to-morrow and to-morrow" lines and those of Persius (SAT. v, 66-9) beginning "Cras hoc fiet" is not a parallel at all. Persius is speaking of procrastination ; Macbeth of his weariness of life. It is surely idle, further, to say that Friar Francis's lines in MUCH ADO, iv, 1,

> "What we have we prize not to the worth
> Whiles we enjoy it," etc.

look very like a paraphrase of Horace (ODES, III, xxiv, 31-2) :

> "Virtutem incolumem odimus
> Sublatam ex oculis quaerimus invidi."

If this be not a piece of proverbial wisdom, nothing in Shakespeare can be so described. And surely the same may be said of the line in CYMBELINE, iv, 2 :

> "Cowards father cowards, and base things sire base," etc.

which Professor Collins again refers to Horace, ODES, IV, iv, 29-32. As it happens, not only Horace's lines :

> "Instillata patris virtus tibi . . .
> Fortes creantur fortibus et bonis,"

but the equivalent lines of Lucretius (iii, 741-3, 6-7), are cited by Montaigne in the APOLOGY, and duly translated by Florio. But if any classical tag whatever might be presumed to have general currency in Elizabethan England it should be this.   It occurs, for instance, in EUPHUES.[1]

9. Concerning the old question of the debt of the COMEDY OF ERRORS to the MENAECHMI of Plautus, it should suffice to point out (1) that a translation or adaptation offered to the theatre may easily have been the basis of the Shakespearean play, whether or not a printed translation then existed ; (2) that the translation published in 1595 had avowedly been long in MS. ; and (3) that the evidence for the existence of a previous play is nearly decisive.[2]   For the rest, the traces of Plautus suggested by Professor Collins in others of the plays do not seriously imply any other possibility than reminiscences of school reading.

10. As regards yet other classic parallelisms in HAMLET and later plays, stressed by Professor Collins, they can be shown to have lain to Shakespeare's hand, like so many other classical quotations, in Florio's Montaigne.   Thus Persius'

> " Nunc non e tumulo fortunataque favilla
> Nascentur violae ? "
>
> (SAT. i, 39-40),

which so readily suggests Hamlet's

---

[1] Arber's rep. p. 59.
[2] See Anders, *Shakespeare's Books*, p. 32.

"From her fair and unpolluted flesh
   May violets spring,"

is quoted textually by Montaigne in the essay Of
Glory, and duly turned into rhyme by Florio.[1]

11. The parallel between Lucretius, ii, 1002-6,
and the lines in Ariel's song, "Nothing of him
that doth fade," etc., might just as well be set
up with many other passages of Lucretius cited by
Montaigne, and translated by Florio ; for instance :

"Nam quodcunque suis mutatum finibus exit
   Continuo hoc mors est illius quod fuit ante "
                              (iii, 519-20 : in Bk. I, Ch. 21) ;

"Quod mutatur . . . dissolvitur, interit ergo ;
   Traiiciuntur enim partes atque ordine migrant "
                              (iii, 756-7) ;

"Quare etiam atque etiam talis fateare necesse est
   Esse alios alibi congressus materiai,
   Qualis hic est, avido complexu quem tenet aether
                              (ii, 1064-6 : in the Apology) ;

"Mutat enim mundi naturam totius aetas
   Ex alioque alius status excipere omnia debet,
   Nec manet ulla sui similis res : omnia migrant,
   Omnia commutat natura et vertere cogit "
                              (v, 828-831 : in the Apology) ;

or again, with one of Montaigne's quotations from
Virgil, also in the Apology :

---

[1] B. II, Ch. 16 : Morley's ed. p. 296.

" Hinc pecudes, armenta, viros, genus omne ferarum,
    Quemque sibi tenues nascentem arcessere vitas
    Scilicet huc reddi deinde, ac resoluta referri
    Omnia, nec morti esse locum "
                                        (GEORG. iv, 223-6).

12. Shakespeare's first-hand study of Lucretius now narrows down to the couplet in Friar Laurence's soliloquy :

" The earth that's nature's mother is her tomb :
    What is her burying grave that is her womb,"

which Professor Collins pronounces to be a " literal version " of

" . . . pro parte sua, quodcumque aliud auget
    Redditur. . . .
    Omniparens eadem rerum commune sepulcrum."
                                        LUCR. v, 258-60.

Here we have one line, of a thoroughly proverbial character, rendered by two, not literally. To make this a basis for the proposed conclusion would be an extravagance, even if the idea were not easily to be found in pre-Shakespearean Elizabethan literature.   But we need go no further for it than Spenser :

" He tumbling down alive
    With bloody mouth his mother earth did kiss,
    Greeting his grave " ;[1]

------

[1] *Faerie Queene*, B. I, c. ii, st. 19.

" But like as at the ingate of their birth
    They crying creep out of their mother's womb,
    So wailing back go to their woful tomb." [1]

In Spenser, we may add, as well as in Montaigne, Shakespeare might have found several suggestions of the Lucretian doctrine of the transmutation of forms of matter.[2]

13. A much better case is that made out by Mr. E. A. Sonnenschein [3] for the derivation of Portia's speech on mercy in the MERCHANT OF VENICE from Seneca's DE CLEMENTIA, I, iii, 3, I, vii, 2, and I, xix, 1. Here the parallels are real, and it is a sound inference that Shakespeare had either read Seneca in the original or in translation, or had met with a similar speech or passage in a previous play or book. But even if we suppose him to have read the original, we are far from having warrant to call him well-read in Latin ; and the possibilities of his having read a manuscript translation, or seen such a declamation in a previous play or book, or heard it in a sermon, are so great as to leave no ground for certainty on the former head. There is a homily on " Mercifulness " in Elyot's GOVERNOUR [4] which

---

[1] *The Ruines of Time*, st. 7.

[2] E.g. *Faerie Queene*, III, vi, st. 37 and 47.

[3] Cited by Mr. George Greenwood in his work, *The Shakespeare Problem Restated*, 1908, pp. 94-5.

[4] B. II, Ch. vii.   One of Seneca's points is here applied.

could suggest many others. Such lines as Spenser's :

"Then know that mercy is the mighties jewel,"[1]

and those in EDWARD III.:

"And kings approach the nearest unto God
By giving life and safety unto men"[2]

tell of a general vogue of sententious thought of the same kind. And Lodge's translation, though not published till ten years later, may have been long current in MS., as were so many Elizabethan writings.

14. Much less warranted than Mr. Sonnenschein's thesis is the proposition put by my friend Mr. George Greenwood àpropos of the parallel between the two lines :

"Not marble nor the gilded monuments
Of princes shall outlive this powerful rhyme,"

in Shakespeare's 55th sonnet, and the familiar

"Exegi monumentum aere perennius
Regalique situ pyramidum altius," etc.

of Horace (ODES, III, 30). "It is quite clear," writes Mr. Greenwood, "that Shakespeare was familiar with the Odes of Horace." Mr. Greenwood cannot mean to affirm that this very inexact

---

[1] Sonnet xlix.   [2] Act v. sc. i. 41, 42.

parallel between two lines of Shakespeare and one
of the most hackneyed quotations from Horace is
a proof of " familiarity " ; yet he cites no other
item of evidence save (later) Hallam's very weak
instance of Shakespeare's use of " continents " =
river-banks, by way of parallel to Horace's *continente
ripa*. By implication he rests his case mainly
upon the parallels drawn by Professor Collins ;
and we have seen how little there is in these. On
the other hand, the Horatian *exegi monumentum*
tag might justly be classed as a literary commonplace. In Spenser's dedicatory sonnets we have :

> " Thy praise's everlasting monument
> Is in this verse engraven semblably,
> That it may live to all posterity "
> > (Sonnet to Lord Charles Howard) ;

> " Live, Lord, forever in this lasting verse "
> > (To Lord Hunsdon) ;

> " Love him that hath etérnizèd your name ; "
> > (To Sir John Norris).

The obvious probability is that a score of
variants of the Horatian phrase had appeared in
current Elizabethan sonnets. And the etymological
use of " continent " is no better a proof of
" familiarity " with Horace or any other Latin
writer. My friend on various grounds refuses
assent to even the solidest proofs of the identity
of the " Stratford actor " with the author of the

plays ; yet he here makes the most illicit inference as to scholarship without a sign of misgiving. I regret to observe that he not only lets the general thesis of Professor Collins pass unexamined, but accepts it as a demonstration *prima facie*, after having recognised the unsoundness of the same writer's reasoning upon other issues. I fear that the desire to buttress the case for a highly cultured " non-Stratfordian " author of the plays has at this point reversed his critical method. " I think, *then*," he writes [1]—without attempting any general corroboration—" it must be admitted that Mr. Collins has made out his case that Shakespeare [2] had undoubtedly the knowledge of Latin claimed for him, and very probably some knowledge of Greek as well." And again : " The works show that Shakespeare was a man of the highest culture, of wide reading, much learning, and of remarkable classical attainments." [3]   Of all contrary argument he thus disposes :

" Never again, let us hope, shall we hear the amazing proposition put forward that Shakespeare had no knowledge of the classics. . . . Should the advocates of the ignorant uncultivated

---

[1] *The Shakespeare Problem Restated*, pp. 101-2.

[2] My friend signifies by " Shakespeare " the pseudonym of the author of the plays, and by " Shakspere " the " Stratford actor," who, he maintains, cannot have written them.

[3] *The Shakespeare Problem Restated*, p. 104.

theory make a cheap retort, . . . I will not vex myself, for I need only refer them to Mr. Churton Collins's illuminating articles." [1]

I of course cannot admit that to deny Shakespeare's wide knowledge of the Latin and Greek classics in the originals is to make him out ignorant and uncultivated. I credit him, not with " no knowledge of the classics," but simply with " small Latin and less Greek." But of that proposition, I fear, my friend is destined to hear much reiteration. It has been shown above, I think, that the thesis of Professor Collins, which he so readily accepts, is untenable ; and when he adds : [2] " It really seems to me that the 'fanaticism' lies with those who deny the learning of Shakespeare," I must be content to leave judgment to the studious reader.

15. When, finally, Professor Collins, after arguing that Lear's " Tremble, thou wretch" can hardly be an accidental parallel to Juvenal (SAT. xiii, 223-6), writes : "Nor can we attribute to mere coincidence the terse translation given of Juvenal's lines (SAT. x, 346-52) in ANTONY AND CLEOPATRA (ii, 1)—

> " We, ignorant of ourselves
> Beg often our own harms, which the wise powers
> Deny us for our good : so find we profit
> By losing of our prayers "

---

[1] *Id.* pp. 101-11   [2] *Id.* p. 126.

—it suffices to point out, first, that Shakespeare's lines are *not* a translation of Juvenal's ; secondly, that they are likely to be an independent expansion of what had become a common saying ; and thirdly, that if we are to suppose him indebted to Juvenal for the idea, we need again go no further for the passage than Montaigne, who gives Juvenal's lines 346-9 [1] textually— to say nothing of the fact that the word "profit" occurs in Florio's rendering. The idea, further, is elaborated and reiterated by Montaigne through two pages.[2]

We have now noted, I think, all that is significant in the case put forward by Professor Collins ; and on analysis we find that it does but strengthen the reasons given by Farmer for the contrary view. Not once, be it observed, do the classicists attempt to meet Farmer's dilemma : "Treat Shakespeare as a learned man, and what shall excuse the most gross violations of history, chronology, and geography ?" [3] Would the scholar of

[1] "si consilium vis,
Permittes ipsis expendere numinibus, quid
Conveniat nobis rebusque sit utile nostris.
Charior est illis homo quam sibi."

[2] B. II, Ch. 12 : Morley's Florio, pp. 295-6.
[3] Preface to 2nd. ed. of *Essay on the Learning of Shakespeare.*

Professor Collins's fancy have made Hector quote Aristotle, or a comrade of Coriolanus allude to Cato ; or would he speak of the Lupercal as of a hill ? In view alike of such mistakes, of the express and explicit testimony of Jonson, of the implications in the testimony of the players, of the opinion expressed in the commendatory verses of Digges, of the judgments of Drayton, Fuller, and Milton, and of the fact that the small pedantries in the plays are almost wholly confined to those in which there is the best reason for recognising other hands, rational criticism is compelled to conclude for the "small Latin and less Greek" ascribed to the great poet by his admiring friend.

IV

Nor is there any good ground for the assertion that it "seems clear" that Shakespeare "had a good reading acquaintance with French and Italian." The very fact that his ostensible study of Montaigne dates (as I have striven to show in the foregoing pages) from the year of the publication of Florio's translation, or at earliest from the few years before, when it was passing round in manuscript (though it is practically certain that he had known Florio, who had long

22

been at work on his version), sets up a strong presumption that he had no facility in French ; for no French book of that age could better appeal to him than Montaigne's. The main ground, again, for attributing to him a knowledge of Italian, is the apparent non-existence of any English translation of the story in Cinthio's collection from which is derived the plot of OTHELLO.[1] It is astonishing that any one who knows the ordinary course of play-writing and play-production should draw such a conclusion from such a circumstance. Any one who could read Italian might have furnished Shakespeare or his partners with a translation of the story ; nay, for all we know, there may have been an earlier play on the " Moor of Venice "—I have shown above some reasons for the surmise [2]—as there was certainly an earlier HAMLET. If Shakespeare really had known Italian we might reasonably look to find in the plays some signs of his having read Petrarch, but no such evidence is forthcoming. Once more, Professor Baynes's assumption that he " no doubt acquired for himself the key that would unlock the whole treasure-house of Italian literature " [3]

1 Professor Baynes's *Studies*, p. 101.

2 Above, p. 239. Cp. Anders, *Shakespeare's Books*, p. 146 ; and H. C. Hart, as there cited.

3 Professor Baynes's *Studies*, p. 103.

is quite unwarranted. In all likelihood Shakespeare knew Florio ; but it is idle to set the mere possibility of his having learned French and Italian from that professional teacher against the solid negative presumption built up by the plays and the sonnets and the facts of the poet's life.

V

THE sooner such argumentation is given up, the sooner will the Baconian theory be abandoned; because the erroneous ideas of Shakespeare's learning fostered by such Shakespeareans as Maginn, Baynes, Fiske, and Professor Collins are so much standing-ground for that theory. The starting-point of Mr. Edwin Reed's popular BRIEF FOR PLAINTIFF : BACON *v.* SHAKESPEARE is that " It is conceded by all that the author of the Shakespeare Plays was the greatest genius of his age, . . . and, with nearly equal unanimity, that he was a man of profound and varied scholarship." Similarly, Mr. Donnelly declares that whereas at one time it was the " universal belief" that Shakespeare was an unlearned man, " the critical world is now substantially agreed that the man who wrote the plays was one of the most learned men of the world " ; and he represents the change of view as having taken place within some fifty years. Mr. Donnelly is much mistaken in both of his statements. When Farmer wrote in 1767, the attitude of the bulk of the commentators was one of tribute to Shakespeare as a classical scholar ; and though Farmer did much to change critical opinion, the new idolatrous movement set up by Coleridge and Schlegel in the early years of this century went far to re-establish the error. The whole influence of Charles Knight went to support it. It is since his time, on the other hand, that, despite the bluster of Maginn, the reasoning of Baynes, and the idealising zeal of other enthusiasts, there has grown up a widespread and reasoned conviction that the author of the plays drew his culture almost wholly from his own language, and from easily accessible sources in that.

The only works of Shakespeare concerning which we can at all safely assume that no other hand than his has wrought in them are the VENUS, the LUCRECE,[1] and the sonnets. The first two, as we have seen, are the work not of a well-schooled student of the original Ovid, but of one who used translations ; and the sonnets not only give no

---

[1] Even in these cases it would not be quite out of the Elizabethan way for a friend to contribute some stanzas.

sign of classic culture, but distinctly avow the lack of it. The lines :

> "But thou art all my art, and dost advance
> As high as learning my rude ignorance," [1]

like the phrase "my untutored lines" in the dedication to the LUCRECE, cannot rationally be supposed to come from the competent classicist pictured by Professor Fiske, and further magnified by Professor Collins and the Baconians. The whole series of sonnets from the 76th to the 86th, and others to boot, tell of a strangely plastic temperament, sustained by no sense of learning in the literary field, and conscious of being there outbraved by the learning of others. But they also evince an easy mastery of English, of rhythm, of the speech of deep reverie and passionate emotion, and of the whole life of the feelings—the true distinctions of the great plays. There is thus no psychological riddle in the case save that created by the determination of the Baconisers—evinced before the appearance of Professor Collins's essay—to find in the dramas even more learning than was ascribed to them by the confuted commentators of the past. One of their favourite pleas proceeds upon an incautious comment by Mr. Richard Grant White concerning the lines :

---

[1] Sonnet lxxviii.

> " Thy promises are like Adonis' gardens
>   That one day bloomed and fruitful were the next,"

in the first Act of HENRY VI, Sc. 6.   In the first
place, the passage in question is in one of the most
palpably *non*-Shakespearean parts of the play—a
consideration never faced by the Baconians.   But
even were it not, the dispute is quite gratuitous.
Deciding that the passage does not properly
describe the κῆποι Ἀδώνιδος of the classics, Mr.
White wrote that " no mention of any such garden
in the classic writings of Greece and Rome is
known to scholars."   The Baconians suppress his
mention of the familiar classical detail, quote the
above clause, and then triumphantly cite the
decision of Mr. J. D. Butler that the couplet
" must " have been suggested by a passage in
Plato's PHAEDRUS, which in Shakespeare's day
was not translated.   Now, the passage in the
PHAEDRUS does unquestionably refer just to the
customary " gardens " of the festival of the
Adonia ; and the Platonic expression does not
conform any more closely to the English couplet
than does the hard-and-fast description of those
" gardens " as consisting merely of lettuces and
herbs set in a wooden tray.   And if Mr. White
had only gone frankly to Anthon he would have
found the sufficient solution of the whole matter

in the record that " the expression Ἀδώνιδος κῆποι became proverbial, and was applied to whatever perished previous to the period of maturity "— as witnessed by the ADAGIA VETERUM, p. 410. The couplet in the play does but make a loose use of the familiar phrase ; and Mr. White's strained cavil has only helped the Baconisers to darken counsel.   As to their independent performances, it may suffice to cite one of Mr. Donnelly's, in illustration of the procedure of the school.   Quoting the familiar lines of Catullus :

> " Soles occidere et redire possunt :
> Nobis, cum semel occidit brevis lux,
> Nox est perpetua una dormienda,"

Mr. Donnelly appends somebody's halting translation, with italics :

> " The *lights* of heaven go out and return.
> When once our *brief candle* goes out,
> One night is to be perpetually slept,"

and points for parallel to the " all our yesterdays have *lighted* fools," and the "out, out, *brief candle*," of MACBETH.   Burlesque could no further go. There is no " candle " in Catullus ; and even the " lights " of the first line is a variant made by the translator.   If Mr. Donnelly had but heard a little more about Catullus, he might have made out a comparatively respectable case for the claim that

> "The undiscover'd country, from whose bourn
> No traveller returns,"

was drawn from the lines on the dead sparrow :

> "Qui nunc it per iter tenebricosum
> Illuc, unde negant redire quemquam."

Even in that case he would be wrong, for Shakespeare did *not* get the suggestion from Catullus ; but the proposition would at least not be ridiculous.

It is doubtless vain to invite the general run of the Baconians to reconsider their position ; but one may in the present connection submit, to such as will reconsider anything, a few critical suggestions by way of challenge. Bacon, a habitual reader of Latin, crowds his pages with Latin phrases and quotations ; whereas even in the pseudo-Shakespearean plays there are but a few Latin tags. Bacon quotes Virgil in his works some fifty times ; Ovid only some ten times ; whereas the classicists among them find but two or three semblances of Virgilian reading in the plays,[1] and rest their case mainly upon Ovid. To

[1] Stress is still at times laid upon the "Most sure, the goddess," of Ferdinand in the *Tempest*, as copying Virgil's "O dea certe," and upon the further parallels in the contexts. Yet Farmer had pointed out that Stanyhurst (1583) translated the phrase "No doubt, a goddess." The point, however, is really too trivial for discussion : "small Latin" indeed would have made Shakespeare acquainted with such a tag ; and he may well have read the passage at school.

Aristotle Bacon refers more than a hundred times, with critical knowledge: in the plays, Aristotle is named only twice—once in a colourless allusion in the TAMING OF THE SHREW, once in what we have seen to be a current misquotation, or adaptation, made by Bacon also. Of Bacon's endless criticism of Aristotle the plays show not a trace. Of Plato, Bacon speaks some fifty times : in the plays he is not once named. Bacon, always playing with metaphors, constantly turns myths into moral lessons : for Shakespeare they are simply tales and tags. Prometheus is for Bacon an allegorical figure, standing for Providence ; in the plays we have only the tags of "Prometheus tied to Caucasus" (TITUS) and "Promethean fire," which Shakespeare could get from Peele, the main author of TITUS. Apart from the article on Atalanta in the SAPIENTIA VETERUM, Bacon six times over makes use of the tale of how she was stayed in her course by the golden balls : it is always for him a figure of the deflection of science from its proper course by the allurements of profit. In the plays we have only "Atalanta's heels" and "Atalanta's better part" : for Shakespeare she is merely the swift runner of fable. In their relation to classical lore, as in their whole psychic cast, the two minds are widely different in their content. In the face of

all this, to found a theorem of identity on the one
or two points of intellectual contact in the plays
and Bacon's works is to turn critical reason out
of doors.   Of the multitude of scientific problems
which occupied Bacon, the only traces in the plays
are those we have noted concerning the motion of
the earth, the substance of the stars, and the relation of art to nature.   In Shakespeare (apart
from two allusions to the power of adamant)
the magnet is not once mentioned, while Bacon
frequently refers to Gilbert.   And Bacon uses
thousands of words that never occur in the plays.
Bacon and Shakespeare had a literary friend in
common ; and Bacon might now and then see a
Shakespearean play : that said, all is said.   And
for one point of contact with the ideas of Bacon,
the plays have a dozen with the diction of dramatic
contemporaries.

VI

On one other issue, unfortunately, the Baconisers have gratuitous support from the Shakespeareans.   Many of these, including Professors
Fiske, Baynes, and Collins, decide that the Venus
and Adonis must have been written about six
years before its publication, " probably before

Shakespeare left Stratford for London." [1] This
view is taken on the ground that Shakespeare calls
the VENUS AND ADONIS "the first heir of my
invention," and that before its publication in 1593
he had had a hand in several of the chronicle plays,
and had presumably written LOVE'S LABOUR'S
LOST, the TWO GENTLEMEN OF VERONA, and
the COMEDY OF ERRORS. Now, this antedating
of the poem makes a much worse difficulty than is
set up by the natural hypothesis that it was written
shortly before its publication. The Baconisers may
well ask how Shakespeare could have produced
such a comparatively polished piece of diction in
the illiterate circle of Stratford.

It would not avail to press Professor Baynes's
proposition that the poet's mother was "of gentle
birth," for she too was illiterate, and her rank as a
well-to-do yeoman's daughter is no guarantee for
her having spoken literate English. But we
might still more pertinently ask how it can
reasonably be supposed that Shakespeare would
have kept such a taking poem by him in manuscript for six or seven years of his London life,
when it was his business and his ambition to make

[1] Baynes, *Shakespeare Studies*, p. 207. This sentence is clearly
inconsistent with the previous statement that "within six or seven
years" Shakespeare produced not only the *Venus and Adonis* and
Lucrece but "at least fifteen of his dramas" (p. 105).

a living by his gifts. Even if he had thus un-
intelligibly withheld it, he cannot conceivably have
omitted to revise and improve his rustic performance, so that in any case it would represent the
results of his six or seven years of effective culture
as an actor in London, before audiences who
would not easily tolerate a provincial accent, in
poetic plays often written by collegians. All the
while he had access to the English *belles lettres*
of his day, and to the society not only of educated
and literary men but of such a cultured aristocrat
as Southampton, whom the dedications, to say
nothing of the sonnets, imply to have been warmly
sympathetic with the literary work of his *protégé*.
Shakespeare had thus had precisely the culture
that, after an average schooling, was needed to
develop his unique faculty of rhythmic and vivid
expression to the level at which we find it in the
poems and the early comedies. And if the phrase
in the dedication be not, as Mr. Barrett Wendell
has suggested, merely a statement that the poem
is its author's first published work, it entitles us
rather to infer that he did not claim to be the sole
or original author of the plays supposed to have
been earlier written by him, than to make the
violent assumption that he wrote the poem in his
native village, before he was twenty-three, and

found no need to recast it in London at twenty-nine. The LUCRECE is avowedly written after the publication of the VENUS, and there is certainly no such difference of style between them as to make it conceivable that in composition they were separated by six or seven of the formative years of a man's life.

VII

IN fine, the one mysterious thing in Shakespeare's work is just the incommunicable element of genius, which is no more incalculable in the son of John Shakespeare than in the son of Queen Elizabeth's Lord Keeper. Given that genius, as Farmer argued, "Shakespeare wanted not the stilts of languages to raise him above all other men." Let it then be left to the Baconisers to do all the forcing and all the evading of evidence, all the straining-out of gnats and swallowing of camels that is done in the controversy they have raised. They have great need of such expedients ; the rational Shakespearean has none.

And there is, finally, a certain needless violence of assumption in Professor Fiske's way of making out that there *could not* have been any contemporary mistake as to Shakespeare's authorship of the plays.

We are really bound to admit that there was some measure of very serious mistake on the subject ; and our confidence must be reached on other grounds. Professor Fiske, citing the high praises bestowed on the dramatist by competent contemporaries, writes :

> " To suppose that such a man as this, in a town the size of Minneapolis, connected with a principal theatre, writer of the most popular plays of the day, a poet whom men were already coupling with Homer and Pindar—to suppose that such a man was not known to all the educated people in the town is simply absurd. There were probably very few men, women, or children in London, between 1595 and 1610, who did not know who Shakespeare was when he passed them in the street. . . ." [1]

The mere transition here from " all the educated people " to " [most of the] men, women, or children " indicates haste in surmise. The truth is, it is because even among the educated people of Shakespeare's day there was so little approach to unanimous appreciation of the greatness of the actor-manager's work as a dramatist—so little serious readiness to conceive that he might fitly be named with Homer and Pindar ; so little capacity to imagine that an actor and playwright could be a great genius—that we to-day know so little about his life. Elizabethan London differed vitally

[1] P. 644.

from Minneapolis in being a capital city of an old monarchy, with manifold metropolitan interests, and a perpetual come-and-go of all manner of notables. Above all, it was not more than half cut free from the code of feudalism ; and the exultant belletrists of the time were really not taken by outsiders at their mutual valuation. What Shakespeare (at times) thought and felt of his theatrical calling we know from himself. In many a sonnet does he tell how his " name receives a brand " from his life, how " vulgar scandal " has clung to his brow, how he is " made lame by fortune's dearest spite," how he must keep apart from his friend lest he carry discredit with him. In view of it all, we are not entitled even to assume that he was fortified against disregard or disesteem by consciousness of real superiority, much less that his superiority was generally recognised in the spirit of Meres. Nay, we cannot even decisively lay the suspicion that with his transcendent gift there went a certain psychic weakness, perhaps definitely physiological. But however that may be, it is clear that we shall understand him, if at all, by defining his psychic cast and the culture he had, not by surmising acquirements and status that he had not.

INDEX

THE END

Printed by R. & R. CLARK, LIMITED, *Edinburgh.*